THE EARLIEST RELATIONSHIP

The Earliest Relationship

PARENTS, INFANTS, AND THE DRAMA OF EARLY ATTACHMENT

T. Berry Brazelton, M.D.

Bertrand G. Cramer, M.D.

A Merloyd Lawrence Book

PERSEUS BOOKS
Reading, Massachusetts

Library of Congress Cataloging-in-Publication Data

Brazelton, T. Berry, 1918–
    The earliest relationship : parents, infants, and the drama of
early attachment / T. Berry Brazelton, Bertrand G. Cramer.
        p. cm.
    "A Merloyd Lawrence book."
    Includes bibliographical references.
    ISBN 0-201-10639-6
    ISBN 0-201-56764-4 (pbk.)
    1. Infant psychology. 2. Parent and child. 3. Attachment
behavior in children. I. Cramer, Bertrand G. II. Title.
BF720.P37B72 1990
306.874—dc20   89-39839

Cover illustration: *Under the Horse Chestnut*, by Mary Stevenson Cassatt (American, 1844–
1926). Color print with dry point and aquatint, 16 × 16 inches. Bequest of W. G. Russell
Allen. Courtesy Museum of Fine Arts, Boston.

Cover design by Cope Cumpston
Text design by Barbara DuPree Knowles
Set in 11-point Aldus by DEKR Corporation

Perseus Books is a member of the Perseus Books Group

8 9 10 11 12 13 14—0201009998

Find us on the World Wide Web at
http://www.aw.com/gb/

For Merloyd Lawrence,
who has brought this book
from a fetus to its full infancy

Acknowledgment

The authors wish to thank Serge Lebovici for his inspiration and for his suggestion that they collaborate on this book.

CONTENTS

PREFACE

As a pediatrician involved in infancy research and a psychiatrist involved for some time in infant psychiatry, we have long been struck by the need to integrate the contributions of our respective fields into theory and clinical work. In 1982 we had the opportunity to work together at the Boston Children's Hospital and there we began to conceive of a book that would apply research in infant behavior and in parent-infant interaction to the growing field of infant psychology and psychiatry.

Parents and their new babies are cared for by professionals from a variety of disciplines, including pediatrics, psychiatry, psychology, nursing, and social work. Some of this care concentrates on the health and development of the infant; some focuses on the parent's problems and anxieties. Our book starts from two assumptions: that the parent-infant pair must be cared for as a unit, and the approach must be transdisciplinary. In the words of D. W. Winnicott, who was one of the first to point out this interdependence: "At this very early state, it is not logical to think of an individual" (Winnicott, 1988a). "If you set out to describe a baby, you will find that you are describing *a baby and someone* [italics his]. A baby cannot exist alone, but is essentially part of a relationship" (Winnicott, 1987). Pediatricians and nurses who care for healthy infants and infants at risk and developmental psychologists who study them can benefit from knowledge of parental emotions and fantasies drawn from psychoanalysis and dynamic psychiatry. Psychiatrists, psychoanalysts, and social workers who treat new parents will find it useful to understand the contributions of the infant to a troubled relationship.

While Margaret Mahler and Selma Fraiberg pioneered in therapy with both mother and infant, and John Bowlby and Louis Sander and others began to combine observations of infancy with psychological insight during the 1960s, the work of integrating these various perspectives has only begun. Meanwhile, individual disciplines have continued to advance. Research into infant development has evolved tremendously in recent years, providing a window into the richness of newborn perceptual, behavioral, and social capacities. Interaction studies, as we will see in Part III of this book, have also flowered, providing an enormous wealth of quantitative data. More recently, the field of infant psychiatry has emerged, offering insight into a parent's representation of the infant and an opportunity to use this in a clinical setting.

Much of the impetus for writing this book has come, for both of us, from personal experience. As a pediatrician, I (TBB) became aware very early that I could help infants toward optimal development only if I involved their parents. Without recognizing the issues which parents bring from their childhood experience and therefore the meaning to them of the child's "symptom," I could do nothing to change their counterproductive responses. I sensed the powerful forces of caring within these parents, but was not able to tap them to bring about change. While training in pediatrics and child psychiatry made me all too able to identify physical deviations and failures in infants' development, I nevertheless felt unable to reach parents as they moved with their baby toward a pattern of failure.

Study and research in child development helped me begin to appreciate the forces for growth and healing in the infant—the marvelous plasticity even after serious physical or psychological insults. This study of the newborn led me to recognize the powerful interaction between all of the systems (motor, affective, autonomic, and cognitive) and how they fueled each other as the infant strove to achieve each developmental task. It also provided me not only with insight into how sensitive infants are to their environment, but also into how powerfully they shape that environment. By seeing them as interactive organisms from the first, I began to understand some of the ingredients necessary for healthy parent-infant relationships.

While developing the research techniques which became the Neonatal Behavioral Assessment Scale (NBAS), I began to understand the specific capacities in the newborn on which early interaction is founded. Observations of parents in our Child Development Unit at Boston Children's Hospital, undertaken with colleagues Edward Tronick, Heidi Als, Barry Lester, and Suzanne Dixon, taught me how mothers and fathers learn to fit the rhythms, the behaviors, and the needs of a new baby. Each of these research opportunities provided another window into the parent-child relationships that I saw regularly in my pediatric practice. While trying to support these families, I began to see the infants' behavior and their responses as a language which we could all share to foster the family's growth and enjoyment. The developmental research helped me identify prospective failures in relationships at an early stage. No longer could I tolerate myself or a colleague saying to a parent, "Don't worry, he'll outgrow it." Babies and parents in difficulty cope as best they can, but often perpetuate problems. With a minimum of understanding and insight, they can usually conquer the difficulty. Even a premature baby or one with a congenital or birth defect can adapt in a sensitive and appropriate environment.

For parents, as well, the turbulent period of pregnancy and first few months with a baby provide an unparalleled opportunity for change and growth. The quest for a better understanding of the "ghosts" from parents' earlier experiences which can arrest such growth led me to work with Bertrand Cramer, whose understanding of these unconscious forces has continuously enhanced my own work.

As a psychoanalyst and psychiatrist (BGC), my clinical practice and research have been focused on infancy for the past twenty-five years. Training in child psychiatry made me aware that therapeutic efforts with a child are often jeopardized by protracted conflict in the child's relationship with parents. Joint parent-infant therapy offered the opportunity to bring about changes in both parties simultaneously at a time when each is extraordinarily open to new learning and change.

Classical psychoanalytic psychotherapy focuses primarily on a patient's verbal accounts; the expression of a problem at the level of behavior is not the direct object of study. Since such a verbal focus is not possible with infants, I was drawn to seek further understanding of infant behavior through developmental psychology and the emerging field of behavioral pediatrics in which Berry Brazelton has been a pioneer. Observed interaction has become a main source of information in the work I do with parent-infant pairs. Studies of infant competence and early interaction have been of tremendous value to me, along with many other psychodynamically oriented child psychiatrists.

In work with parents and infants, another problem with traditional psychiatry is the focus on severe pathology and maladaptive patterns. My work with Berry Brazelton has helped me to recognize and enlist the strong positive forces that are inherent in each side of the parent-infant relationship. Long experience in mother-infant psychotherapy has convinced me that intervention at this early stage is one of the best chances we have for prevention of child psychopathology.

With this background, *The Earliest Relationship* brings developmental psychology, infant research, and psychoanalytic insight to bear on the period from conception through the early months of life. We attempt to integrate research in infant development and mother-infant interaction on the one hand and clinical work with parents and infants who are having problems, on the other.

Part One of our book traces the birth of attachment back to the first stirrings of the desire for a child, through the fantasies and work of pregnancy. It is intended as an overview, to set the stage for the chapters that follow. The effect of the new imaging techniques which make the fetus a visible presence and new knowledge about the responses of the fetus in the womb on a parent's relationship to the child-to-be is also explored. An expectant father's fantasies and expectations are compared and contrasted with that of mothers-to-be.

Part Two introduces the other participant in the relationship, the "armful of anatomy and physiology" (Winnicott, 1988), who will influence the relationship from day one. What we have now learned about all that the newborn brings to the relationship—reflexes, sensory capacities, and states of consciousness—is described from the point of view of developmental psychology and infant research. We outline methods of assessing the behavioral repertoire of newborns, their strengths and skills—in particular the applications of the Neonatal Behavioral Assessment Scale.

In Part Three we first review interaction studies, historical and current. Our own systems model for interaction is described, as well as the contributions of "still-face" studies. In this part, we analyze the stages of early interaction and key ingredients such as synchrony, contingency, and entrainment.

Part Four balances these objective observations of interaction with a look at the fantasies and dramatic representations often underlying them. Here we present new data on the various kinds of "imaginary interaction": the "ghosts," the replayed battles, the reincarnated relatives, and ways of eliciting and interpreting these.

Finally, in Part Five, in cases drawn from both our clinical practices, we set out to weave these threads together. We illustrate our complementary approach—observation and interpretation—in nine case narratives of the sort which might present themselves to anyone caring for young families. The problems and situations described: crying, prematurity, depression, overstimulation, sleep difficulties, and a minor birth defect, etc., involve common, perennial issues. We hope that readers from many disciplines will draw inspiration from these cases as they meet real situations in their work. The entire chapter is intended to illustrate our dual point of view and also the way in which assessment, in itself, becomes an early intervention.

PART ONE

Pregnancy: The Birth of Attachment

The same soul governs the two bodies . . . the things desired by the mother are often found impressed on the members of the child which the mother carries at the time of the desire.

—LEONARDO DA VINCI, *Quaderni*

Introduction

For all parents-to-be, three babies come together at the moment of birth. The imaginary child of their dreams and fantasies and the invisible but real fetus, whose particular rhythms and personality have been making themselves increasingly evident for several months now, merge with the actual newborn baby who can be seen, heard, and finally held close. The attachment to a newborn (whose contribution to the relationship will be explored in detail in Part II) is built on prior relationships with an imaginary child, and with the developing fetus which has been part of the parents' world for nine months.

In order to understand the "earliest" interactions between parent and child, we must step back briefly to examine these still earlier relationships. The forces, biological and environmental, that lead *Ask* women and men to desire children, and the fantasies to which these desires give rise, can be seen as the prehistory of attachment. Then, during pregnancy and the nine months of adjustment, physical and psychological, to the growing fetus, there is a progression of stages which might be described as the dawning of attachment. Because the drive toward parenthood, the fantasies, and the experience of pregnancy are necessarily not parallel in men and women, we will look at the ways in which a father adjusts to an unborn child in Chapter 3.

1

The Prehistory
of Attachment

Each woman's pregnancy reflects her whole life prior to conception. Her experiences with her own mother and father, her subsequent experiences with the oedipal triangle, and the forces that led her to adapt to it more or less successfully and finally to separate from her parents, all influence her adjustment to this new role. Unmet needs from childhood and adolescence are part of the desire to become pregnant and, then, to adapt to the condition of pregnancy. After examining how these early experiences and needs are reflected in the desire for a child, we will look at the transformations brought about by pregnancy itself, and at the further reshuffling of emotions and fantasies as a woman develops her new identity as a mother.

Gender Identity

Many forces act together to bring about a sense of identity for each gender. Most people have a mixture of these feelings, but a core identity predominates. This "core gender identity" (the subjective sense of belonging to one sex) appears to develop from the beginning of life, under the influence of both biological and environmental forces.

1 / HORMONAL INFLUENCES. Sex chromosomes determine the differentiation of the ovary and the testes in the developing fetus. Then, at "critical" moments of fetal development, high levels of cir-

culating androgens determine the formation of typical male external genitalia. A dominant level of androgens will give a genetically female fetus male external genitalia. The clitoris will be enlarged at birth and appear to be a penis. The testicular sac is developed, and the baby's physique is masculinized.

John Money and Anke Ehrhardt (1972) have also demonstrated that behavioral and emotional sex differentiation may be influenced in the uterus in the same way. Sex hormones have a direct influence on the brain, affecting the formation of important neurotransmitters as well as fostering the growth of nerve cells. Sex hormones affect the hypothalamus, an area of the brain closely related to behavior regulation. Both male and female animals exposed to high levels of prenatal androgens exhibit mating and other behavior characteristic of the male. In human beings, however, while hormones play a role in the development of external genitalia and, possibly, in brain development, it is the interplay between such biological forces and environmental factors that determines behavior.

2 / ASSIGNED SEX. At birth, a sex is assigned to the baby on the basis of the appearance of the external genitalia. This assignment plays a determinant role in developing gender identity. Money and Ehrhardt have shown this dramatically in their study of children born with external genitalia that differ from their chromosomal sex orientation (Money & Ehrhardt, 1972). This is the case with the female fetuses mentioned above, who were exposed to androgenic hormonal influences and who demonstrated "male" genitalia at birth. These children are raised as boys, and the perceptions and behavior of those around them determine their subjective conviction of being boys. Money and Ehrhardt showed that by age two, gender identity is fixed in the child's mind.

Similarly, a genetically male fetus that is insensitive to the influence of androgens during fetal life will look female at birth, with a vagina and the external characteristics of a female. Such children will be raised as girls. From the first, parents will treat them as female, and they will grow up thinking of themselves as female. Only when puberty or infertility leads them to seek medical attention is their true genetic sex discovered. Meanwhile, having thought of themselves as female, they have behaved as such.

These "experiments of nature" demonstrate how powerfully parental and social expectations based on assigned sex can reinforce intrauterine hormonal influences. For these children, childrearing practices are influenced by the appearance of genitalia, and not at all by the genetic sex. Social pressures, role assignment, and parental expectation determine their subjective sense of gender identity and subsequent behavior.

3 / INNATE BEHAVIORAL DIFFERENCES. Although many researchers have tried to differentiate inborn behavioral differences in newborn boys and girls, few differences have been shown consistently. Newborn boys do not exhibit more motor activity than girls, but the quality of their motor behavior may be different. The male infant's motor activity seems to be more vigorous, but short lived in the duration of each motor act, while the same motor behavior is smoother and peaks more slowly in females. While boys tend to show higher levels of irritability, this may be related to a higher incidence of prenatal and birth complications in males (Parmelee & Stern, 1972). Newborn boys seem to look at objects for shorter but more active periods, while newborn girls are slower in buildup of attention, but pay attention for longer periods. Female infants may be more sensitive to touch, taste, and smell and show more oral activity and behavior (Maccoby & Jacklin, 1974; Korner, 1974). While these innate sex differences are less pronounced than individual differences unrelated to sex, they can influence early interaction (Cramer, 1971).

4 / PARENTAL ATTITUDES. From the first recognition (or assignment) of the baby's sexual identity, parents feel differently toward a baby boy and a baby girl. A mother must see parts of herself more easily in a girl and is likely to set the boy up as a counterpart to herself. Fathers cannot help but wish for a male child to identify with, a girl to feel more tenderly about. These unconscious labels determine to some extent how they will treat the new baby. Since our cultures have fostered strong sex-stereotyped behavior for so long, it is almost inevitable that a boy will be played with more vigorously and a girl

will be nurtured more gently. A father is more likely to toss a boy baby into the air; a mother is likely to protect her daughter from such play. Our vocal behavior is also set by past experiences of our own. We are likely to talk softly and soothingly to a girl, to attempt to excite and stimulate a boy with the same words. The rhythm of interaction between parent and child is likely to be low-keyed and slow for a girl, with more dramatic ups and downs and shorter intervals for boys. There is increasing evidence that mothers tend to talk to and to handle girls more than they do their boy babies. These labelled behaviors are so deeply ingrained in all of us by our own parents' handling that we are unlikely to be able to change them by conscious determination. How parents feel about maleness and femaleness will have a powerful influence on gender identity, and will be transmitted to the infant in subtle ways through every interaction. Identification with her mother's behavior toward her and a father's participation in a little girl's nurturant behavior may reinforce her wish to become a mother in later life.

5 / BODILY SENSATIONS AND IMAGERY. The developing infant's sensations—especially around the genitals—may influence the psychic concept of the self belonging to one sex or the other. Since boys' genitals are more exposed and more available to self-handling as well as to handling by the caregiver, the early experiences of exploration, masturbation, and of valuing one's genitalia can lead to more exhibitionism and externalizing of sexuality in the male. In the female, privacy, wonder at her genitalia and its meaning and value, and internalizing of sensation are more likely. These differences in sensual experience based on differences in the sexual characteristics of the body will deepen and grow throughout life and continue to influence gender identity. A girl's questions about what her genitalia and breasts are expected to do will recur often as she grows up. When she reaches the age of menstruation, these questions become heightened all over again. Her unseen and untested reproductive organs will be woven into her fantasies of pregnancy. Robert Stoller has described these fantasies as vital to a female's development of her identity and argues for the concept of primary femininity (Stoller, 1976). In his view, a girl develops a feminine identity from early infancy. This notion of

the primacy of feminine identity has altered Freudian theories of penis envy. In Freud's view, a girl sought to replace what she did not have, the penis, by using her body to generate a baby. Females needed the material evidence of the intactness of their bodies that came from creating a child. A healthy baby became reassuring proof that a woman's internal organs were productive and healthy and resolved her "inevitable" penis envy. Freud also pointed out that a little girl's fantasies about having a baby of her own allow her to imagine herself the equal of her all-powerful, life-giving mother. These assumptions of early psychoanalytic theory were generated in a sexist society which not only segregated male from female psychodynamics, but interpreted female psychology from the point of view of a woman's longing to be male. Until the psychoanalyst Helene Deutsch wrote her two-volume analysis *The Psychology of Women*, little actual attention was devoted to woman's psychological development. In her volumes, the emphasis is still on the woman's envy of the dominant male. Not until fairly recently have analysts begun to look for a "feminine core identity" in young girls' development which is not determined by "penis envy." Bodily sensations and the imagery of the female child form the early foundations. Much later, the psychological work done during pregnancy and the early adjustment to the baby will fulfill the nurturant aspect of this evolving identity.

The Wish for a Child

A woman's desire for a baby is fueled by many different motives and drives. In any individual woman, it would be impossible to tease all these apart. However, to give a sense of the power and complexity of this desire, and to help in understanding the turmoil of pregnancy, we will attempt to identify some of the most important of these ingredients. They include identification, the fulfillment of various narcissistic needs, and attempts to recreate old ties in the new relationship to the child.

1 / IDENTIFICATION. All women have experienced some form of being mothered. As a baby girl is nurtured, she is likely to engender

the fantasy of becoming the nurturer rather than the nurtured. As her own autonomy develops, she will begin to assume the postures of women who are close to her. She will learn by imitation how mother figures behave. Those around her are likely to delight in her imitations, reinforcing them, and strengthening her unconscious identification with her mother and mothering figures.

Early in the second year, a toddler will cuddle a doll or a toy animal. She will hold the "baby" close to her left breast, nurturingly, as her mother has done. As she cuddles it, she will rock it gently, look down into its face with soft eyes, a receptive expression, and a crooning voice, as if she expected the doll to look up at her and to croon back. As she walks around with "her baby," she walks taller. Her gait becomes more adult, with more certain steps. A toddler's feet are generally wide apart and tentative at times as she explores her world, but when she picks up her beloved toy, she becomes the adult she is imitating. Her gestures, her rhythms, her facial and vocal behavior could not have been taught to her. She has absorbed them by imitation, through her own experiences of being cuddled and carried and by identification with her mother or other mothering figures to whom she has been exposed. It is no coincidence that this behavior peaks in the second year, coinciding with the toddler's thrust toward autonomy. As her need to be on her own alternates with her desire to be treated like a baby, she acts out each of these roles: the independent mother and the helpless baby. When asked to name the "baby" she is carrying, she is most likely to name it after herself. As the second and third years progress, the words she uses for the baby will express the ambivalences of her developing identity—at one time, the "good baby" she wants to be and at another, the "bad baby" she also wants to be. As her identity evolves, her nurturant play makes clear that she is incorporating important parts of her mother.

By the age of five or six, a girl may begin to deny this nurturant role from time to time. She may begin to identify with more masculine behaviors, to disavow any desire to play with dolls or a "baby," and to prefer trucks or climbing. In our present society with its trend toward unisex treatment of small children, we are likely to see girls who will only wear trousers, or, given an audience, who stagger around with the "macho" gait often adopted by little boys. But, often, more nurturant play is likely to reappear when girls are alone together, or with their mothers.

2 / THE WISH TO BE COMPLETE AND OMNIPOTENT. Among the narcissistic motives that fuel the wish for a child are the wish to maintain an idealized view of oneself as complete and omnipotent, the wish to duplicate or mirror oneself, and the wish to fulfill one's ideals. We use the term "narcissistic" to refer to this work of developing and maintaining a self-image and also to the degree of investment in that image. Narcissistic work is expressed in psychic life by fantasies, among which is the fantasy of being complete and omnipotent. One of the basic postulates of the psychoanalytic theory of narcissism is that there is a tendency to gratify these fantasies of completeness and omnipotence, and that on this gratification is built a human being's ultimate sense of self. This tendency will be in continuous interplay with opposing tendencies, such as the wish for object-relationships, objects representing essentially what is not the self and what is separate from it. The need to be omnipotent is also in conflict with sexual drives, with the need for stimulation from others, and with acknowl-edgement of reality, since we need others to fulfill our needs and are constantly confronted with our insufficiencies and incompleteness. These opposing forces create conflicts that can be solved only by compromise. The kinds of compromise will be determined by the choices of investments, of love objects, of interests and pursuits. In this way, conflict is a main force behind development, creating oppor-tunities for new relationships, for new functions, for new solutions (whether normal or pathological).

The desire to be complete is fulfilled both by the condition of pregnancy and by a child. For some women, the wish to be pregnant predominates: pregnancy offers an opportunity to be full, to be com-plete, to experience the body as potent, productive. Pregnancy makes up for feelings of emptiness and for concerns about the body's being incomplete. This pregnancy wish is already seen in the play of small children. Girls *and* boys try to portray a pregnancy by inflating their abdomens with pillows or by puffing out their stomachs. Abdominal pain, stool retention, or difficulties in gastrointestinal function may be an unconscious but related part of this identification with the adult role of pregnancy.

The narcissistic wish to complete oneself through a *child* is more differentiated: the mother will view the desired child first as an extension of her own self, as an appendage to her body; the child bolsters her body image, giving it an added dimension which can be proudly displayed.

3 / THE DESIRE FOR FUSION AND ONENESS WITH ANOTHER. Along with the wish to be complete is the fantasy of symbiosis, of fusion of oneself and the child. Together with this wish for oneness with the child is a wish to return to oneness with one's own mother. This desire is a vital phase in normal development, a fundamental fantasy in the maintenance of self-esteem, and an important part of adult love life. The opportunity for gratifying such fantasies of symbiosis during pregnancy makes it a time for dreaming and for revelling in fantasies of union. After birth, the development and maintenance of maternal attitudes of attachment depend on a woman's recapturing these fantasies of oneness with her own mother. The child-to-be holds the promise of a close relationship, a fulfillment of childhood fantasies.

4 / THE WISH TO MIRROR ONESELF IN THE CHILD. Mirroring is a fundamental dimension of narcissism, of the development and maintenance of a healthy self-image. One tends to love one's own reproduced image. A woman's wish for a child is bound to include the hope that she will duplicate herself. This hope keeps alive a sense of immortality: the child will be a living testimony of one's continued existence. This wish for a mirror image extends to ideals and family tradition: the child represents a promise of continuation, an embodiment of these values. The child is seen as the next link in a long chain that unites each parent with his or her own parents and ancestors. The power of such filiation creates endless expectations: the child will bear the family features, the family name; he or she may assume a trade that characterizes the family, or the name of a famous ancestor. The many rituals surrounding birth, such as baptism, and other traditions strengthen this strong and necessary feeling of identity between children and their families.

The term "mirroring" has generally been used to describe a vital function of the *mother*, that of providing the infant with an image of his or her own self. Infants see on their mothers' faces the effects of their behavior, thus learning about themselves (Winnicott, 1958). Here we use mirroring to refer to a woman's dreams of the perfectly responsive baby who duplicates her ideal self and who will let her know how successful she is as a mother. Any fear of an imperfect baby threatens this self-image and must be repudiated. The wish for a child includes a wish to see reflected on the child the marks of one's creativity and one's capacity to nurture.

5 / FULFILLMENT OF LOST IDEALS AND OPPORTUNITIES. Parents imagine the future child as succeeding wherever they failed. However young they may be, by the time they conceive a child, parents are confronted with limitations and the need for compromise. They know they cannot realize all the dreams of power, beauty, and strength that they entertained in childhood. Young adults must come to grips with the acknowledgement that they are mortal, limited in their options and capacities, and committed to a particular career and life choice.

The child-to-be represents, then, a chance to reverse this series of compromises and limitations. The imaginary child enshrines the parent's ego-ideal. She will be a token of perfection. She will carry on the sorely tried quest for omnipotence. The future child is not only an extension of the mother's body, he or she is an extension of what Kohut (1977) called her *grandiose self-image*. The fantasy child must, therefore, be perfect, must realize every potential dormant in the parents.

Evidence of these wishes abounds, both in everyday experience and in the offices of child psychiatrists. Parents become very involved in a child's looks, motor performances, and, later, scholastic achievements. Values that have been highly prized by the parents may become an "obligation" for the child. The more they have failed, the more they must press the child to succeed. If a mother wishes to be more independent, the infant will have to be autonomous. If a father saw himself as unintelligent, the child will have to go to Harvard. However hidden and grandiose the wish, the future child will have the mission to fulfill it. The reverse of such grandiosity is the inevitable fear that the baby will be a failure. This fear, too, must be suppressed, for it threatens to confirm the parents' own failures all over again.

While it is easy to see how these narcissistic wishes may interfere later with a child's development, it is vital to understand that they are indispensable as well. They prime the mother for attachment: she must see her child as unique, as a potential redeemer of lost hopes, and as all-powerful in fulfilling her wishes. How else could she develop the feeling that her baby is the most precious thing in her life, worthy of all of her attention? How else could she develop what Winnicott has called "primary maternal preoccupation," made up of an otherwise totally unacceptable state of complete altruism and self-denigration?

A mother's tremendous neglect of her own narcissistic needs after birth is possible because *they are now allocated to the baby.* She can disregard them in herself, because the child will gratify them all later on. Mothers can tolerate the tremendous selfishness of babies because in caring for them, they are vicariously catering to their own selfish needs and wishes. The more a mother succeeds in giving to a future child, the more she will fulfill her own wishes and expectations for herself as a successful adult.

Nature gave mothers nine months to entertain doubts, fears, and ambivalence about the child to come. Counterbalancing these feelings is this important fantasy of the perfect child. When the time comes, the baby will offer the mother the certainty that she can create, that her body functions well, and that her unfulfilled ideals and hopes will finally be realized. This hope helps to keep mothers in a state of positive, anticipatory illusion during pregnancy and to protect them against overwhelming doubt and anxiety.

6 / THE WISH TO RENEW OLD RELATIONSHIPS. The wish for a child also includes the wish for a new partner with whom to replay old relationships. A child holds the promise of renewing lost ties, the loves of childhood, and thus will be endowed with attributes of important people in the parent's past. This potential is dramatically illustrated when a child appears to be a replacement for a dead parent, sibling, or friend. It is fascinating to see how often a pregnancy is started after a woman has lost a close relative (Coddington, 1979).

Children always carry the potential for renewing old relationships. In Part IV, we will see how this affects early interaction. The promise of renewing past attachments is an incentive for having a child. The child of fantasy is endowed with magic powers: the power of undoing the old separations, of negating the passage of time and the pain of death and disappearance.

A new child is never a total stranger. Parents see in each baby-to-be a possibility of reviving attachments that may have been dormant for years, a new opportunity to work them through. The feelings contained in these previous relationships will once more be played out, in an effort to resolve them.

In an analytic situation, we would call the child-to-be a transference object, that is, unconscious feelings and relationships of the parents will be transposed onto the child. The process of transference in itself has curing effects, precisely because it revives old, lost bonds. To this extent, we could describe the child to come *as a healer:* he or she holds the promise of re-creating dormant relationships that provided gratification in the past.

7 / THE OPPORTUNITY BOTH TO REPLACE AND TO SEPARATE FROM ONE'S OWN MOTHER. In her wish for a child, a woman experiences a unique form of *double identification.* She will simultaneously identify with her own mother *and* with her fetus, and thus will play out and work through the roles and attributes of both mother and baby, on the basis of past experiences with *her* mother and *herself* as a baby. By bearing a child, she will achieve a long-cherished dream of becoming like her own mother, making her own the magical and envied attributes of creativity. She will now match her all-powerful mother, reversing her submissiveness to her and her sense of inferiority in the oedipal rivalry. She can now become the Earth Mother, realizing her creative potentials, often while her real-life mother is mourning her own lost capacity to bear children. While this may involve guilt, it also provides sources of renewed self-esteem. The wish for a child may also include a wish to restore images of her mother, whom she felt she had damaged because of her envy. A woman may dream of offering her new child to her mother, as a token of gratitude. The reemergence of the relationship to her own mother is a very

intense process during pregnancy. It can be revealed in dreams, in fears, and in a *rapprochement* to her mother. A new relationship can emerge. In cases where this relationship was fraught with heavy conflict, this evolution can be impeded, and the conflict may be intensified.

The yearnings and fantasies just described do not exhaust the varied forces and social pressures that weave together into the wish for a child. But we hope that they are enough to suggest the power and complexity of this wish. The identifications, the healthy narcissistic needs, the longing to re-create old relationships will all energize a woman's capacity to mother and nurture. As they rearrange her dreams and emotions, they set the stage for attachment to the baby.

2

The Dawn of Attachment

The Work of Pregnancy

The nine months of pregnancy offer parents-to-be the opportunity for psychological as well as physical preparation. The psychological preparation, unconscious as well as conscious, is closely interlocked with the physical stages of a woman's pregnancy. After nine months, most parents feel a sense of completion and of readiness. When this time is cut short, as it is in premature labor, parents feel raw and incomplete. When there are physical complications, they endanger the psychological adjustment.

The psychological work of pregnancy may surface as turmoil or anxiety. Emotional withdrawal or regression to a more dependent role in other relationships within the family are common in this period. The prospect of responsibility for a new baby lends a sense of urgency. A parent-to-be needs to withdraw or regress in order to reorganize. The anxiety within both parents may carry them back to the struggles and ambivalent feelings of earlier adjustments. This mobilization of old and new feelings provides the energy necessary in the huge job of adjusting to a new baby.

Both expectant parents and those who care for them must understand the power and ambivalence of the feelings that accompany pregnancy. Prenatal visits, whether with obstetricians, nurses, pediatricians, or, in certain cases, psychiatrists, must allow for the expression of a wide range of positive and negative feelings. In the authors' experience, pregnancy—like many other critical phases of life—is perceived differently by psychiatrists and pediatricians. The former are consulted in cases of crisis and troubled outcome and thus are alert to the potential for neurotic or psychotic problems in pregnancy. The latter are more likely to be impressed by a mother's amazing capacity to rearrange her whole life toward the welfare of her child. By looking at the stages of pregnancy from our dual point of view, we hope to illuminate this remarkable period and also to trace within it the birth of parental attachment.

The work of pregnancy can be seen as three separate tasks, each associated with a stage in the physical development of the fetus. In the first stage, the parents adjust to the "news" of pregnancy, which is accompanied by changes in the mother's body, but not yet by evidence of the actual existence of the fetus. In the second stage, the parents begin to recognize the fetus as a being who will eventually be separate from the mother. This recognition is confirmed at the moment of "quickening," when the fetus first announces its physical presence. Finally, in the third and final stage, the parents begin to experience the coming child as an individual and the fetus contributes to its own *individuation* by distinctive motions, rhythms, and levels of activity.

Stage One: Accepting the News

"I'm having a baby!"

In the past, a mother waited after a missed period for further confirmation of pregnancy from her own body. Changes in the color and sensation of the nipple, "morning sickness," or weariness made the fact of conception gradually more certain. Nowadays, parents are likely to receive the "news" from a physician after a pregnancy test, or even from a chemical reaction in a home pregnancy test.

However and whenever the news comes, parents will know that they have stepped into a new phase of their lives. Their feelings of dependence on their own parents must give way to responsibility. Their one-to-one relationship with each other must evolve into a triangle.

Initially, both parents are often euphoric. But almost at once the euphoria is replaced with a dawning awareness of future responsibility. When conception is planned, this awareness may have been faced already to some extent, but the reality of pregnancy requires a new level of adjustment; soon there will be no turning back.

The "work" of pregnancy now begins in earnest. The prospect of parenthood throws adults back to their own childhood. No adult looks back on childhood as unmitigated pleasure. The struggles of growing up are mobilized each time an adolescent or young adult faces a crisis and, in pregnancy, these struggles are raw once again. The first fantasy of most parents-to-be is one of avoiding the struggles of their own childhood and of becoming perfect parents. "Not one like my mother." "My father tried, but he got everything wrong." "I certainly hope I can do better than they did!" What is it that parents wish to do better? Is it to protect their child from an imperfect world, or from the perceived negative sides of themselves? The latter is the more likely. As we mentioned earlier, all parents hope that they will be able to shield the new infant from their own feelings of inadequacy, or from the perceived failures of their own lives. With this magical wish that their own inadequacies can be conquered, parents-to-be see themselves as completely nurturant, completely positive—ready to create the perfect child.

Behind this fantasy is also ambivalence. At some point, all parents-to-be begin to wonder why they ever let themselves in for such an adjustment. "Do I really want to be a mother, a father? If I don't, have I hurt this baby already? Can I hurt an unborn baby with my fears, my negative feelings?" Especially for a pregnant woman, the depth of the caring involved in this adjustment makes her so vulnerable that her magical thinking about hurting her fetus becomes very real. All pregnant women dream about the possibility of having a defective child. Not only do they dream of all possible aberrations, but in waking, they rehearse what they would do if their child were born handicapped. Any danger to the fetus that they may have read or heard about will be called up at some time during pregnancy. The barrage of information now available about the effects of drugs, food, tobacco, alcohol, or pollution on the developing fetus only exacerbates the fears that universally haunt pregnant women.

In order to overpower such fears and her underlying ambivalence, a mother-to-be must mobilize more and more defenses. She must begin to idealize the infant, to visualize the baby as perfect and as completely wanted. The work of overpowering the negative forces escalates the positive wishes for the baby and for being the perfect parent.

As a pregnant woman struggles through this turmoil of ambivalent emotions, she will be especially available to the support of others. A physician or nurse or friend who is an experienced mother will be accepted readily. An expectant mother often develops a strong transference to any supportive professional at this time. She yearns for understanding of her powerful emotions, for mothering as she prepares to be a mother. Professionals or family members who can accept this temporary dependency on the part of a mother without being overwhelmed will be helping to launch a stronger family.

During this time, many women tend also to withdraw into themselves. The rebalancing of hormones and other physical processes is paralleled by emotional adjustments, and a great deal of time and energy is needed to achieve a new stability. Days may be spent in daydreaming, nights in sorting out strongly ambivalent dreams. When this inner work is successful, a mother can eventually look forward wholeheartedly to her new role. But she may spend a great deal of her own and her family's energy in the attempt. In the process, she will, in all likelihood, withdraw somewhat from her previous relationships. She may even unconsciously blame her husband and others for her condition, even while, simultaneously, feeling a sense of elation. Now and then, she is likely to feel that she has been forced into this role. Such feelings may represent her effort to share or displace responsibility for the overwhelming adjustment, and may also represent a realistic reaction under certain social and economic conditions.

A woman's most immediate task is to accept the "foreign body" now implanted within her. She may experience the embryo as an *intrusion* by her mate, and may temporarily want to withdraw from the man who has impregnated her. Just as her body lowers its defenses against this "foreign body" and comes to accept and shelter it, the mother, too, must come to experience the child-to-be as a benign part of herself.

Often, in an effort to accept her new condition, a woman will turn to her own mother or her mother-in-law. But here, too, she may feel ambivalent. Morning sickness and other physiological symptoms may serve to express the negative side of her ambivalence, while consciously she may be adapting with enthusiasm to her role. All pregnant women face this ambivalence, which surprises and disappoints them. Feelings of helplessness, of inadequacy, may even express themselves in the wish for a spontaneous abortion. While the disappointment and feelings of guilt that accompany either the bleeding of a threatened abortion or the reality of one belie this ambivalence, they are always there. Only gradually does the drive toward motherhood, with all the powerful components that we saw earlier, transform this ambivalence into fuel for the work of pregnancy, into the positive anticipation and energy of the later months.

Stage Two: First Stirrings of a Separate Being

At some point during the fifth month of pregnancy, a mother will feel the first butterfly motions of her baby-to-be. These delicate, stroking sensations will gradually turn into vigorous activity. After the confirmation of pregnancy, the moment of quickening is the next landmark event for expectant parents. This news, too, will be eagerly shared with husband, family, and friends.

Until this moment, mother and baby-to-be are one. Until this first fluttering of life, a mother can entertain the narcissistic image of total fusion with her child. Now, psychologically speaking, the baby has begun to "hatch." The earliest attachment may be said to begin here, for there is now a separate being, the possibility of a relationship. Quickening is the child-to-be's first contribution to the relationship.

When the mother begins to recognize the life of her fetus, she will unconsciously put herself in its place, identify with it. Her fantasies will be based on her infantile relationship to her own mother. Dinorah Pines reported a vivid instance of this two-layered fantasy. One of her patients had a series of dreams in which she became progressively younger as the pregnancy progressed; shortly before birth, she dreamt of herself as a baby sucking at the breast, "thus combining the representation of herself as the mother and as the newborn child" (Pines, 1981). The new concreteness of the baby, supplemented by ultrasound images and the now visible body changes in the mother, brings both a new reality and new fantasies to the pregnancy. The mother can identify with the now evident fetus and also replay her own wishes of fusion and symbiosis with her mother. This fantasized "return to the womb" allows for yet another working through of unfulfilled dependency needs and symbiotic wishes. It is as if—through the mediation of her unborn child—the mother can "plug back into" the rewarding aspects of her early relationships with her mother, refueling and revitalizing herself. Curiously, this resembles the way toddlers dart back to their mothers, finding in that contact new energy to pursue their development toward individuation (Mahler et al., 1975). Pines points out that pregnancy offers mothers a new opportunity for working through separation conflicts, promoting a new phase in their process of disengagement (individuation) from the original symbiotic relationships (Pines, 1981).

This regressive trend can also activate conflict and pathological reactions. It may be experienced as a threat to identity, for it reawakens strong feelings of fusion between the mother and her own mother. If the mother's need for dependency is too great and unfulfilled (in some teenage mothers, for example), she will experience her fetus—and later, her baby—as a rival, and may treat the infant as an envied sibling. In this case, mothering will seem a heavy burden and even a frustration of her own needs. When things go well, however, this regression to symbiotic identification with the baby will lead to renewed psychic energy and also a source of empathic knowledge of what a baby is all about.

Recognition of a father's role helps a mother see the baby as separate from herself. If she remains aware that her pregnancy resulted from an act on the father's part as well as her own, and, ideally, of the father's wish for a child, she will avoid falling prey to the illusion that she alone produced the baby. When a woman chooses single parenthood, and especially when she chooses artificial insemination, these issues may be clouded. A woman who uses a man simply to fertilize her, or uses a sperm bank, is more likely to entertain the illusion that the baby is the result of her own omnipotent creativity. Her fears and doubts, as well as her hopes, will be heightened.

Acknowledging the father's role not only helps a mother-to-be with the job of separating from the fetus, and of differentiating it from her fantasies, but reassures her that she alone will not be responsible for any successes or failures. This can cushion her fears of inadequacy and her anxiety about her new role. If the relationship with the father has been fraught mainly with resentment and conflict, this may be projected onto the child-to-be. But if the relationship is sound, if the father endorses his responsibility as a co-creator and doesn't flee from his role, the mother will have a better chance of recognizing that the child is a separate being, with a separate potential for growth. As we will see later, the wish for a child also holds many promises for the father, thus bolstering his own attachment to his future offspring.

The beginning of fetal movement, and the recognition that the baby is a reality, heighten the mother's self-questioning. Periods of depression and elation may come over her unpredictably. Her fantasies about the baby become more specific. During this period, she may begin to dream about the perfect boy or the perfect girl. Her preference for one or the other may begin to surface, or she may repress her real wishes for fear of endangering the fetus. The traditional belief in the "evil eye" and the superstitious rituals surrounding pregnancy are expressions of the universal desire for a perfect baby and the associated fear that the mother will do something to endanger the fetus. So concerned are mothers-to-be with their own struggles that intelligent women often express surprise and gratification when told that all women worry during pregnancy.

The rehearsal for an abnormal infant continues during this period. By the time the infant is born, a woman will have worried about every possible kind of problem her baby may present. She will have rehearsed in her dreams and fantasies what she must do if she is presented with a Down syndrome baby, or a cerebral palsied infant, or one who embodies any of the abnormalities that she has heard of in either her own or her husband's family. Hence, a premature or an impaired infant comes less as a surprise to a mother than as a disappointment for her lack of success in all the effort she has made during pregnancy. She will have rehearsed and even mobilized forces for helping her deal with the failure, but she must still face her grief at losing the "perfect" baby she dreamed of as a reward for her work.

The experiences of diagnostic amniocentesis and of ultrasound techniques for visualizing the fetus have a complex effect on this work of adjusting to a baby and a new role. Although mothers (and fathers) profess a hunger to know the sex of the baby (which can be determined by amniocentesis), a surprising number (about 40 percent) do not wish to be told. The pregnant woman's curiosity and amazement at seeing her baby visualized on a screen in the third month is accompanied both by awe and by a fear of looking too deeply below the surface. The work of adjusting to her ambivalent feelings and fears about the fetus has just begun. She is not ready to face the baby as a reality yet. Many first-time expectant mothers who watch the screen on which the fetal movements are being visualized express mixed emotions. They see the fetus as inadequate, fearsome, or incomplete. They turn away from the screen as if it were too frightening or overwhelming. "Is that a real baby?" "He looks so tiny and helpless." They find unbelievable the obstetrician's reassurance that the fetus is normal and need to hear it over and over. Until they themselves feel the fetus's movement in the fifth month, this poorly visualized, shadowy creature is likely to be seen as unreal, vulnerable, fearsome. Such feelings are a reflection of the mother's struggle with her own ambivalence. She needs more time to get ready for the baby.

Elizabeth Keller, a Child Development Fellow at Boston Children's Hospital Medical Center, compared mothers and fathers who were told the sex of the baby after amniocentesis or ultrasound with parents-to-be who didn't know the sex of their baby until birth (Keller, 1981). One might expect attachment to, and early personification of, the newborn baby to be enhanced by foreknowledge of the baby's sex. Not at all. The parents who knew the baby's sex took longer to personify and recognize the individuality of the baby after birth. It seems there may be a protective system at work—protecting the parents and the baby from a too-early attachment. The work of attachment to an individual baby takes time and early attempts to consolidate it may be rejected. Once again, this points up the problem of adjusting to a premature infant, for whom this work of attachment has been foreshortened.

Stage Three: Learning about the Baby-to-Be

During the last few months of pregnancy, parents see the fetus as increasingly separate and increasingly real. Names are often chosen during this time, houses are rearranged to accommodate the baby, and plans are made for leave from work and for childcare. As parents muse about names, select baby clothes, or paint the nursery, they begin to personify the fetus. During this same time, the fetus is now also playing its role. As fetal motion and levels of activity begin to fall into cycles and patterns, the mother can recognize and start to rely on them. Her response can be seen as a very early form of interaction. She will begin to read into these patterns, giving the baby-to-be a temperament, a personality, sometimes even assigning a sex (Sadovsky, 1981). A mother with older children will compare the behavior of this fetus with that of her earlier ones. She will label these perceived characteristics "quiet," "aggressive," "like a dancer," "like a football player," and so forth, giving meaning to them in the process. It is as if the mother needed to personify the fetus so that he or she will not be a stranger at birth.

Many of the observations of pregnant women over the centuries are being confirmed by modern ultrasound. In order to understand the rich variety of fetal activity to which parents are responding as they endow their unborn baby with an individual personality, we will look briefly at what is now known about fetal development.

1 / FETAL MOVEMENTS. The full repertoire of movements of the newborn baby can be seen before birth, in the fetus (Milani Comparetti, 1981). A great deal of motor development takes place during pregnancy, preparing for adaptation after birth. For instance, breathing movements are now known to be present as early as 13–14 weeks. These rapid, irregular breathing movements are associated with low-voltage, high-frequency "electrocortical" activity in the brain (Boddy et al., 1974). Fetal movements have been the object of particular attention, because they can be studied by noninvasive methods and because they have diagnostic value. As an extreme example, marked decrease and cessation of fetal movements indicate impending fetal death. Fetal movements are affected by various agents: alcohol, tobacco, sedatives, maternal emotional stress.

Fetal movements evolve in intensity and form during pregnancy.*

*Because of new imaging techniques, this chronology is being refined all the time.

Around 6–7 weeks, smooth, circular movements of the body are seen. These movements become more complex as time goes on.

Around 13–14 weeks, flexion and extension movements, opening and closing of the hands, swallowing, and breathing movements are present. Mechanical stimuli produce a startle response, and the fetus's ability to habituate to stimuli can be demonstrated.

Around 15 weeks, a fetus will suck on its fingers.

Between 16 and 20 weeks, mothers first perceive fetal movements.

Around 20–21 weeks, one can see isolated segmental movements of fingers, foot, eyelids.

Around 26–28 weeks, a stimulation by sound will induce a startle response or trunk and head rotation, and an increase in heart rate (Janniruberto & Tajani, 1981).

There can be great variations from one fetus to another. While recordings have shown that the mean number of daily fetal movements increases from about 200 in the 20th week to a maximum of 575 in the 32nd week (then to a mean of 282 at delivery), the number in an individual fetus can range from 50 to 956.

Mothers' reports concur with objective measures of fetal movements in 80–90 percent of cases. Fetal movements are affected by various stimuli, increasing after exposure to sound, and also after light stimulation. Ninety percent of fetuses move more during ultrasound exposure. Touch and pressure on the mother's abdomen also trigger an increase.

2 / CYCLES OF ACTIVITY. The states of consciousness observable in the newborn—quiet, alert, sleep, REM sleep, and so on (see Part II)—are observable in the fetus. These states appear to occur in cycles. During maternal sleep, a rhythmic rest–activity cycle of 40–60 minutes was observed over twenty years ago (Sterman, 1967). A rhythmic rest–activity cycle of 40–80 minutes has been noted more recently, in both awake and sleeping mothers (Granat et al., 1979). A marked circadian rhythm of fetal movements has been shown as well (Roberts et al., 1977). This periodicity in fetal activity was not found to be correlated with gestational age, nor with fetal sex, birth weight, or with assessment of newborn behavior such as the Apgar score. Rather,

it seems to be connected to intrinsic physiologic properties of the fetus, and may be affected by maternal activity.

In the later months of pregnancy, any woman can tell what times of day her fetus will be active. Most women predict that peaks of fetal movement will occur at times of inactivity for them. Although this association has been attributed to their available awareness during rest periods, there is reason to believe that the observation is correct. The fetus may begin to "adjust" to the mother's rest–activity by reciprocal activity and inactivity. When she is active, it will be quiet. When she is quiet, it will begin to "climb" the uterine walls. The lactic acid of muscular activity, which peaks as the mother rests after activity, has been thought to stimulate fetal movements. A fetus's predictability and adjustment to its mother's rhythms become further evidence for the mother of his or her existence as a person, a person who can "adjust to her," as well as to the pressures of her life.

When asked to keep a record of a fetus's rest and activity, mothers can make extremely accurate predictions after two or three days of conscious attention to these cycles. Such regular, organized cycles dominate fetal behavior. Distinctions between states of activity in the fetus become more and more evident to the mother. In the last trimester, women can tell when their baby is in (1) *deep sleep* (quiet and essentially unresponsive to outside stimuli with, at most, an occasional jerk of an extremity), (2) *light sleep* (quiet, but with bursts of repetitive movements of the extremities, hiccoughs, and, occasionally, slower thrusts of the arms or legs, or trunk), (3) *active awake* ("climbing" the uterine wall, with bursts of thrusting, vigorous movement), and (4) *alert but quiet* (apparently waiting and receptive to external stimuli, with smoother, more directed movements, often in response to external events).

3 / RESPONSES TO STIMULI. Of the species that are helpless at birth (altricial), humans are the only one in which all the sensory systems are capable of functioning before birth (Gottlieb, 1971). Immature neural tissue functions before nerve-ending receptors are present, before myelinization is complete. Stimulation apparently plays a role in the maturation of sensory organs. This maturation appears to

be accelerated or slowed down by increased stimulation or lack of stimulation, respectively.

As early as day 49 after fertilization, the fetus will bend its head away from the site of stimulation when the face is touched lightly near the mouth. Sometime between day 90 and day 120, the so-called "righting reflexes," in which the fetus attempts to keep its head in balance, begin to appear. At about six months, the fetus is capable of responding to auditory stimulation. At this time, fetal heart rate changes in response to sound stimulation have been recorded.

In the last trimester, there are discrete evoked responses of the fetal cortex that can be measured with noninvasive techniques (Rosen & Rosen, 1975). Electrodes applied directly to the fetal scalp after rupture of the membranes demonstrate a rich range of responses to sound, touch, and visual stimuli. Observing whether the fetus is able to habituate to these is one way of measuring fetal well-being; if the fetus keeps on responding with no change, it may be under stress (Hon & Quilligan, 1967). Using maternal reports and confirming them with fetal behavior during ultrasound monitoring, we [TBB] became convinced that the fetus in the last trimester responds reliably to visual, auditory, and kinesthetic stimulation (Brazelton, 1981a).

When a bright light is shone on the mother's abdomen in the fetus's line of vision, it will startle. If a softer light is used in the same position, the infant turns actively but smoothly toward it. A loud noise next to the abdomen will also produce a startle, while if a soft noise is used, the baby will turn toward it. When stimuli are offered while the fetus is in a quiescent state resembling sleep, the responses are less predictable, more subdued, and the fetus habituates to them more rapidly. These differentiated responses to external stimuli can be perceived as signals by the mother. If these signals coincide with her own responses, they may initiate the beginnings of synchrony between mother and child.

While in the womb, the fetus is being preconditioned to maternal sleep–wake rhythms and to the mother's style of reactivity. Not only have newborn babies experienced their mother's rhythms in the womb, but auditory and kinesthetic cues from her are now "familiar." No wonder a newborn already prefers a female to a male voice at birth (Brazelton, 1979). The fetus's reaction patterns are shaped and made ready for "appropriate" cues after birth.

Meanwhile, the parents are learning about their baby. Toward the end of pregnancy, mothers report more and more differentiated responses. They say that their babies react one way to a Bach concert—with smooth, rhythmic kicks—and an entirely different way to rock music—sharp, jerky movements. When they announce this, they are proudly stating that the baby is an aware, competent being already. The baby is not only aware of the environment, he or she is demonstrating a readiness to meet it. Parents now begin to see their babies as strong enough to survive in the outside world. The more parents can imagine an unborn child as a competent, interacting individual, the more confident they can be about the baby's ability to survive labor and delivery.

As a mother gets closer to delivery, however, her fears about having damaged her infant once again weigh more heavily. In fact, so raw are these fears that few women can even speak of them in the last month. They *must* be repressed or they can become overwhelming. To balance these fears, the parents continue to personify their child. The fetus's characteristic movements and responses become of heightened value in demonstrating its integrity. The more a mother can see her unborn baby as a separate person, the more protected she feels from her own imagined inadequacy and incompetence. Mothers who can see their child-to-be as strong and resilient may even perceive the child as an ally in the difficult task of delivery.

The Task at Birth

During the forty weeks of pregnancy, the growth of the fetus is paralleled by a progressive development in the mother's image of the baby. As we have seen, this image is based both on narcissistic needs and yearnings and also on perceptions of the fetus's development: quickening, activity, patterns of response. Thus, when birth occurs, the mother has long been prepared to cope with (1) the shock of the anatomical separation, (2) the adaptation to a particular infant, and (3) a new relationship which will combine her own needs and fantasies and those of a separate being. Not only is pregnancy a period of rehearsal and anticipation, it is also a phase during which old relationships have a chance to be reshuffled, as well as a continuing confrontation between wish fulfillment and the acknowledgement of reality.

When the moment of delivery arrives, the mother must be ready to create a new bond, and also to be amazingly available to enter that condition Winnicott described as a form of "normal disease," a state of total involvement in which mothers become able to "step into the shoes of the baby" (Winnicott, 1986). Among the formidable tasks that face the mother at birth are:

1. An abrupt ending of the sense of fusion with the fetus, of the fantasies of completeness and omnipotence fostered by pregnancy;

2. Adapting to a new being who provokes feelings of strangeness. Michel Soulé has described these as feelings of *unheimlichkeit* (Soulé & Kreisler, 1983);

3. Mourning for the imaginary (perfect) child, and adapting to the characteristics of her specific baby;

4. Coping with fears of harming the helpless child (often experienced in new mothers, for instance, as the fear of drowning the baby in the bath);

5. Learning to tolerate and *enjoy* the enormous demands made on her by the total dependency of the baby; in particular, she has to withstand the baby's intense oral cravings, and gratify them *with her body*.

All this represents a major psychological upheaval. It is as if a new mother must go through a complete "shake-up"; her previously held positions, her attachments, her image of herself are all subject to change. So pervasive is this upheaval, in fact, that it can resemble a transient pathological state. The result is a new maternal identification, a focusing of her affections, and an ability to acknowledge and adjust to an inescapable new reality (Brazelton, 1981b).

During this time, others (husband, family, doctor) can play a vital supportive role. For instance, a prenatal visit with the future pediatrician can be of great help. Young parents are particularly eager to establish a positive relationship with a benevolent figure interested in the future child's welfare (Bibring et al., 1961). Even one short visit will do much to allay parental fears and to prepare for mutual cooperation in later routine visits. One of the unconscious factors often involved here is a desire for the physician to allay a mother's guilt by "allowing" her to have a child, reassuring her that her body is capable of carrying and delivering a healthy fetus.

Apart from her pediatrician or an understanding obstetrician, a mother, of course, has two important allies as she summons her energies to face these tasks. As we will see in the next chapter, the father of the baby is experiencing many upheavals, some different, some parallel to her own. And as we will see in Part II, their newborn baby will be a powerful force in their new lives, capable from the start of contributing to the growing relationship.

3

Attachment in Fathers-to-Be

As it is with women, a father's attachment to his baby is influenced by his own experience in childhood. In infancy, a boy may first identify with his mother, identifying with her childbearing and nurturing capacities. She seems all-powerful to him, the source of all gratification, stimulation, and care. Wishing to become as powerful as she, he identifies with her. Many boys simulate pregnancy with pillows and tenderly act out their capacity for childcare with dolls. In this make-believe play, they develop a core of identification with their mothers. Meanwhile, they are also beginning to identify with their fathers. Out of this interplay of opposing forces, a boy's identity develops. A young boy must integrate his core maternal identification with his growing identification with masculine behavior. The solution of this dilemma, the "paradox of masculinity" (Bell, 1984), will shape both his gender identity and his future fatherhood. Many resolutions are possible, including difficulties with sexual identity or a stern refusal to acknowledge any feminine attributes, as in the "macho" complex. A balanced resolution, however, makes possible a boy's future acceptance of his nurturing role, a capacity both to identify with a woman's pregnancy and to contribute to childrearing as a father. The conflict leads to adaptive solutions, preparing a boy for his role as a caring father.

Traditional fathers from our past have often been described as "aloof," absent, and not showing emotion (Bell, 1984). Whether this has been really true or not, in the past most boys remembered their fathers as non-nurturing. Has this been an assigned role or a real observation? Have fathers in the past been more nurturing than reported? Have their so-called feminine inclinations and behaviors been merely shielded by an aloof or distant surface? Have there always been hidden nurturing forces in men which men, until recently, have not been permitted to express? Could the fathers of the present display such evident positive attachment to their pregnant wives and to their infants had they not perceived models in their fathers as well as in their mothers? In all likelihood, their fathers' model for nurturing played some role, though in no way parallel to that of mothers. Will this change in the future, or does this imbalance serve a lasting purpose?

The main developmental task of the boy, in the gradual achievement of fatherhood, is to relinquish his wish to be just like his mother and to bear children as she does. Not all men accomplish this task. Some persist in envying women's childbearing capacities and never accept that they must be excluded from this process. Unconsciously, they compete with their wives, exhibiting symptoms similar to the *couvade* of primitive tribes (in which men exhibit symptoms of pregnancy and labor), or else flee from these wishes by absenting themselves during their wife's pregnancy. Men who can successfully sublimate these wishes may feel renewed creativity, or increased professional productivity during their wife's pregnancy. Such rechanneled wishes may even become the incentive for choosing a career in a childcare profession.

The Wish for a Child in Men

A man's wish for a child, first grounded, as we said, in the desire of the boy to be like his mother, was described by Freud in the story of little Hans, a five-year-old boy who imagined that he too could bear his father's child. Other determinants, similar to those we described in women, are active. The narcissistic wish to be complete and omnipotent by producing and identifying with one's child is universal, as is the wish to reproduce (mirror) one's own image. This is certainly one reason why fathers are likely to prefer to have a boy. In India, the very name for the son, "putra," means "one who delivers from the hell called put" (Kakar, 1982). In the *Mahabarata*, one of the

34

fundamental sacred texts in India, it is said that the father himself is born as the son, and in the placing of his own seed in the womb, he has conceived his own self. This wish to reproduce one's own sex is stronger in men than in women; it may reveal a greater need in men to bolster and confirm their masculine identity, which is so constantly challenged. In one author's experience [BC]), nearly all children who are referred to psychotherapy for evaluation of cross-gender behavior are boys.

For fathers, sons are more likely to become the carriers of the father's unfulfilled ambitions than daughters. Fathers are more likely to be concerned about their sons' achievements, their progress in the areas of motor development, cognition skills, and scholastic achievement. A son often has the mission of shoring up a father's doubts about his masculine self-image. This is why fathers become so anxious when they see signs of weakness, insecurity, and lack of drive in their sons. Such weaknesses seem to reflect, in an amplified and socially visible form, the father's insecurity about himself. Possibly contributing to this strong identification is a man's deep-seated feeling that he can influence his son's masculine identification but not his daughter's outcome.

A woman, as we have seen, longs for a child to quiet doubts about her own fertility and reproductive capacity. The equivalent, in a man, is expressed in doubts about his potency, his power to make his wife pregnant. An extension of this is the father's need to raise a boy who shows all the signs of future manhood. While these stereotypes about sex roles are changing, the wish of fathers to duplicate their masculinity and power in their sons is still strong.

Fathers, like mothers, also need to renew old relationships with important persons of their past, and they expect their children to provide this link. Fathers wish to ensure the continuity of their lineage, "our only path to immortality," said Freud in *The Interpretation of Dreams* (Freud, 1955). Freud named his own sons after men he admired and loved; beloved teachers and admired historical figures. The practice of giving one son the first name that the father himself inherited from his father is a testimony of the powerful drive to maintain filiation and to find in one's child the loved attributes of one's ancestors.

A man's wish for a child is also influenced by his old oedipal rivalry;

not only does having a child provide a way to equal one's father, but raising him provides an opportunity to do better than one's father. Each new father resolves to be a better father. Today, he turns to the abundant literature on child raising to provide himself with the technical know-how of fatherhood, in the hope that his informed fatherhood will be totally new, surpassing past methods.

All the threads described above weave together into the incentive to have a child, stirring new conflicts as well as offering new solutions to old conflicts. A wife's pregnancy is an important time for the consolidation of a man's identity. With it will come all the anxiety and self-questioning that besiege mothers. Each stage of pregnancy is a new challenge, as it is for women.

A Father's Feelings during Pregnancy

When a father first learns that his wife has conceived, a flood of different emotions assails him, some joyous, some anxious, many conflicting. Both the strength and the nature of these emotions will come as a surprise to most fathers.

One of the first reactions of the new father-to-be is a feeling of exclusion. Even though, when a child is wanted, both husband and wife share in the euphoric announcements to friends and relatives, the expectant father will soon feel upstaged. Not only does his wife begin to focus her attention—her energy and concern—on the unborn child, but she herself becomes the center of others' attention. Everyone asks about her mood and health; no one cares about his. Those around a pregnant woman are drawn to take care of her, and she expects the same solicitous concern from him.

This sense of exclusion is complicated by a father's feeling of responsibility for the pregnancy. He feels displaced, but at the same time, he feels that he has only himself to blame. Whatever his wife experiences, nausea or fatigue, appears to him to be his own fault. He takes responsibility to an irrational degree.

Now that fathers are more involved in planning for a baby—participating in prenatal visits to the obstetrician and the pediatrician, for instance—a natural competition between new mothers and fathers begins early. Competition for the nurturing role is added to competition with the unborn baby for each other. This kind of competition can be alarming, unless both parents understand that it is a natural, and also a necessary, part of their growing attachment to their future child. Not only do these feelings stir up attachment, but they can strengthen rather than weaken the parents' bond to one another.

As the pregnant mother begins to make her inner adjustments, to slip into the fantasy world we have just described, the expectant father has his own adjustment to make. Will he be a good provider? Will he be able to free up time from his career, to be a nurturing father as well as a strong, dependable support for his wife? All these doubts, this turmoil, emerge when pregnancy is first acknowledged and help to prepare the father for his changing identity.

While women cannot flee from the facts of pregnancy, fathers have more leeway in the extent to which they will get involved. They can choose to withdraw, ignoring what is going on, while women have to submit to the physical process of pregnancy. Some fathers may be so shaken up by a pregnancy that they prefer to distance themselves from it, running to extramarital affairs, developing alcoholism, or sexual impotence. This kind of acting out may be based on the reawakening of bisexual conflicts. It also reflects another important force—the man's sense of being displaced. A prospective father may experience the child to come as a rival who robs him of his wife, the way his father or a sibling had robbed him of his mother in his own childhood. Since, as we pointed out earlier, a boy first identifies with his own mother, and then must repudiate this identification, these feelings are likely to be revived. For all these reasons, men are bound to have ambivalence about the child-to-be.

James Herzog described expectant fathers as falling into two groups (Herzog, 1982). One group acknowledged their feelings about the arrival of a first child by becoming empathic with and invested in their wives. The other group was made up of fathers who expressed little awareness of their feelings. The "attuned" men felt compelled, toward the end of the first trimester, to feed—in fantasy—the mother and the fetus. Making love was imagined as a form of nutriment to their pregnant wives, and somehow nurturing the growing fetus. Less attuned men complained that their sexual needs were not being fulfilled.

By saying things like "I am hungry for it all the time," they betray their own wish to be fed, in competition with the fetus. The expectant fathers were thus divided between those who nurtured their wives and those who felt disappointment at not being nurtured themselves and who were jealous of their wives and the baby.

As pregnancy progresses into the second trimester, the father-to-be is likely to show an increased concern with his own body. His unconscious identification with his wife intensifies, sometimes leading to bisexual and hermaphroditic fantasies. This shift again provides an opportunity for the reshuffling of forces that contribute to his masculine identity (Gurwitt, 1976).

In many Third World cultures, this increased identification with the pregnant wife is expressed in the *couvade* syndrome mentioned earlier. Men simulate the process of delivery, going through its various phases and manifestations. Those around them treat them as if they were suffering; they are catered to. Through this "play," they dramatize their envy of the procreating woman and their disappointment at being left out. As they take onto themselves the pain of the laboring woman, they participate in her process and are seen to be protecting her. More benign forms of this identification are found in the developed world, in the form of various aches and pains. Expectant fathers experience more nausea, vomiting, gastrointestinal disturbances, and toothaches than nonexpectant men.

Such turmoil and symptoms show convincingly that a man's wish to be pregnant, to be like the mother and the wife, is reawakened during pregnancy. When it takes the form of pains and symptoms, it is because this identification is unconsciously full of conflict and cannot be expressed. As men repudiate their feminine side, they feel angry at the pregnancy. Once they resolve these conflicts, they are able to feel an empathic identification with their pregnant wives.

In the last part of the pregnancy, fathers tend to sort out their relationship to their own fathers. Just as women tend to plunge back into their early relationships to their mothers, fathers need to turn to their own fathers (in fantasy or in reality) to bolster their emerging parental role. This anchoring of new roles with old childhood models is a theme that comes up again as parental identity unfolds during pregnancy. A man who enjoys *a solid bond with his father is protected against fears of becoming too much like his mother.*

In the third trimester, fathers, like mothers, experience anxieties about the future baby's health. They too have doubts that their offspring was adequately protected against their ambivalence, their rivalry, and their resentment. They feel anxiety about the future baby's normalcy and completeness and are in need of assurance. A father who "flees" at the end of pregnancy will do so either in reality (abandoning the family) or—more frequently—simply by showing emotional indifference or lack of involvement. This turning away is a defense against feelings of hostility against his wife—whom he experiences as preferring the baby—or against unresolved fears of identification with her.

These feelings are acknowledged by many fathers:

I began to think at this point that I might really be harboring some secret anger toward the baby. Before she was born, I used to joke in rather sadistic ways about birth defects and about child abuse, and finally my wife asked me why I did this. I came to realize that it was my way of ridding myself through humor of the fantasies which I carried around and couldn't verbalize in any other manner. . . . Basically, I have come to understand that these were fairly primitive feelings against the baby for displacing me. For a man, having a baby entails being denied a certain sense of specialness, and it means losing out as the center of attention (Bell, 1984).

The coming of a new member of the family, the baby, forces the father to accept the transition from a dual relationship to a triangular one. This awakens feelings of being the left out, third party, as we all experience in childhood when confronted by the intimacy of our parents, or when a sibling is born.

The "Absent" Father

Despite great advances in involving fathers during pregnancy and delivery, the forces that have historically excluded fathers are still strong. They are based on cultural recognition of fathers' natural ambivalence, as well as the fathers' own powerful doubts about being able to be protective and nurturant. We are gradually seeing that those factors can be modified by programs fostering fathers' involvement in pregnancy and delivery, including childbirth education, Lamaze classes, prenatal visits, and family support programs (Samaraweera & Cath, 1982). Nevertheless, we must recognize that the lingering traces of exclusion which fathers still experience have deep roots in widespread historical and cross-cultural practice. The "gatekeeping" seen even in working mothers today still serves to keep fathers at a distance.

In only 4 percent of sample cultures is a "regular, close relationship" apparent between fathers and infants (West & Konner, 1982). Strict separations are enforced between men and women during labor and in the days following delivery in many cultures; in 79 percent of world societies, the father sleeps apart from mother and infant during the nursing period (Hahn & Paige, 1980).

Apart from the employment of the majority of mothers in our society, childbirth education groups and medical personnel are also important agents of change. They can have a powerful future impact in determining the new models for fatherhood, in promoting more active participation, and in enhancing nurturing proclivities in men.

The Father's Role in Supporting His Pregnant Wife

The process of pregnancy, the delivery, and early attachment is strongly influenced by the father's attitudes. The husband's emotional support during pregnancy contributes to his wife's successful adaptation to pregnancy, and the presence of the husband during labor and delivery is associated with reduced need in pregnant women for pain-relieving medication and with a more positive labor experience (Parke, 1986). A mother's competence in breast- or bottle-feeding is also influenced by her husband's attitude (Pedersen et al., 1982). The nature of marital relationships during the first trimester of pregnancy is strongly predictive of the mother's postpartum adjustment (Grossman et al., 1980). Perhaps most significant is the correlation between a mother's report of the father's involvement during pregnancy and clinical observations of the extent of her own involvement with the child throughout the first four years (Barnard, 1982). Many other more recent studies confirm clinical observations, not to mention everyday intuition: a father-to-be's presence and loving support help a woman develop her maternal role. As modern families rarely allow for the maintenance of the support system based on the extended family (the mother's own mother, aunts, etc.), fathers play an increased role in the development and maintenance of maternal capacities. If the father also stays involved in a close love relationship with his wife, this will help prepare her to renounce the gratification of an exclusive attachment to her baby.

In turn, of course, fathers' involvement in pregnancy and delivery reinforces their own identity as participative, active agents, lessening the likelihood of their exclusion (Barnard, 1982). They are preparing for a more direct role after the baby's birth. Their continuing presence is thus rewarding in two ways: their own bond with their wives is maintained, and they begin to taste the joy of fatherhood.

Giving Fathers Their Due

Psychoanalysis has been concerned with a fantasized or mythical father: the bearer of the law, the forceful spokesman of reality, the holder of the knife that cuts the umbilical cord and threatens castration. Though the father could become an object of love (the negative Oedipus), little was said about a primary preoedipal infant love for the father. Even less was said about fathers showing positive, early attachments to the infant. Only mothers were studied—psychoanalytically—in dyadic love relationship with infants. More recently, studies have shown that the father has a *direct* influence on the child's development, enhanced by his attachment to the child from infancy on. This attachment is mediated by the mother's attitude toward the role of the father. Some mothers, in order to fulfill their own needs, tend to interfere with the reciprocal bond between infants and fathers, as if they were threatened by the infant's emancipation from the symbiotic unit. Mothers are gatekeepers, capable of enhancing or dampening father–infant attachment. If they promote a triangle, this opens the way for the child's future attachment. The mother's own experience of the oedipal triangle influences her child's opportunity to become close to his or her father.

One may wonder if the neglect of the father's role in so many studies for so many years—all of which placed the emphasis on the early mother–child dyad—didn't itself reflect the tendency to exclude the father from the mother–child relationship, such as is revealed by the historical and ethnological studies. Perhaps a universal fantasy of the father threatening the mother–baby relationship influenced even those studying that very relationship, blinding them to benign aspects of a father's role.

Since learning to be a father is a developmental process, it is determined simultaneously by basic psychic energy and experience and by environmental forces. Basic psychological attitudes are supported or undermined by events, social pressures, and institutions (Klaus & Kennell, 1982; Brazelton, 1981b). Crucial touch points, such as the prenatal visit, prenatal classes, and support during labor and delivery, provide opportunities for fostering the development of fathering. And as we will see in Part II, newborns themselves are capable of distinguishing between parental responses and appear ready to captivate a father's attention, however uninitiated.

PART TWO

The Newborn As Participant

It is fortunate for their survival that babies are so designed by nature that they beguile and enslave mothers.

—JOHN BOWLBY
"The Nature of the Child's
Tie to His Mother"

Introduction

Newborn babies are beautifully programmed to fit the parents' fantasies and to reward the work of pregnancy. From the first, they are active participants in shaping their parents' reactions to them. Parents are hungry for responses from their newborn. During pregnancy, they have dreamed of a smiling baby who snuggles neatly into their arms. They need a responsive infant to fuel the work ahead. The now outdated image of a baby who could neither see nor hear for several weeks after birth made parents blind to the very responses that can swiftly strengthen attachment. Today, the newborn's developed sensory powers are better known, and those of us who work with parents can help point out the extraordinary range of behavior in the repertory of an individual infant. Parents who appreciate and value this responsiveness are ready for a richer dialogue with their baby.

Part II will outline the complex capacities that are available in the normal human newborn, ready to reward adults for appropriate responses. These capacities, programmed into the baby, match universal expectations in parents. The baby's behavior and the parent's instinctive nurturing responses meet in the newborn period to fuel the growth of attachment between them. Energy is high at this time and the newborn is equipped to capture it.

When a mother holds her newborn in a comfortable, cuddled position, the infant molds into her body. On her shoulder, the infant lifts his or her head to scan the room, then settles a soft, fuzzy scalp into the crook of her neck. As she automatically pulls the infant to her, a newborn will burrow harder into her neck, molding his or her body against hers, legs adjusting to fit her body. All of these responses say to her, "You are doing the right thing." If she leans down to speak in one ear, the baby turns to her voice and looks for her face. Finding it, the infant's face brightens as if to say, "There you are!" A newborn will choose a female voice over a male, as if to say, "I know you already and you are important to me."

As we will see, newborns' states of consciousness are responsive to mothers in similarly reinforcing ways. When they are crying, as their mother speaks to them, touches them, or holds their arms, they will quiet. Both mother and newborn feel the thrill of having "done the right thing." Each time something she does brings a response, whether quieting or waking or becoming alert, a mother feels her competence confirmed. If, on the other hand, an infant's ability to respond is disturbed or impaired, she feels her expectations violated. Both her attachment and her future relationship with this infant are put at risk.

Insecure new parents look for signals from their baby to reassure them that their caring attempts are on target. They need the baby's responses as a continuous confirmation of the appropriateness of their parenting. At a time when no extended family system provides advice and monitoring, the baby's behavior is the parents' best guide to each new effort.

4

The Appearance
of the Newborn
and Its Impact

The baby's appearance stimulates parenting responses. The soft, rounded face; the fuzzy, fine hair and delicate skin with an incredibly soft feel; the short limbs and relatively long torso; the beautifully molded tiny hands reaching helplessly out—all of these are markers of "babyishness." We know now that there is a program in adults of many species that makes them want to reach out for and take care of any small, helpless member of their own species with certain specific physical characteristics.

The initial, bluish, rather mottled appearance of a newborn is due to dependence on the mother's oxygen in the uterus. The presence of a special kind of fetal hemoglobin has made it possible for the fetus to maintain a lower oxygen level. Until its lungs and circulation take over effectively, the newborn will be somewhat blue. This transition is miraculously short in most cases. All babies are born with "poor" color and with gasping, irregular respiration. The fact that babies are blue at birth has worried obstetricians unnecessarily, and they have too often instituted drastic measures to make the baby "pink up" or to get deep, regular respirations. This in turn has aroused anxiety in parents. With a little patience, the baby's color will improve anyway. Spanking babies or immersing them in cold-water baths to "shock" them into crying may not be necessary. Crying improves the air exchange more rapidly so that color and circulation improve. In a normal, healthy baby, this will happen rapidly and without harm.

When a new mother and father see their baby limp and blue in the delivery room, they may imagine brain damage. Reassurance by a professional that this color and initial unresponsiveness is "normal" can be critical as they start to reach out to the baby. The battered appearance which most babies have after delivery can also arouse a mother's fears that she has damaged her baby in labor and delivery. She needs to hear that the molded head, the bruised, mashed areas are common, that they will heal and are not a sign of damage to the brain. The rapid changes in the initial appearance can be used to reassure parents that their baby's head is resilient and "normal."

5

Reflexes in the Newborn

Primitive automatic movements, called reflexes, are present in an active fetus for many months before delivery, as if in preparation for the coming event. The patterns of these reflexes are often remnants from our heritage, our monkey and amphibian ancestors, but they may also serve a purpose. The fetal activity appears to keep the uterus contracting (Milani Camparetti, 1981). When *dystocia* (the slowing down of the uterine contractions) occurs, an inactive fetus may be a contributing factor. Until fairly recently, obstetricians have usually laid the cause of dystocia to an inefficient uterus, but there is more and more reason to suspect an interaction between an inactive fetus without reflex movement patterns and an understimulated, underreactive uterus. Reflexive behaviors also seem to play a role in the writhing necessary to help the fetus work through the cervical opening. Among these reflexes are:

1. *Tonic neck reflex.* With head turned abruptly, the fetus assumes a fencing-like position, arching the body, extending or stretching out all muscles on the face side of the body, and flexing on the other side. As labor progresses, the head turns to make the body arch one way, then the other, so that the baby swims its way along through the cervical canal.

2. *Spinal cord reflex.* If the back is stroked along the spinal cord, the entire body curls up toward the stroke. The trunk will switch back and forth in reptilian movements if there is enough stimulation along the

49

spinal cord. In labor, the touch of the birth canal wall keeps the baby arching back and forth, inching forward (Galant, in Saint-Anne D'Argassies, 1974).

3. *Moro or startle reflex.* As the head is extended backward, the arms extend outward, then flex, and the legs are thrust outward. These movements are suppressed in the cervical canal but would free the baby from a "stuck" situation if his or her head became arched suddenly.

4. *The step reflex and the standing reflex.* These emerge as the baby's feet press on a stable surface and are good examples of the stretching extensor reflexes of all muscle groups. As labor proceeds, the alternating flexion and extension of extremities is likely to play a major role in stimulating the uterus.

5. *Crawl reflexes.* When newborn babies are placed on their bellies, they automatically try to pick up and turn their heads to free the airway. Their arms come up beside the head and they attempt to get their hands into their mouths. Their legs push back and forth in vigorous crawling movements. These are precursors of crawling later on. Parents can see that the baby is already programmed to move forward in bed, and also that the baby will raise his or her head to free it from bedclothes, when lying face down.

Reflex motions are programmed at a very primitive level in the brain. Apart from being adaptive in labor and delivery, they may play a role in programming motor behavior in a way that makes it predictable to parents. For example, in the tonic neck reflex, each side of the baby's body behaves differently. One side will respond with flexion, the other with extension movements. The Moro causes a baby to reach out, then grasp onto the mother's body. Parents may be unaware of this patterned behavior at first but will rapidly learn to depend on it as they play with their baby. Of course, all of these reflexes become a base for learned, complex behavior later on. The step or standing reflex sets the stage for future learned behavior of walking and standing. When parents or the pediatrician or nurse hold newborns to a standing position, their faces will often brighten and they appear to be attempting to participate. This, in turn, delights and rewards the adult, setting up feedback for future learning.

Swaddling is used in many cultures to replace the constraints offered by the uterus and then by a mother's holding and containment. Such control over disturbing motor responses allows newborns to attend to and interact with their environment. The Navaho Indians used cradleboards and swaddling. Observers noticed that their babies quieted as soon as they were wrapped onto the cradleboard. Clyde Kluckhohn (1948) felt that this custom led to quiet, passive, but internally frustrated infants. When we [TBB] have worked with Navaho babies, we have seen the quieting, but not the frustration. Mothers handled the swaddled babies easily, propping them up to watch as they worked in the fields, laying them down to sleep wrapped on their cradleboard. Essentially, Navaho babies became observers and thus participants in the lives of the adults around them because of the cradleboard. The present use of baby chairs seems comparable in certain ways.

6. *Sucking and gagging reflexes.* Initially, newborn babies need to rid themselves of the mucus in their airways. At this point, gagging reflexes compete with sucking. As a result, a baby's response to a nipple or finger will often be to gag and spit up before he or she can begin to suck. An eager new parent who puts her baby to breast will feel rejected if she finds the baby gagging or refusing to suck. The sucking reflex must be gradually brought out and reinforced—often it takes several days.

This gradually improving sucking reflex parallels the mother's milk production. A new mother doesn't get milk for four or five days. Meanwhile, her breasts produce a milky, whitish fluid full of protein and antibodies, but in small amounts. The first few days at the breast can be seen as a "learning" or practicing period. Adjusting to each other is the big job. Learning to suck is the baby's task. Learning how to hold and encourage the baby, to feel comfortable in nursing, is the mother's. This early practicing period takes the first week with a first baby. If hospital personnel or family try to rush this process, thinking that a new mother should know instinctively how to nurse a baby, they are likely to endanger her confidence in her ability to nurture her baby.

Feeding Behavior

Rooting and sucking are among the most reliable activities of newborn babies. When a breast is offered and touches a newborn's cheek, the infant will search for it by a few head turns, then almost gobble to mouth the nipple. An awake, hungry newborn exhibits active searching movements in response to any stimulation in the region around the mouth. This reflex is set off by touch as far out on the face as the cheek and sides of the jaw and head. The rooting reflex is present in a premature infant even before sucking itself is effective.

Sucking is made possible by the thorax when the infant breathes in and by fixing the jaw between breaths. Swallowing and breathing must be coordinated, and the depth and rate of breathing are handled differently when the baby is engaged in nutritive and non-nutritive (such as on fingers or a pacifier) sucking. In the latter, the chance of inhaling milk is not important. This whole process has been studied by Albrecht Peiper who argues for a hierarchical control system in which swallowing controls sucking and sucking controls breathing (Peiper, 1963).

There appear to be three components of sucking: a lapping motion of the tongue, a milking movement at the back base of the tongue, and suction from the upper esophagus. One can feel all three of these by putting a finger in the new baby's mouth. There is a brief delay before these become coordinated in an effective milking mechanism.

The infant sucks in a more or less regular pattern of bursts and pauses. During non-nutritive sucking, this rate averages about two sucks a second. Bursts seem to be arranged in groupings of 5–24 sucks per burst. The pause between bursts has been looked upon as a rest and recovery period as well as a time during which information is being processed by the neonate. These pauses, as we have mentioned, are important in the early mother–child relationship, since they are used by mothers as signals to stimulate the infant to return to sucking. Mothers tend to look down at, to talk to, and to jiggle babies when they pause between bursts of sucking. The infants, in turn, come to expect these responses. The mothers' jiggling actually prolongs the pause as the infants attend to the signals from their mothers (Kaye & Brazelton, 1971).

6

The Five Senses in the Newborn

Sight

One of the first questions a new mother asks is "Can my baby see?" When parents first lift the baby to face them, the eyes of an unmedicated baby will open and search the parent's face. Few responses on a baby's part have a more powerful impact on parents.

Picking up or rocking a baby will both soothe and alert a newborn (Korner & Thoman, 1972) and set off a reflex response of eye opening and attention to a visual stimulus. A semi-upright (30° angle) position appears to produce the most prolonged alertness in newborns (Madansky, 1983). Parents can see that when they rock or bring a baby up to their shoulders, the baby quiets and becomes more alert. When held out in front of them and rocked gently in a semi-upright position, the baby's eyes will come open, "ready" for interaction. Both the newborn and the new parent seem to become intensely involved, as if saying, "Finally, there you are!"

A newborn's ability to see and hear in the delivery room may be as important to the "bonding" process as the act of putting the baby to breast to suckle. The silver nitrate treatment, once routine, causes immediate swelling of the eyelids and is now postponed in many hospitals. Some hospitals use a less irritating antibiotic ointment. In a controlled experiment, postponing this treatment for thirty minutes after delivery allowed new parents to interact visually with their babies in the delivery room (Butterfield et al., 1982). Thirty days later, parents were significantly more sensitive to their babies' visual and auditory cues than were a matched group of parents who had not had opportunity for visual interaction right after delivery. All new parents have a hunger for visual interaction with their newborn after delivery.

Face-to-face interaction in the newborn period may be as critical as any other kind, such as breast-feeding, holding, or cuddling. Right in the delivery room, mothers want to hold their babies in an *en face* (face-to-face) position (Klaus & Kennell, 1982). Mothers attempt to elicit eye-to-eye contact with premature infants even while they are in their isolettes, in order to reassure themselves that the baby is all there, and in order to feel that he or she belongs to them despite the separation and the baby's difficulties. Visual ability in the newborn has powerful adaptive significance, attaching the mother to her baby.

A baby seems to be programmed for learning about human faces from birth. The visual stimuli that appeal to newborns the most seem to be the shiny eyes or the mouth, as well as the edges of the face (Salapatek & Kessen, 1966). This allows for very early learning about his or her caretakers and the human world surrounding the baby. Robert Fantz (1961) first pointed out the newborn's preference for certain kinds of complex visual stimuli. By pairing two pictures, he judged preference by how often the baby looked at one versus the other. This way he found many preferences in the newborn. For instance, he found that sharply contrasting colors, larger squares, and medium brightly lit objects were more appealing. These brought the newborn to a prolonged alert state of fixation. He and others found that the neonate preferred an ovoid object the size of a human face and one in which there were eyes and a mouth. The baby fixed on the picture's shiny eyes, the red mouth, and the edges of the face. A three-dimensional face was even more preferred.

Immediately after birth in the delivery room, babies will not only fix on a drawing that resembles a human face but will follow it for 180° arcs, with eyes and head turning to keep it in view (Goren et al., 1975). A scrambled face does not get the same kind of attention, nor do infants follow the distorted face with their eyes or head.

Preference for a responsive adult's face is shown by the newborn's increasing excitement as he or she follows it back and forth and even up and down in the delivery room. In fact, if one gets serious and presents a flat face after this, a brand-new baby will look worried and turn away. The responsiveness of an adult's face may be a critical factor in keeping the newborn's attention. Learning about important visual cues proceeds rapidly. A mother can tell that her baby has begun to recognize her face by the age of three weeks, and is responding differently to his or her father or another familiar adult by four to five weeks. Visual recognition quickly becomes a rewarding signal for both parents. The fact that a newborn learns about each of them so rapidly tells them that all the baby's faculties are intact and that they are important to the baby already.

For professional caregivers as well as parents, visual behavior in the newborn is one of the most reliable signs of an intact central nervous system (Sigman et al., 1973). The ability to become alert, to maintain an alert state, to fix on and attend to a visual display appears to be correlated with the infant's stage of maturity. It also signifies an optimal condition of the baby's central nervous system (Brazelton et al., 1966). Absence of visual responses, however, need not be thought of right away as necessarily signifying brain damage, since these are so dependent on whether the infant is in an appropriate state for visual interaction. Ordinary conditions can interfere with the newborn's capacity to come to an alert state—such as the usual exhaustion of the nervous system that follows delivery. Low oxygen or the usual stresses that occur in normal deliveries, such as premedication given the mother, can delay the baby's responsiveness. Other common conditions, such as hunger, fatigue, or being in an overlit delivery room or newborn nursery, can make a baby unresponsive. Mothers and fathers need to know this, so that they don't feel that the baby is damaged or impaired. Those who care for new parents can help them avoid disappointment by showing them how to rock their baby up and down and to each side in order to set off the reflexes that will alert the baby so that he or she can interact visually. This can be exciting for the doctor or nurse as well as the parents.

How far can a newborn baby see? This is difficult to determine. An early experiment measured infants' responses to a moving drum which circled over their heads as they lay in bed (Gorman et al., 1957). Ninety-three of 100 infants responded preferentially to stripes at certain visual angles. The newborns were relatively nearsighted, and they preferred objects at 10–12 inches in front of them. By three months, a baby can see farther than 8 feet and an adult ability appears to be reached by six months of age (Dayton et al., 1964). The newborn infant's inability to register a good image beyond 3½ feet is due to smaller eye size and a greater relative depth of the eyeball. As the baby grows, the eyeball becomes rounder and more flexible. We have found that prematures see, too. Their sight is less reliable, and they are even more nearsighted, but they can also fix on and follow the lines on a moving drum.

Newborns are relatively myopic with only 20/150 vision, as determined by this same technique (Dayton et al., 1964). It does not seem that newborns are able to accommodate well to a moving object. They have a fixed focal length of about 19 cm (10–12 inches) and cannot follow unless the object is moved very slowly. In order to capture a newborn's interest with an object, an examiner must present the object at 10–12 inches, move it up and down slowly until the baby alerts. Then the examiner can move it slowly to each side, waiting for the newborn to follow it.

Sight in a newborn is more than a passive ability. From the research just described, it is clear that newborns will actively try to prolong their attention to an attractive object. As a bright object is brought into a newborn's line of vision and is moved slowly up and down to attract his or her attention, the baby's pupils contract slightly. As the object is moved slowly from side to side, the baby's face begins to brighten, eyes widen, limbs become still, and the baby stares fixedly at the object, beginning slowly to track the ball from side to side. A newborn will actively maintain this stilled posture in order to attend to the ball. A newborn's eyes first track in small arcs, moving past the target, but as the baby becomes more invested, the eye movements become smoother and more efficient. The baby's eyes move, tracking the object. The baby's head begins to turn from one side to the other. A newborn is able to follow an object for as much as 12° to right and left and will even make eye and head movements to follow it 30° up or down. Meanwhile, interfering body movements and startles are actively suppressed. The baby can often maintain this intense visual involvement for several minutes before startling, becoming upset or dull, losing the alert state that is necessary to this kind of visual behavior. When watching a human face, the newborn's involvement is more prolonged. Normal newborns in the proper alert state can fix on and follow a face, moving their eyes and head in long, slow arcs and brightening as they do so.

The seemingly simple act of watching a face or a ball is not possible without coordination between an alert state, the motor capacity to turn the head, suppression of distracting motor reflexes, and the visual behavior itself. This coordination implies a complex and highly developed nervous system. It is difficult to believe that the cortex is not involved in maintaining the alert state and controlling the motor behavior. Newborns without this capacity to maintain alertness have less opportunity to learn about their environment.

The ability to watch and follow an object should be distinguished from a fixed stare that does not change and which does not change over time. This is not a good sign. It may mean that the baby cannot cut down on visual input. After several minutes of stimulation, a normal baby will begin to shut down and turn away. The baby who cannot do this is at the mercy of such stimulation. A healthy response to visual stimuli in a newborn is thus more than alert attention and might be described in four stages: (1) an initial alerting, (2) an increasing attention, (3) a gradually decreasing interest, and (4) a final turning away from a monotonous presentation. (See discussion of habituation later in Part II, Chapter 7.)

An interesting experiment by Lauren Adamson (1977) revealed how important sight is to the newborn baby. She covered an alert baby's eyes with first an opaque and then a clear plastic shield. He swiped frantically at the opaque shield and attempted vigorously to remove it. When it was removed, he instantly quieted. When a clear shield was substituted, he calmed down to look through it. Being able to see seemed to outweigh the disturbing aspects of something covering his face, thus implying a real investment in vision, even at birth. This dovetails nicely with the parents' eagerness for visual response from their babies, as described earlier.

Hearing

Newborn babies' hearing capacity is also evident at birth. They show a clear preference for the female voice, brightening and turning toward it in preference to a male voice. When this is demonstrated to mothers, their attachment seems to take a great spurt. With an interesting auditory stimulus, such as a rattle or soft voice, an infant will move from sleep to an alert state. Their breathing becomes irregular, their faces brighten, their eyes open, and when completely alert, their eyes and head will turn toward the sound. Head turning is followed by a searching look, a scanning motion of the eyes, to find a source for the sound.

In the past, our ways of assessing hearing in newborns have been insensitive and have led us to miss certain abilities. For example, the clackers used for detection of central nervous system defects were ineffective in loud, noisy nurseries. A large percentage of newborns tested this way were unresponsive, having shut out all loud noises in the nursery. Under these same conditions, a soft rattle might have caused them to turn.

Eisenberg (1976) has determined that there are differential responses to different ranges of sound. The preferred range is 500–900 cycles per second, the range of human speech. For sounds in this range, newborns are more likely to inhibit motor behavior and demonstrate heart rate deceleration. A preference for the female speech range is demonstrated by the way newborns turn repeatedly and preferentially to a female voice when paired with a sound of the same intensity in any other range.

Parents of newborns quickly learn the pitch that arouses and captures their baby's attention. With sounds that are too high pitched or loud, infants will startle initially, turn their heads away from the sound, their heart rate and breathing accelerating as they do, and their skin will redden. If the sound is repeated, they will attempt to shut it out and, if that is unsuccessful, will start to cry in order to control their startling and the other motor reactions, which are the result of disturbing auditory input. With a soft, gentle, insistent auditory stimulus, the newborns' movements will slow down and their heart rates will decelerate as they turn slowly toward the attractive sound. A hypersensitive baby will overreact to most sounds and will be unable to contain motor overreactions. A mother will have a more difficult time to find such a baby's range.

The newborn's response to sound illustrates a rule called the law of initial values. Lacey (1967) pointed out that any stimulus will press the newborn's response toward a mean level. Using heart rate responses as a measure, he demonstrated that when the rate was high when the stimulus was presented, the response brought the heart rate down, and when the rate was low, the response brought it up. This same pattern can be seen in behavior—for example, if a baby is active or crying, an interesting sound will make the baby quiet down, and turn toward it. When quiet or asleep, the baby will startle initially at the sound and become more active, trying to attend to the stimulus. Each response leads in the direction of a mean. In each case, the baby moves toward an alert but quiet state particularly conducive to learning and interaction. Parents talking to the infant will interpret this pattern of alerting and attending as responses to them, a sign that the baby "knows me." Alert parents will also notice, sooner or later, that their babies synchronize their motions to the rhythms of their parents' voices, and vice versa.

William Condon and Louis Sander (1975) showed that, immediately after birth, newborns will synchronize their movements to the rhythm of a mother's voice. This is an example of the great mutual power of adaptation in early infancy. The baby's movements match the mother's, who, in turn, adapts her speech to the baby's movements. Parents learn the pitch, the rhythm that captures their baby, who begins to dance, as it were, to the accompaniment of their voices.

Newborns prefer human to nonhuman sounds. G. F. Cairns and E. C. Butterfield (1975) were able to demonstrate the differences in the neonate's responses to human versus nonhuman sounds by observing patterns of sucking as various sounds were offered. When they used a nonhuman sound, the baby stopped sucking to attend to it, but then resumed sucking. When they used human sound, the baby stopped sucking to attend to it, then resumed sucking in a pronounced burst–pause pattern—as if waiting for more human signals. In the observations of one of the authors [TBB], a particular burst–pause pattern of sucking is very commonly associated with human interaction at feeding time—as if the newborns pause to gather more information from the person feeding them. This response in their new baby reinforces the parents' attempts to communicate.

Sense of Smell

Newborns have a highly developed sense of smell, ready to distinguish the appealing and unappealing odors that will help them adapt to their new world. For example, infants act as if they are offended by vinegar, asafetida, and alcohol but are attracted to sweet odors, such as milk and sugary solutions (Engen et al., 1963). Seven-day-old babies can reliably distinguish the odor of their mother's breast pads from those of other lactating mothers, although this ability does not seem to be present at two days (MacFarlane, 1975). They turn their heads toward the smell of their own mother's breast pads with 80 percent reliability, after left-right preferences are accounted for. This amazing ability uses surprisingly little information from the environment to distinguish an important person. In our own clinical work, we have both seen that breast-feeding infants at three weeks may refuse to accept a formula from their mothers. This refusal seems to be based on the infant's ability to smell the nearby breast. Fathers are successful in giving a bottle to these same babies. When a mother recognizes such a preference, her attachment to her baby is likely to deepen.

By two to three weeks, babies will begin to fall into a businesslike rooting behavior—as if expecting to be fed—when in their mother's arms. In their father's arms, they are more likely to be in an alert, playful state. There are, of course, many other cues—rhythms, level of speech, differences in patterns of handling—in addition to smell that make up the total gestalt of a mother versus a father. Whatever sensory mode we focus on, it is clear that the newborn baby is already doing a lot of "work" to learn what to expect from each caregiver.

Sense of Taste

Newborns can recognize subtle differences in taste. Their complex taste preferences have been demonstrated (Johnson & Salisbury, 1975). When infants are fed different fluids through a nipple, their sucking pattern has been recorded on a running paper. Salt water causes so much resistance that the baby chokes on it. With a cow's milk formula, the baby sucks in a rather continuous fashion, pausing at irregular intervals. If breast milk then is fed in this same way, the baby registers recognition of the change in taste after a short interval, then sucks in bursts with frequent regular pauses. This burst–pause pattern seems to indicate that the breast milk evokes other expectations. The baby seems to expect other kinds of stimuli (such as social signals) to be added to the feeding situation in the pauses. In other words, it seems as if human infants are programmed with a special kind of sucking pattern which they come to associate with breast milk. The babies in this study expected more social interaction on the breast than with a bottle.

Lewis Lipsitt (1977) has shown that the baby requires only two sucks before recognizing a change in sweetness of liquids. Recognition of changes in taste is registered by rapid changes in depth of sucking (increasing for sweeter fluids) as well as changes in the effectiveness of each sucking burst. With sugar water, the pauses decrease and the sucks increase in number as sweetness increases. Quickly, a new mother begins to "see" these different patterns of response and uses them to interpret the infant's needs and desires. As she learns her baby's patterns of response, she learns the signals that register recognition of the environment. As babies get repeated chances to "learn" about feeding, their behavior becomes clearer and clearer. The burst–pause pattern, though subtle, may be a powerful means for babies to elicit more interactive behavior from their mothers.

Touch

Touch is the first important area of communication between a mother and her new infant. Mothers respond to upset babies by containing them, shutting down on their disturbing motor activity by touching or holding them. By contrast, fathers are more likely to jiggle or rock babies in a playful, rhythmic fashion (Dixon et al., 1981). Touch is a message system between the caregiver and the infant—both for quieting and for alerting and arousing. We [TBB] have found that a slow patting motion is soothing whereas more rapid patting becomes an alerting stimulus, and that the threshold is very specific. With patting any faster the baby becomes upset (Barnard & Brazelton, 1984). As with auditory stimuli, the law of initial values seems to be of primary importance. When babies are quiet, a tactile stimulus serves to alert them and bring them up to an alert state. When babies are upset, a slow, modulated tactile stimulus seems to serve to reduce their activity. The area in which the newborn is touched also determines the response. Stimulation around the mouth elicits rooting and sucking, as well as motion of the upper gastrointestinal tract. Pressure on the palm of one of the hands elicits head turning and mouth opening to the same side (Babkin reflex). Stroking on one side of the mouth also stimulates the hand on the same side to flex and be brought up to the mouth. These hand-to-mouth responses to touch are established before birth and serve several purposes—for self-comfort, for control over motor activity, and for self-stimulation.

7

States of Consciousness

Not so long ago, the newborn infant was thought of as neurologically insufficient, subcortical in behavior. Nothing in this description fits the kind of predictable, directed responses one sees in a newborn when in a social interaction with a nurturing adult. When positive rather than intrusive stimuli are utilized, the newborn has amazing capacities for alerting and attention, and for suppressing interfering reflex responses in order to attend. Newborns respond to and interact with their environment from birth. But in order for an adult to engage this response, a knowledge of the newborn's ongoing states of consciousness is necessary. These states are the necessary context for understanding a newborn's reactions. Depending upon the newborn's state, stimulation is either appropriate or inappropriate. When appropriate stimuli are offered in appropriate states, an intact and adaptable central nervous system can be observed even in the most premature infant. To say that newborn babies function by controlling their state of attention or consciousness may be going too far, but such control seems to be within the capacities of a healthy, normal newborn (Brazelton, 1984).

Labels for states of consciousness refer to the level of availability of the newborn. States range from deep and light sleep states, to a semiconscious, then to an alert and very available state, on to fussy, and then to unreachable crying. In research at the Child Development Unit at Boston Children's Hospital, we [TBB] have found that state range and state control in the newborn are the best predictors of cognitive and social performance at eighteen months (Lester et al., 1985). Not only does state determine the capacity of babies to take in information and to use it, but it will also affect the kind and degree of response they will make. A trained observer quickly becomes able to predict which response a baby will make to a negative and to a positive stimulus in each state of consciousness. Newborns will not be unpredictable if one accounts for the states within which they are reacting. State, then, appears to be a basic regulatory system. If newborns can maintain control over their states, they can regulate when and whether they take in and respond to the world around them. For example, in a noisy, overstimulating environment, newborns will either go into a deep sleep state or cry in an unreachable way.

One of a parent's first jobs is to learn to recognize and predict their baby's states of consciousness in order to know whether he or she will be available—for feeding, sleeping, and for interaction. The six states, as we currently understand them, are as follows:

The Six States

1. *Deep sleep.* Eyes are firmly closed, breathing is deep and regular, and there is no motor activity. At regular intervals but many seconds apart, the baby may have brief startles, but will not rouse. In this state, the baby is relatively unreachable to outside stimuli. This state occurs in roughly four-hour cycles in full-term newborns. Premature infants have less well defined cycles of this kind of sleep, and its occurrence is a sign of maturity and of good nervous system function in a disordered or high-risk baby. Obviously, this state serves an important purpose, to rest and organize an immature and easily overwhelmed nervous system. Its recurrence in short cycles over the day serves babies well. As they mature, they can postpone the need for deep sleep longer and longer. (See *Sleep cycles*, below.)

2. *Active sleep* (REM, or rapid-eye-movement, sleep). In this light or active sleep, babies are more vulnerable to the outside world. Their eyes will be closed, but slow, rotating movements may be apparent. Body activity ranges from minor twitches to short bouts of writhing and stretching. Breathing is irregular, rather shallow at times, and faster

than that seen in sleep. Facial movements will include frowns, grimaces, smiles, twitches, mouth movements, and sucking. The predominance of REM sleep in normal newborns has led to the hypothesis that in this state brain growth and differentiation occur.

3. *Drowsy, in-between state.* The infant's eyes may open and close, or they may be partially or fully open, but they will be dazed in appearance. At times, there may be rather smooth movements of the arms and legs. Breathing is regular, but faster and shallower than that observed in sleep. Stimulation in this state is likely to arouse a baby to a more alert, responsive state.

4. *Awake, alert state.* The infant's body and face are relatively quiet and inactive, with eyes that are "bright and shining" in appearance. Visual and auditory stimuli will bring predictable responses. In early infancy, this state is likely to be short-lived, but by 2–3 weeks, a baby may be able to maintain it for as much as 20–30 minutes at a time. For parents, the deepest rewards occur in these times.

5. *Alert but fussy state.* This is a transitional state to crying. Babies are available to external stimuli and may still be soothed or brought to an alert state by attractive stimuli. If the stimulation gets to be too much, they are likely to break down to fussing again. Movements are jerky, disorganized, and make infants fuss even more when they set off massive startles in themselves.

6. *Crying.* Crying serves many purposes for the baby. From the first, it is the most effective mode for attracting a caregiver. Not only are there at least four types of cries (pain, hunger, boredom, discomfort) which are distinguishable early in the baby's life, but it seems as if the baby were programmed to try to communicate by crying in these various ways. A crying baby sets off an automatic response of concern, responsibility, and guilt in parents. They feel compelled to respond, to settle the baby's reason for crying. When they are able to, they feel reinforced as parents.

A mother can recognize her baby's cry from that of other newborns by the third day (Boukydis, 1979). She can begin to distinguish between pain, hunger, and boredom cries by the end of the second week. A father recognizes them by three weeks. Crying is, obviously, an important communication system for all of them, a complex signaling system in which babies express themselves differentially from the first (Lester & Zeskind, 1982).

By the second or third week, a kind of fussy crying occurs periodically throughout the day—usually in a cyclic pattern—which seems to discharge and help to regulate the states that ensue. After a period of such crying, the newborn may be more organized for a while and may sleep more deeply.

Although parents learn early to distinguish the various kinds of crying, they may also attribute many inappropriate meanings to it. We will see the results of this misinterpretation in Part V.

Sleep Cycles

The length of sleep cycles (REM-active and deep sleep) changes normally with maturation of the nervous system. As we mentioned, in a full-term baby, sleep and waking occur in approximately 4-hour cycles. Within these cycles, a baby is in deep sleep for 45–50 minutes and will then rouse to become active but still in light sleep. After awhile, he or she will settle back down to deep sleep. These cycles go on all day and night whenever the baby is asleep. A lack of regularity in these cycles may indicate problems in the development of the nervous system (Thoman, 1975). Learning to sleep for a 4-hour period already involves some learning of handling REM and deep-sleep cycles.

Learning to sleep longer than three to four hours at night is a more complicated process. First of all, the nervous system must mature so that the baby can handle stimuli from the environment without waking up. In order to sleep beyond these 3–4-hour cycles, babies must develop reliable behavioral patterns which serve to comfort them when they are trying to get from light sleep into a deeper sleep. Sucking fingers and scrabbling about for a comfortable spot are among these self-comforting measures.

Immature or hypersensitive babies take longer to stretch out their sleep at night. Not only are the sleep cycles of these babies shorter, but their ability to shut out stimulation in order to return from light to deep sleep is impaired. They will need extra time and pressure from the environment before they become able to keep themselves from waking at short intervals every time they come up to REM sleep.

Learning to sleep at night is tied to daytime patterns. Regular naps and regular feedings help. Babies who start to manage for themselves when frustrated during the day are more likely to learn patterns necessary for nighttime. Once parents understand a baby's needs and responses, they feel more confident in holding off for feedings in the daytime and in gradually encouraging the infant toward a regular, predictable pattern. This will help the infant learn to stretch out at night. As we will see in Part V, if there is a mismatch, and parents do not understand the baby's patterns, the interaction can become more and more anxious and disordered.

Habituation

Habituation is a protective response, a closing down of the nervous system against too much stimulation from the outside. It is essential to newborns' capacity for survival, helping them deal with potentially overwhelming demands on their immature nervous systems. When presented with a series of bright lights, babies first startle, then gradually respond less and less. Observable motor responses eventually cease. The heart rate and respiratory changes seen after the initial stimulus gradually diminish. The babies begin to breathe deeply and regularly until they appear to be in a deep sleep. An electroencephalogram will show changes similar to sleep in their brains.

This habituation response can be brought about by auditory, visual, or tactile stimuli. When these are repeated, the newborns will show gradually decreasing responses and appear to go to sleep. However, if the stimulus is varied slightly, they begin to become interested again, alert, and their heart rates increase. In fact, one can document a newborn's capacity to detect differences in duration and intensity of a stimulus by monitoring heart rate at such a time.

Although habituation produces a state similar to sleep, there are differences. These infants have *tightened*, flexed extremities, with little movement except jerky startles, and no eye blinks. The babies seem to be actively maintaining control over their environment, rather than relaxing into sleep.

In impaired or immature newborns, the capacity to habituate is not as effective, and these infants are more at the mercy of environmental stimuli of all kinds. This ability is also affected by medication, such as barbiturates given to mothers at the time of delivery. Not only is habituation an important means of self-protection but it suggests active regulation of state control in the newborn period. The infant shuts out intrusive stimuli and can attend more effectively to appropriate ones. Early interaction between parents and infants is greatly enhanced when a parent understands this important protective response.

8

Assessment of the Newborn

If we accept the notion of the newborn as an active participant in early interaction, the careful assessment of an individual infant should help us to understand the infant's side of the dialogue. Also, any professional who wants to support early attachment will find it useful to illuminate the nature and capacities of the baby for the parents.

A newborn's behavior will have already been shaped for nine months in the uterus. We need to be aware of the powerful influences on fetal development of acute infections, toxins, and maternal bleeding, as well as more prolonged intrauterine influences such as nutrition, hormones, medication, drugs, alcohol, caffeine, smoking, and even of maternal activity and attitudes. Although many of these factors can affect the developing brain, the nervous system of the fetus is marvelously plastic and may have recovered from an insult and appear to function normally. Nevertheless, with careful observation, subtle "soft" signs, such as hypersensitive behavioral responses or problems in state organization, may show up which call for special vigilance and care.

Sometimes the most valuable use of assessment is in reassuring parents that events beyond their control have *not* impaired the baby's future. Fortunately, it is rare that one event or one factor will affect the baby's development. Ordinarily, the synergistic interaction of several factors is necessary to create real problems in development of the fetal nervous system. However, parents must be informed of any important variations in the baby's behavior that might call for special attention and consultation.

Gestational age is important in understanding the baby's behavior (Dubowicz et al., 1970). Immaturity of even two weeks can result in behavioral differences that can in turn influence the parents' reaction to their baby if they don't understand the reason for them. Acute depletion of fat, sugar, and liquid stores resulting from an inadequate placenta will produce a long, lean, peeling, jittery baby who looks worried and anxious. The infant may well be hypersensitive to all usual stimuli and may overreact by withdrawing from his or her parents' ministrations—by sleeping, crying, or frowning. Parents can be alerted to the reasons for their baby's hypersensitivity and hyper-reactivity, so that they will not take it personally. They will be able to nurture the baby with more gentle handling, knowing that time will help restore the balance.

Apgar scores reflect a newborn's immediate responses to labor, delivery, and to the new environment, but they cannot be used alone as an index of stress at birth. The likelihood of future neurological problems is increased if these scores are low at 1, 5, and 15 minutes, and are also an index of a difficult delivery. However, we now know that a baby who is in good condition as a fetus before a difficult delivery can withstand an amazing amount of stress and even a lack of oxygen without resultant brain damage. The condition of the brain with which a fetus faces a difficult delivery may be more critical than the stressful events themselves.

As long as the newborn was thought to function at a brain stem level, essentially not using the brain's cortex or higher centers, as-sessment of newborn infants did little to predict later outcome. Once it was understood that the newborn arrives with a complex, highly developed nervous system, more sophisticated ways of assessing in-fants have been developed. A neurological assessment that taps mid-brain behavior does not give enough indication of the potential for recovery. Behavioral assessments seem to offer more useful informa-tion and a more reliable way of predicting later development.

Neonatal Behavioral Assessment Scale

The Neonatal Behavioral Assessment Scale (NBAS) was designed to capture newborns' behavioral responses to their new environment

(Brazelton, 1984). In order to record and evaluate some of the capacities of newborns when handled by a skilled observer or parent, we developed a behavioral examination that tests an infant's responses to environmental events in the context of states of consciousness. It is a means of scoring interactive behavior. The infant is not assessed alone, but as an active participant in a dynamic situation. While a few basic neurological observations are included, the NBAS is not a formal neurological assessment.

The NBAS emphasizes and tracks changes in states of consciousness over the course of the examination—their lability and direction. The infant's use of state, in order to control and interact with the environment, points to a capacity for self-organization. The assessment measures newborns' ability to quiet themselves as well as the way they handle stimulation.

The stimuli used in the NBAS include the kinds of stimuli—touch, rocking, voice, facial behavior—that parents use in their handling of infants as they attempt to help them adapt to a new environment. There is a graded series of procedures—talking, placing a firm hand on the newborn's belly, holding and rocking—all designed to soothe or alert the infant. The newborn's responsiveness to human stimuli—for example, the voice and the face—and to inanimate stimuli—for example, a soft rattle, a bell, a bright red ball, a bright light, handling, and temperature changes—are assessed. Estimates of vigor and excitement are measured as well as the kind of motor activity, the muscle tone, and color changes as the infant changes from one state to another.

There are twenty-eight behavioral items. These assess the newborn's capacity (1) to organize states of consciousness, (2) to habituate to disturbing events, (3) to attend to and process simple and, in some cases, complex environmental events, (4) to control motor tone and activity while attending to these events, and (5) to perform integrated motor acts, such as putting a hand in the mouth, maintaining the head upright while sitting, or knocking off a cloth which covers the face. All of these reflect the range of the behavioral capacities of the normal newborn. They seem to demand control over cardiac and respiratory systems and to be dependent on either the cortex or higher brain centers. For newborns to achieve this control, they must have successfully managed the physiological demands of the early adjustment period after delivery. The newborn's ability to attend to, to differentiate, and to habituate to the complex stimuli of an examiner's maneuvers may be an important predictor of future central nervous system organization, as well as of individual temperament.

The behavioral items are:

1. Response decrement to light (a flashlight shone briefly into infant's eyes)

2. Response decrement to rattle (shaken 10–12 inches from infant)

3. Response decrement to bell (rung 12–15 inches from infant)

4. Response decrement to a light pinprick on heel

5. Orienting response to inanimate visual stimulus (a red ball)

6. Orienting response to inanimate auditory stimulus (a soft rattle)

7. Orienting response to animate visual stimulus (examiner's face)

8. Orienting response to animate auditory stimulus (examiner's voice)

9. Orienting response to inanimate visual and auditory stimuli (red rattle)

10. Orienting responses to animate visual and auditory stimuli (examiner's face and voice)

11. Quality and duration of alert periods

12. General muscle tone, in resting and in response to being handled (passive and active)

13. Motor maturity (how smooth and vigorous the newborn's motions are)

14. Responses of arms, shoulders, and head as newborn is pulled to sit

15. Cuddliness (responses to being cuddled by the examiner)

16. Defensive movements (reaction to a cloth over face)

17. Consolability (number of maneuvers examiner must make to quiet the upset newborn)

18. Peak of excitement and capacity for self-control (during whole exam)

19. Rapidity of buildup to crying state

20. Irritability during the examination

21. Kind and degree of activity (during whole exam)

22. Tremulousness (during whole exam)

23. Amount of startling (during whole exam)

24. Changes in skin color

25. Number of changes of states during entire examination

26. Self-quieting activity (observable efforts and successes)

27. Hand-to-mouth activity

28. Smiles (both grimaces and replicas of social smiles, occurring at apparently appropriate moments)

The NBAS has been used extensively since 1973 in the United States and abroad. It was designed to help newborns produce their best available responsiveness to stimulation and to measure newborns' capacity to handle the stress of labor, delivery, and a new, demanding environment. Since any single assessment should be seen in the context of a curve of recovery from stress, it is not sufficient to predict future adaptation. Several exams, plotted against the known stressors which a newborn encounters (such as length of medication and anesthesia given to the mother, stresses of low oxygen, duration of labor, difficulty of labor and resuscitation), are better evidence of the baby's ability to handle future stress. Together with colleagues (Lester et al., 1985), we have used recovery curves of behavior over the first few weeks to predict development at eighteen months. Certain behavior, such as motor activity reflexes, is stable and less available to shaping from the environment. The way a newborn handles states of consciousness and social stimulation is more responsive to environmental input and changes most significantly over the first few days and weeks. These responses predict cognitive and affective development at eighteen months with significant reliability. The NBAS has been used in many different situations and cultures to measure influences that might affect a baby's future. For instance, it has been used in Guatemala to investigate the effect of maternal malnutrition. In the U.S., it has been used to measure the effects of medication given during labor, and the effects of alcohol and narcotics addiction during pregnancy. The impact on newborns of phototherapy given for elevated bilirubin levels has also been studied by means of the NBAS (Brazelton, 1984).

For the purposes of the present book, however, two uses of the assessment—to help parents understand their particular baby, and to identify newborns whose behavior may make them difficult to handle—are most pertinent. For example, a quiet newborn who takes a long time to respond will not be easy for parents to read. If such babies do not become clearly alert, the parent will inevitably worry about brain damage. If they do not cry in protest, parents may not feed or tend them appropriately. Delayed changes from state to state make for a sluggish baby, and adults are likely to turn away from such a baby in subtle as well as in important ways. Hypersensitive, disorganized babies can be almost impossible to understand. Not only do they overreact to stimuli, but they may react negatively with relentless crying or habituation in the attempt to control input from the environment. State changes will be abrupt, and such babies may "shoot" from one state to another—sleep to crying and down again, without any time for parents to reach them for consoling or for response (Brazelton et al., 1971). A parent will feel shut out and ineffective with either of these extreme kinds of babies. Their future interaction may well be endangered unless parents are helped to understand them. The NBAS was designed to help professionals judge the baby's style of response and thereby support parents in their effort to reach out. Its best use may be not as a test but as a way of demonstrating the newborn's behavior to parents so that they can understand the baby and their own job better from the beginning.

9

Individual Differences

Over years of experience in assessing newborn babies, we have been struck by the pronounced individual differences between them. These differences affect both the way an infant will participate in early interaction, and the way parents will respond. The importance of these individual differences to the early parent–child relationship must not be underestimated. Fortunately, because of the psychological energy which is churned up during pregnancy, the parents' capacity to understand and empathize with a baby is enhanced. Parents seem to be programmed to look for and value the individuality of their particular baby. The more that fathers and mothers can be encouraged to use this powerful psychological energy for recognizing characteristic responses and strengths in their babies, the firmer their early relationship will be.

The most fortunate families are those who enjoy a fit between the baby's individuality and the family's capacity to nurture. There are major differences in wishes and expectations from one set of parents to another. Parents also have personality characteristics limiting the kind of baby they may be able to handle. Energetic, intense parents are likely to feel more comfortable with an active child. A quiet, sensitive parent might feel overwhelmed and angry with the same infant. A quiet baby who waited to demonstrate a reaction might suit them better. While some responsive, well-organized babies would be easy for any parent, most parents must work to achieve an understanding of their baby in order to achieve a good fit. The following three cases suggest the range of possible parent–baby combinations and the challenge they present.

Robert* was a well-muscled, well-proportioned baby who was active right after delivery. He weighed nine pounds and was heavy-boned and sturdy. His mother had been prepared for a big baby, but when she first saw him on the delivery table, she said, "My God, was all that baby inside of *me?*" He had a shock of dark, matted hair, a round face with big, searching eyes, and he looked around the delivery room hungrily. His face and head were slightly pushed to the left because of his position in the womb, and both ears were flattened against the side of his head. His big, soft features were appealingly babyish, more like a one-month-old baby.

As he was placed on his mother's belly for her to inspect him, he quieted down. Before that, he'd been moving arms and legs continuously in slow cycles; his face had been wrinkled as he scanned the room around him. Now, as he lay face down, head on his mother's chest, he made crawling movements with his legs, settling finally with his hand up next to his mouth. His mother picked him up to look him in the face, his eyes came open, and he looked at her eyes with an eager expression. His face softened as she spoke softly to him, and his body tensed as he looked even more intently at her. She said, "I think you're seeing my face and hearing my voice already! What a wonderful fellow you are!" She laid him on the bed to inspect him all over. He grasped her fingers with his fists, brought his legs up to his abdomen to push off her hand, and when she pulled him up to a sitting position, he responded with vigorous head control, keeping his head nearly upright and in the midline. As he sat there, again his eyes came open and he surveyed the room.

Everyone in the delivery room was struck with how competent and controlled this alert little boy was, moments after birth. His father leaned over, talking to him in one ear. Immediately, Robert seemed to grow still, turning his head to the sound of the voice, his eyes scanning for its source. When he found his father's face, he brightened again as if in recognition. His father said, "Oh, what a great, big handsome boy!" He picked Robert up to handle him. As he was cuddled, Robert turned his body into his father's chest and seemed to lock his legs around one side of his father. Robert reached up to grasp and hold onto his father's gown, looking up into his face. By this time, his father was about to burst with pride and delight. When he put Robert up on his shoulder, the brand-new, still-slippery baby nestled against his father,

*Names and identifying details have been changed in case histories throughout this book.

his legs still seeming to hold on, his hands and arms up on his father's shoulder, his head cocked and nestling in the crook of his father's neck. His beaming father pulled him in even closer to contain and cuddle him. Although he'd been undressed by now for fifteen minutes, Robert's color remained pink, and he seemed contented at being handled and played with. He was not upset by any of these maneuvers.

The nurse finally took him to clean off the slippery material, called "vernix," which helped him get out of the birth canal. As she washed him, he began to fuss, to startle, and then he cried even louder. His cry came out with a rather low, but lusty, wail. She said, "It's good for him to cry. It opens up his lungs," as if she were apologizing for breaking into this idyllic family situation. She rushed to give him the required injection of vitamin K, to place the identification bands on his wrist and ankle, and to instill silver nitrate in each eye. With each intrusion, Robert slowly built up to a louder protest. By the third maneuver, he was pretty upset, crying vigorously. His color was an even brighter red by now.

When she wrapped him in a swaddling blanket, he calmed down, brought his right fist up to his mouth as if to suck, and began to settle into a quiet, peaceful position. He seemed relieved to be left alone. His regular breathing, his peaceful-looking face, his body at rest suggested that he had achieved his goal at last. His hand remained up near his mouth as if ready for self-comfort if he needed it. His red flushed color disappeared.

Both his parents had been hungrily watching each of the nurse's maneuvers. When he settled down, they sighed with deep relief. His mother turned to look at her bare belly and the rumpled bed, as if to say "Now I can take care of myself." His father realized that they'd both been so caught up with Robert's behavior and the miracle of watching him that he'd neglected to pay attention to his wife's needs.

A well-organized baby like Robert exudes a sense of reassurance and comfort. His appearance of strength, of perfection, of wholeness reinforces the parents' every move. Even in this first, short period, he tells his parents that he can "manage." They can be intrusive (as is the nurse); they can make mistakes with him; they can force him to respond even at a difficult time for him (right after delivery). He can manage all of this without disintegrating or falling apart. For an experienced observer, the way in which he moves slowly but surely from one state to another is his most reassuring behavior. For the parents, the remarkable ability to look at them, to register a response, to listen to their voices, and to lock his auditory and visual responses together as he finds their faces is a priceless reward for the long work of pregnancy. His competent movements begin to give them the feeling that he is already a person who can handle himself. His ability to settle down, with their help, but also by himself, is sure evidence of this. It would be difficult not to be off to a good start with this baby. He will do his part.

Consider a very different newborn who may well set the stage for failure in early interaction unless the parents are given guidance and support.

Chris was a long, lean baby when born at forty-one weeks, one week overdue. His mother knew she'd not gained for the past three weeks, but the ultrasound showed a perfectly normal baby, and no one paid particular attention to her comment, "He's slowed down." At birth, weighing six pounds, three ounces, he looked like a famine victim. His skin was loose, peeling on his hands and feet and a bit on his belly. His hair was fine and rather sparse. But the most striking thing about his appearance was his old-man face with a very worried look. As he lay in his crib, his eyes were wide open, staring anxiously off into the room. He lay quietly, but his breathing was deep and relatively noisy. He almost sounded as if he had a cold, and he breathed more rapidly and deeply whenever he was handled, talked to, or stimulated in any way. One had the impression that he wanted to be left alone.

When he was first born, the nurse and obstetrician were concerned about his color and lack of response. They checked him carefully, wrapping and stimulating him before handing him to his parents. The delay heightened their anxiety, making them wonder, "What might be wrong?" Assured by the nurse and doctor that he was intact, their hearts nevertheless sank when they saw his wizened face, with ears which protruded and a dome-shaped, nearly bald head. His mother felt like crying and, without expressing it, she began to wonder what she'd done to her baby. Quietly, each began to look for confirmation of his normalcy. "Poor baby," said his father, who also wondered if they'd done something to make him appear so pitiful. As he lay wrapped in their arms, he looked peaceful enough. But when he was moved even slightly, his face wrinkled up into a frightened animal-looking expression, and he let out a piercing, high-pitched wail. They were relieved when the nurses took him away "to take care of him."

Over the next few days, his pattern of reactions became clearer, but not more reassuring. His mother struggled to get him to nurse, but the combination of no breast milk yet and his poorly organized sucking patterns made that an unrewarding time for them both. Startles dominated his motions. He became so jittery that the medical team insisted he be fed sugar water every few hours to counteract his low blood sugar. They explained to his mother that he was a typical dysmature baby with low fat and sugar stores. Due to no fault of hers, her placenta had "given out" and had not served him at the end of her pregnancy. Hence, he'd probably lost weight in the past three weeks and now his energy stores were too low to fuel him. Although they tried to reassure her, their very questions fueled her guilty feelings about him as they searched for causes—Was she smoking, on alcohol or drugs? Did she have an illness? Her insistent "no" became almost a cry for help as she, too, interrogated herself for why she'd produced this rather frightening "old" baby.

As long as he was allowed to lie in his crib, he seemed to be able to manage—looking off into the distance with wide, empty eyes and heavy breathing. His face continuously wore the worried, frowning look. If anyone came close to his crib, or rocked it, or touched him, or even spoke to him, either he seemed to sleep through it or, if he were awake, his frown deepened, he startled, and he seemed to want to withdraw. When his mother handled him, he invariably turned away from her. He seemed to avoid her face, her voice, her touch. If she continued to try to reach him by cuddling or talking to him or by rocking him, he became mildly blue around the mouth or spit up and arched away from her. Every response seemed to be a negative one. As his jitteriness increased and the worry about his hypoglycemia increased, everyone tried to help him. The nurses fed him hourly; his sucking on the breast became weaker. They roused him when he was sleepy. They swaddled him and left him alone when he was alert and active. Everything he did seemed to be "wrong" and the general worry about him heightened his parents' concerns. He was hard to rouse out of sleep, but when he finally woke, he quickly shot into an agitated state. There was no time in which his mother could see him as alert and receptive to her. Her heart ached. When he cried, he screeched in a piercing, painful way. When he stopped crying to gasp for air, he literally fell exhausted into a deep, unreachable sleep.

At Children's Hospital, we [TBB and colleagues] studied a sample of small-for-gestational-age babies who were below the fifth percentile in the height:weight ratio (Als et al., 1976). These infants suffered from acute placental insufficiency at the end of a healthy pregnancy. In a comparison with full-weight babies, their behaviors were seen as significantly different on days 1, 3, 5, and 10 in motor reflex behaviors (such as crawling, rooting, sucking, Moro, walking), but more importantly perhaps to parents, in scores of attractiveness, use of external stimuli, and the interactive measures of visual, auditory, and tactile communication. These babies seemed to be extremely hypersensitive and difficult for their parents to understand from the first. They cried inconsolably and excessively over the first four months and were still hypersensitive, distractible, and intensely overreactive when they were tested at nine months. Although their sensory abilities were equal to the full-weight control group, they were much more difficult to test because of their distractibility and overreaction to stimuli. Their parents described to us the enormous difficulties they had had in adjusting to these infants. This study helped us understand the high incidence among such babies of failure in parent–infant interaction, evidenced in failure-to-thrive, child abuse, and psychological disorders.

In these babies, the intrauterine stress has led to poor energy stores and hypoglycemia, coupled with other probable endocrine imbalances. These in turn lead to a kind of hypersensitivity to sensory stimuli, poor state controls with a long, protective latency before the babies can "allow" themselves to respond, then an overreactivity which invades their sensory, motor, gastrointestinal tract, and autonomic systems. Every response is painful to these babies and creates a painful reaction in the parents around them.

We have found that the behavioral correlates of this metabolic imbalance last long after the baby's sugar storage has been corrected. Whether the sensory hypersensitivity, the poor state control, and the motor overreactivity which continue are based on neurotransmitter difficulties which persist, or to exacerbation by anxious parents and other caregivers, cannot be determined as yet. If the baby's condition can be shared with parents in the newborn period, they at least see that this is not "their fault" and have an opportunity to shape a revised role with this difficult baby. Otherwise, their raw feelings of complicity make them even more vulnerable to a sense of failure.

Robert and Chris are extreme cases: the babies who seem to take care of themselves or those for whom it seems impossible to care. The vast majority of babies present some challenges, but ones that alert and caring parents are equipped to meet.

Emily, the third baby, was the first daughter of a twenty-four-year-old black woman who had "not anticipated this pregnancy" as she was a full-time schoolteacher. Although her husband had a job, her salary was necessary for them to survive with any kind of independence and comfort. Both had grown up in relative poverty, and they had worked hard to establish themselves. They wanted a real future for their children. The boys were six and four, launched in school and nursery school. Before this pregnancy, the family had finally been in balance. Now they had to work out new plans: maternity leave for four weeks, sick leave for another four—and then, they'd have to make it with substitute care. The father could help a lot when his job didn't demand him.

By the third day of Emily's life, the contrast between her and her brothers was striking. The boys had both been a pound heavier. Emily had small bones and an expressive face, with huge eyes, open and searching. She lay in her bed with her delicate arms and legs pulled up close to her body as if to conserve energy. When disturbed or undressed, she'd throw out all four extremities in a startle. She'd come awake suddenly with a cry, her arms and legs active with jerky and trembling motions. As she built up steam rapidly, she made unsuccessful attempts to quiet herself. She'd get her hand up close to her face, but a startle would send it flying. Then her outstretched arms would set her whole body off into uncontrolled movements. In the hospital, the nurses had found that swaddling or placing her on her belly kept her under control. They called her "little dynamite."

Her mother was already a bit intimidated. She'd had such an easy time with her boys that she wasn't prepared for anything else. And the thought of a demanding baby at this time in their lives when they were already close to the limit of their endurance was more than she could contemplate. A feeling of desperation came over her which she tried hard to push away.

When Emily was brought to her to feed, she wrapped up this tiny girl in layers of crib sheets and a blanket. The startling, jerky limbs disappeared and were contained. Her mother noticed that Emily became a different person. As if relieved to be rid of her startles and jerky movements, Emily would look around and listen to everything around her with almost-perceptible hunger. She'd look at her mother's face while nursing. If her mother moved, or talked, or if Emily heard any other sound, she'd stop to listen and turn away from the breast.

Emily preferred gentle handling and subdued noises. Whereas she might turn away from a loud noise or an abrupt stimulus, she'd turn toward a gentler, softer one. Her mother wondered how she'd ever manage at home with two active, noisy brothers. She began to test Emily's ability to take in sounds and touching. If she spoke gently to her as she built up to crying, she could "bring Emily down" to a quiet, alert state. If she stroked her gently or gave her a finger to suck on, Emily used it to keep herself quiet. Even when she was awake and upset, her mother soon found that handling her, rocking her in a containing embrace, or standing her up to bounce gently on her legs became ways that organized Emily and calmed her upset, driven states. She began to worry less but wished she had more time with Emily alone to be sure that this chance for learning about each other could continue. She knew what chaos awaited them when they went home.

This baby's ability to use the stimuli that her mother can offer her is her major asset. Her response to her mother's attention contrast with her own apparent inability to quiet herself, and this makes her appealing to her mother. Her delicate appearance and her need for help in handling state changes make her a rewarding baby to mother. If her disorganization should become predominant, their relationship could deteriorate. But if her mother can find the time and energy to work with her, and if Emily's controls improve over time, she will continue to be a rewarding baby, and they will have a constantly improving relationship. In the following part, we will look more closely at this early interaction as well as the stages through which these individual differences in temperament and fit will evolve.

PART THREE

Observing Early Interaction

A baby cannot exist alone, but is essentially part of a relationship.

—D. W. WINNICOTT
*The Child, the Family,
and the Outside World*

Introduction

The dialogue of cooing and smiling which charms an observer of three-
or four-month-old infants with their parents is both a new beginning
and an achievement with a history all its own. As we have seen, this
history begins even before conception, in the dreams and desires of
parents-to-be. At birth, the elaborate sensory and motor program of
the newborn and the powerful fantasies of the parents meet and seek
a new balance.

Both adult and baby bring powerful resources to this major adjustment. As we saw in Part I, the turmoil of pregnancy has mobilized
the emotional energy of the parents. Ambivalent feelings during this
period fuel them to seek and accept the baby's individuality, even
when it does not fit their dreams. This effort is evident in the way
parents fasten upon every detail of the baby's appearance: "She's the
image of your mother." "He's got my family's ears." The baby's
behavior is scrutinized with equal intensity.

The newborn is equipped with all of the complex sensory and motor
behaviors described in Part II. Nine months of intrauterine conditioning readies babies for the particular environment into which they are
born. The maternal cues they have received *in utero* have shaped their
responses and prepared them to be responsive to their mother's
rhythms and signals after delivery.

The remarkable capacities for attention and interactive behavior of the newborn when held and cared for by an adult have become more and more evident to us in our own research and clinical work, as well as in that of many others. We see the infant not as helpless, chaotic, or unpredictable, but equipped with highly predictable responses to both positive (appropriate to the infant) and negative (inappropriate or overloading) stimuli from the outside world. These responses in turn shape those of the caregiver to set up a mutual feedback system appropriate to that baby. Nature and nurture become inseparably entwined by the opportunities for reciprocal feedback in each interaction from the moment of birth.

10

Interaction Studies: An Overview

Before offering our own observations and model of the development of parent–infant interaction, we would like to review briefly some of the important studies which have opened up an understanding of the neonatal period and furthered our own research. The observation and analysis of parent–infant interactions has a fairly brief history—less than fifty years.

Psychoanalytic Studies

In the psychoanalytic field, direct observation of children and mothers has been developing since the late 1940s. René Spitz and Anna Freud studied children's behavior in situations where they were separated from parents, in institutions and under war conditions respectively (Spitz, 1946, 1964; A. Freud, 1936). Their studies alerted observers to the defensive operations that these stressful situations triggered in children. Thus the first insights into the nature of the child's dependency on important adults came from studies in which mothers were absent. These drastic experiments of nature underlined the powerful nature of the bond between mother and child. Descriptions of the severe pathology which resulted from the deprivation of mothering gave us deeper insight into the critical nature of this earliest relationship.

This deprivation model remained strong and motivated research until the mid-sixties. Among the most influential studies were those by Sally Provence and Rose Lipton (1963), James Robertson (1962), John Bowlby (1958), and Myriam David and Genevieve Appell (1961). Heinz Hartmann (1958) drew from similar studies to formulate his concept of ego development in the infant, seeing it as dependent on the quality of attachment to the parents.

Margaret Mahler was one of the first to study the observable, interactional correlates of interpersonal relations in very young children, especially in what she called the "symbiotic phase" (Mahler et al., 1975). While Mahler did not study infants under four months, many of her descriptions deal with interactional issues relevant to an earlier age. A typical example is the notion of "refueling." While analysts have always favored the term *relationship* over that of *interaction*, their object of study was the *intra*psychic aspect of relations. Spitz (1965) wrote that the "moulding" process "consists of a series of interchanges between two partners, the mother and the child, which reciprocally influence each other in a circular manner." These interchanges have been called by some authors "transactional," a description which fits what we call interaction today.

Psychoanalysis has also contributed to an appreciation of the enormous turmoil aroused in parents as they adjust to any baby, whether labelled difficult or not. As we will see in Parts IV and V, this turmoil creates not only a need for support but also a unique opportunity for change and growth.

The term "interaction" itself was first used by Bowlby in a famous paper, "The Nature of the Child's Tie to His Mother," which appeared in 1958. His work, which has had enormous influence among all who study attachment, led to an increasing use among researchers of the observational or ethological model in parent–infant studies. Bowlby, unlike earlier psychoanalysts, maintained that the exchange with the mother is not based solely on simple oral gratification and its concomitant tension reduction. In his view, there are many basic, *primary* modes of response to human partners. He called these "component instinctual responses," emphasizing their inborn patterning. He borrowed from ethology the idea of "species specific" innate mechanisms. For him, sucking, clinging, grasping, crying, and smiling are basic and innate modalities of interaction with, and attachment to, the mother.

He linked his assumption of primary attachment to Melanie Klein's later work which, he pointed out, saw "more in the infant's relation to his mother than the satisfaction of physiological needs" (Bowlby, 1958).

The work of D. W. Winnicott emphasized the crucial nature of what occurs between mother and infant in fostering the child's development. He used the word "breast" to stand for "the technique of mothering" as well as the "actual flesh." Food to him was only one among other important areas of interaction. He emphasized the importance of the experience of mutuality between infant and mother (1970). He also stated that babies have to be studied *with* their mothers. "I would not like the task of describing what is known about the newborn solo. . . . I like to assume that if we see a baby, we also see environmental provision and behind this we see the mother" (Winnicott, 1986). Bowlby's emphasis on the newborn's preadaptedness to play a role in social exchange with his caregiver, and Winnicott's view of mother and child as a single, interlocking unit have deeply affected interaction studies, including our own, until this day.

Ethological Observations

The ethological point of view has led us to appreciate the newborn's capacity and active adjustment to the interaction. Bowlby looked to ethology in his description of the very active nature of the child's attachment behaviors. From ethology comes the notion of the infant's competence and influence on the caregiver. Earlier psychoanalytic thinking, in contrast, stressed the infant's *dependency* on the mother, the need for gratification in order to hold drive tension in check. Since the mother was seen as the main source of gratification, when there was a failure in the interaction, it was seen as due to failure in the mother.

The emphasis on close observation derived from animal studies led researchers to recognize the infant's role in releasing the mother's maternal responses (by crying, etc.). The accent is on activity rather than helplessness; on eliciting behaviors, not passivity. In this light, the infant came to be seen as an active participant in forming the parent–infant relationship. Similar observations led to the recognition that infants create gratification for themselves, enhancing the perception of the infant as an agent in the relationship with a degree of independence.

Among other contributions of animal studies are Konrad Lorenz's concepts of *critical phase, imprinting,* and *innate releasing mechanisms* (Lorenz, 1957). Critical phases are times when energy is high in the infant and the parent for receptivity to each other's cues as well as for adapting to each other. The hours right after birth, as well as other periods of rapid change, can be seen as "critical phases." The phenomenon of "imprinting" derives from Lorenz's observations of goslings which follow and remember in a heightened way all the cues received from a parent figure immediately after hatching. Innate release mechanisms represent the built-in, hereditary, behavioral responses triggered in the baby by the parent's appropriate cues. These ethological terms, observed in mother–infant animal studies, have been applied to advantage in human infancy. Though the human infant and parent are much more plastic and open to adaptive change, these terms capture the powerful innate forces and heightened energy in the new parent and small baby which lead them to attach to and learn about each other.

The method of study in ethology was as influential to parent–infant research as were the concepts. Naturalistic observation, in natural surroundings, with particular attention to the exchange of signals, has yielded a wealth of insights. "Ethograms," catalogues of the behavioral repertoire of a species, are formulated from detailed analysis of observed behaviors. They have led to human studies which utilize microanalytic techniques for observation and recording behaviors. Robert Hinde, a leading figure in this field, observes that "the first stage in the study of interactional relationships should be one of description and classification." He stresses that in animal studies, "meshing of goals"—reciprocity and complementarity, terms relevant to human interactional studies—are basic (Hinde, 1976).

The influence of ethology led to interaction studies limited to descriptions of overt or surface behavior, without extrapolation of hidden motivation or meaning. However, Hinde emphasized that ". . . we must also remember that objective behavioral data can be misleading if devoid of meaning, and the quickest—and sometimes only—way to meaning may lie through the use of introspective evidence." As the present book makes clear, the student of interpersonal relationships must walk along a knife edge: objective data are essential for purposes of description and communication, but there is always a danger in neglecting the complexity and intersubjectivity inherent in relationships. As an example, the observation of self-gratifying behavior such as finger-sucking in an infant must be accompanied by insight into what this independence, this early loosening of the symbiotic tie, means to the mother. This challenge is a continuing one in all parent–infant studies.

Hinde also suggested that a description of interactions must include not only *what* the partners do but also *how* they are doing it, since the *qualities* of human interactions can be more important than what actually takes place. Ethological studies also reveal the necessity to describe how those interactions are patterned in time—that is, their absolute and relative frequencies and how they affect each other.

Learning and Interaction

Concepts derived from learning theory have also contributed to the understanding of early parent–infant interaction. Although, in our view, early interaction involves much more than classical learning theory could encompass, such concepts as imitation, positive and negative conditioning, reinforcement, and memory clearly apply.

Olga Maratos, in a 1973 doctoral dissertation, and more recently Andrew Meltzoff and M. K. Moore, have established the ability of newborns to *imitate* or match the facial movements of an adult as they get involved in interaction (Maratos, 1982; Meltzoff & Moore, 1977). The baby must be in a quiet, alert state; the adult must carefully match the baby just as he or she matches her. Then it is apparent that they can get locked in imitative behavior—both tongue-thrust and facial gesturing.

Conditioning and *reinforcement* are clearly involved from the earliest days. The infant produces a behavior (a smile, a vocalization, or a movement) initially accidental; the parent reinforces it with a positive response. The infant then receives feedback that his or her behavior was important. When newborn babies begin to recognize the nipple or bottle as a source of food and gratification, they then prepare themselves for gratification with all the behavior necessary for feeding—posture, attitude, attention, sucking, and coordination of breathing patterns. Later, they will lock in interactional behavior as well, and be ready for positive interaction from the caregiver as the source of this gratification.

One of the earliest studies of conditioning in newborns was done by Anderson Aldrich (1928), who sounded a bell while pricking the sole of an infant's foot with a pin. The infant, of course, withdrew his foot from the pinprick. After a dozen pairings, the sound of the bell alone was effective in producing the foot's withdrawal. H. Kaye (1967) used the Babkin reflex to study conditioning. This reflex, defined as a set of movements in which newborns bring their hands up to their mouths to suck on, can be triggered by pressing the newborn's palms. Kaye moved the arms from the infant's sides up to the head just before applying the palm pressure. Soon, this arm movement alone brought on the total reflex pattern, without the usual pressure on the palms. Kevin Connolly and Peter Stratton (1968) also conditioned this reflex by using a bell as they moved the baby's hand up to the mouth. Soon, it was possible to trigger hand-to-mouth movement by sounding the bell. While these studies and later ones demonstrate the possibility of conditioning in early infancy, they ignore the emotional responses that may be stored in the baby with each stimulus-response. How early these matter is as yet unknown.

The baby's ability to recognize the importance of even very minor reinforcers is already present at birth. A variety of studies using positive incentives has brought about changes in the normal sucking behavior of newborn babies. For example, by alerting the newborn and changing the degree of negative pressure in the mouth (Sameroff, 1968), by changing from plain to sweet fluids (Kobre & Lipsitt, 1972), the newborn infant can be induced to increase sucking activity.

One of the most impressive studies illustrating the quick learning ability of the newborn was done by Ernest Siqueland and Lewis Lipsitt (1966). On the first day after birth, newborns mastered head turning to one side 83 percent of the time, when sugar water was offered them after they turned. Once head turning was established, these newborns were taught to turn their heads to the left at the sound of a bell or to the right to the sound of a buzzer, by offering sugar water reinforcement only in response to the "correct" turns. The task was then complicated by reversing everything; bell and buzzer were switched and reinforcement made available only for the opposite turns. This was a challenging task calling for discrimination between the different sounds, left and right head turning, and learning a new arrangement in order to be reinforced by the sugar water. Infants who had learned bell-left, buzzer-right now had to forget this and learn bell-right, buzzer-left. All infants were able to accomplish this in short order— in about thirty minutes. This impressive study demonstrates the power of positive conditioning in reinforcing learned behaviors in the first few weeks of infancy.

For the parents, in turn, the infant's immediately available responses act as reinforcers. Evidence of recognition on the baby's part is deeply rewarding. Parents learn to rely on such responses from the infant— a state change from drowsy to alert, a brightening of the face, a smoothing out of motions in response to their response—as guides to their own behavior. When the responses from the infant are negative or are not present, a parent's anxiety is bound to increase. If the parent then overloads the baby with stimuli, the chance of reinforcing a lack of response is rapidly magnified. Although the resulting failure in interaction stems from the parent's hunger to reach the baby, it will appear to an observer (and to the baby) as the result of insensitive and inappropriate approaches.

The faculty of *memory* is implicitly involved in all activities in which newborns learn from experience. When they express their preferences, or when they become habituated to a stimulus, they are demonstrating a kind of primitive memory. Testing the memory of neonates for particular words, Peter Eimas, Ernest Siqueland, and colleagues (1971) had mothers repeat unfamiliar words (e.g., tender or beguile) ten times in a row at six different times during the day for two weeks starting at fourteen days of age. After a 42-hour delay at the end of training, the infants showed clear signs of recognition of these words as measured by eye activity, head turning, and raised eyebrows. Since they recognized and responded to these words (and didn't to their own names during this same period), it is thought that the frequent and regular exposure to the words was the critical factor in encoding and storing the information.

Experiments with infants a few months old have revealed the infant's capacity for both short- and long-term memory (Cohen & Salapatek, 1975). Attempts to interfere with memory deliberately by inserting irrelevant material has shown that (1) infant memory is relatively robust and insensitive to a host of interfering stimuli; (2) memory can be retained for a long period of time; and (3) infants tend to retain longest those characteristics of objects that are most salient and important to them.

None of these laboratory studies can be as effective in reinforcing an infant's memory as are the times when parent and infant are involved in spontaneous, reciprocal interaction, each giving and receiving rewarding cues from the other. When the mother presents a cue, such as a bright vocalization, which has worked before, she has already built up an expectation that it will produce a brightening of the baby's face, stilling of random movements, and head turning to her voice. When the baby turns immediately and responds as if from memory, she feels doubly reinforced. "He *knows* my voice!" "See how she listens!" Her efforts to produce these responses are redoubled. As her ability to do so increases, her motivation and the rewards she offers the infant are fueled.

Quantitative Research in Infant Interaction Studies

The quantitative study of infant and parent behavior has tended to separate researchers from pediatric clinicians and psychoanalysts. Researchers are likely to endeavor to restrict their observations to the measurable aspects of behavior; clinicians are likely to be concerned with the quality of behavior and the deeper nuances of meaning that elude attempts at quantification. Reliability ratings between observers are necessary in any research, and they often reveal that observable behavior is difficult to quantify. For clinicians, the incidence of a certain behavior may be less important than its meaning, its intensity, its significance in eliciting reactions or responses from the other member of the dyad.

Early quantitative studies were mainly concerned with incidence of various kinds of behavior. For instance, Harriet Rheingold used a checklist to record what infants were doing and the nature of the caretaker acts (Rheingold, 1961). The observations were time-bound: every fifteen seconds for the first ten minutes of every consecutive quarter hour for four hours. Frequencies were recorded. For example, a mother may speak ten times in an hour to her baby, the baby may respond three times with vocal behavior. Her work was typical of early interaction studies.

As such work became more sophisticated, the active role of the infants themselves in shaping the interaction became increasingly recognized. Richard Bell pointed out that "the basic model of socialization, the action of a parent on a child, is too limited to accommodate data emerging from recent studies. The effect of children on parents has to be recognized" (Bell, 1968). He emphasized, for example, the influence of babyness (from a newborn's uncontrolled thrashing movements to the shape of the head, etc.) in pushing a new parent toward the job of protecting and gently nurturing the new, fragile offspring. He first criticized attachment theory for not paying enough attention to the detailed nature of each interactant. This led to interest in subtler but perhaps more important behavioral competencies in babies which could be influential in capturing a parent. The evident necessity for objective, quantified descriptions of each partner gave the impetus to develop microanalytic techniques of assessing mother–infant interactions.

Quantification brought essential dimensions to a study of interaction. Quantification of behavior reveals trends and sets the base for *qualification* of behavior (intrusive, avoiding, hyperactive, reciprocal, etc.). Objectification of *sequential interactional behavior* gives insight into "cause and effect" relations between partners and between separate items of behavior. Time distribution allows for the uncovering of cycles and rhythms. Finally, quantification can help to interpret "intentions" or "meanings." Various frequencies of gaze aversion, for instance, can indicate contact avoidance, shutting off of interaction, or autistic-like behavior. Subtle variations may even reveal conflicts or aggressive intentions. Quantified data obviously need to be supplemented by other kinds of observation to confirm these interpretations.

Some behavior is not seen by the naked eye. It is revealed only through analysis of discrete time units, such as is done, for example, in video film frame analysis. Analysis of interactional data led to the use of more sophisticated machinery. Description of voice intonation is made with sound spectrographs. Sequences of interactive behaviors are examined in frame-by-frame analysis of film. Some patterns of behavior emerge *only* when such mechanical recordings are applied. In studying movements, Colwyn Trevarthan noted, "Until the invention of cinephotography, the details of movements were as far from human vision as were the planets before the invention of the telescope" (Trevarthan, 1977).

11

Interaction in Context

More current studies of parent–infant interaction, including our own, have moved away from analysis of molecular behaviors and discrete time units to more global and contextual approaches. When single behaviors are added together, patterns of behavior and response begin to take on significance. Clusters of behavior from the parent can be seen as a stimulus and clusters of behavior from the infant as a response. Embedded in particular phases of the interaction (as well as the emotional reactions of each participant), the behaviors take on a shaded meaning. For example, an interaction can be broken into periods of initiation, regulation, maintenance, and termination. The same behavior in each of these periods is of different significance. Hence, an interaction must be looked at as a process, with cycles of engagement and disengagement. Within each cycle, behavior can be labelled for quality—intrusive, reciprocal, empathic, or violating.

In this model is an assumption of mutual influence—one member acting on and shaping the other, but also acted upon and shaped *by* the other. Each member stores a memory or expectancy of the other that shapes his or her responses. All the individual differences in infants described in Part II affect parents, whose history and fantasies, as described in Part I, determine their ability to be shaped and respond in turn.

The communicative dimension of interaction has also been studied. Behavior can be seen as a signal that determines the partner's response. Facial expressions, play, pitch of voice are used as indicators by each partner. Intensity of affective display has communicative value. These messages have two aspects: a content aspect and a regulatory aspect (Brazelton, 1976). The content refers to an event or object and is similar to what Watzlawick, Beavin, and Jackson (1967) call a "report." The regulatory aspect contains information about a communicant's acceptance, rejection, or modification of the current state of the interaction. It is a "metacommunication" (i.e., a communication about a communication).

While each separate gesture or expression is a communication, the timing and the sensitive clustering of behaviors communicates more than the behaviors themselves. For example, a mother will lean over her baby, reach for a flailing extremity, hold the baby by the buttocks, enclose him or her in an envelope made up of her intense gaze and her soft vocalizations. Out of this cluster of five behaviors, she will heighten one of them, her voice, to elicit a response. As her voice increases gently, the infant responds with a cluster of behaviors—relaxation of the whole body, softening of facial features, intense looking at her, then a soft "coo." The mother's clustering of behaviors around each vocalization is as important in producing the response as her voice alone. A baby must be "contained" in order to attend to her. The mother also must learn her baby's system of clusters. The capacity of a mother to form a behavioral envelope to contain the baby, to maintain the baby's alert state, and to allow the necessary rhythms of attention–withdrawal becomes critical to her ability to communicate. Then, being able to alternate roles becomes important. If she can create an expectancy or predictability within which the infant can learn relevance and nonrelevance of cues, she will have provided the necessary base for learning to communicate with her.

Nonverbal communication demands a level of control in the infant over neuromotor and psychophysiological systems. Infants must be able to alert and to pay prolonged attention to cognitive and affective cues from the outside. At the same time, infants must know enough about themselves not to be overwhelmed by outside stimuli. The central nervous system, as it develops, drives infants toward mastery of themselves and their world. As they achieve each level of mastery, they seek a kind of homeostasis, until the nervous system presses them on to the next level. Internal equilibrium is always being upset by a new imbalance created as the nervous system matures. Maturation of the nervous system, accompanied by increasing differentiation of skills, drives infants to reorganize their control systems. At each step, parents must also readjust, finding a new, more appropriate way of reaching out.

This interlocking feedback in a mutually regulated system still seems to be best captured by the concept of cybernetics (Walcher & Peters, 1971). Within a continuous feedback cycle, the mother-infant and the father-infant dyads can be depicted, as well as the mother-father-infant triad (Tronick et al., 1977; Brazelton, 1979; Dixon et al., 1981). The baby learns about synchronization as well as differentiation with each partner, and they, in turn, with the baby. Each disruption of the system allows for separation, differentiation, and individuation for each member of the triad. With reorganization, the feeling of equilibrium and of resynchronization is achieved by each member.

Sources of Fueling

There are two sources of fueling for the costly maturation in this feedback system (Brazelton & Yogman, 1986). Loops that close on completion of an anticipated performance affect the baby from within. In brief, anticipation generates energy; preconscious realization that the step is completed creates a satisfying reward. In this way, a sense of mastery is incorporated by the developing infant, freeing up energy which drives the infant toward the next achievement.

At the same time, the environment around the infant, when it is nurturant, fuels infant development and enhances each experience. If the baby says "ooh," for instance, parents say, "That's right," and after a third "ooh," they are likely to say, "Aren't you wonderful!" Each vocalization on the part of the infant is reinforced by an encouraging response. Not only do parents recognize and approve an infant's achievement, but they often add further signals to their approval. Coupled with the positive reinforcement, these signals fuel infants and lead them to match the adult's expectation. When an infant vocalizes with an "ooh," a parent might add, "Oh, yes!" to it. In this way, parents offer the infant positive reinforcement and add on a goal to reach for.

Under ideal conditions, these two sources of energy—from within and without—are in balance and provide the energy for future development. The infant's experience of each of these sources adds to a preconscious recognition of mastery, a developing sense of competence. This internal representation, together with the closure of feedback loops for steps within autonomic and central nervous system control, becomes a precursor of emotional and then cognitive recognition of competence and contributes to the infant's developing ego (Brazelton, 1981).

When all goes well for infants, achieving each new act has these double rewards. Genetic endowment, however, determines the kind of internal and external feedback systems that are available. When either system is deficient, the infant's control over affective and cognitive states can be impaired. This occurs when (1) an infant for a number of reasons is unresponsive to stimuli, or (2) has a low threshold for the intake of stimuli and is thus overwhelmed. If the environment is also inappropriately responsive to the infant (either over or under), interactions will not be rewarding. When failure is consistent, the infant may fail to develop in certain critical ways, and may become withdrawn, apathetic, or even fail to thrive.

The power of another sort of fuel for these earliest interactions, the past experience of the parents, has been discussed in Part I. In Part IV, we will explore the variety of parental fantasies and their impact, as well as the various scenarios in which these fantasies can be played out.

Infant and Object

The regulatory system which underlies attention to any object was first defined by T. G. Bower (1969), Jerome Bruner (1969), and Colwyn Trevarthan (1977), as they elicited the behaviors involved in early reaching. They studied infants paying attention to an object in "reach space" (10–12 inches in front of them in the midline). As infants watch an object, they found, all their behavior reflects their intense, rapt attention. Not only do they have an observable, predictable "hooked" state of attention as the object is brought into this space, but also their entire bodies respond in an appropriate and predictable fashion as they attend to the object.

In these studies, six-week-old infants stare at the object with wide eyes, fixating on it for as long as two minutes without disruption of gaze. Their expressions are fixed, the muscles of their faces tense, with eyes staring and mouth and lips protruding toward the object. This static, fixed look of attention is interspersed with little jerks of facial muscles. Their tongues jerk out toward the object and then withdraw rapidly. Occasional short bursts of vocalizing toward the object occur. During these long periods of attention, the eyes blink occasionally in single, isolated blinks. The body is set in a tense, immobilized sitting position, with the object at its midline. When the object is moved to one side or the other, the infants tend to shift their bodies. Their shoulders hunch as if about to "pounce." Extremities are fixed, flexed at elbow and knee, fingers and toes aimed toward the object. Hands are semiflexed or tightly flexed, but fingers and toes repeatedly jerk out to point at the object. Jerky swipes of an arm or leg in the direction of the object occur from time to time. During this period, the infant seems to hold down any interfering behavior that might break into this prolonged state of attention. Tension gradually builds up in all segments of the infant's body until finally an abrupt lapse of attention comes as an inevitable and necessary relief.

The behavior described here becomes more striking by 12–16 weeks, but can be observed as early as four weeks of age, long before a reach could be achieved.

Infant and Parent

The contrast between infant behavior and attention when attending to an object and when interacting with a parent can be seen as early as four weeks of age.

Of course, the expectancy engendered in an interaction with a static object, as opposed to a responsive person, is very different (Piaget, 1951, 1954). What is surprising is how early this expectancy seems to be reflected in the infant's behavior and use of attention (Brazelton, 1976). When infants are interacting with their mothers, there seems to be a cycle of attention followed by withdrawal of attention—a cycle used by each partner as he or she approaches and then withdraws and waits for a response from the other participant. Within this cycle, clusters of behaviors rather than simple behaviors are the stimuli that control the timing of each interactant's response to the other. A smile alone does not necessarily produce a smile, nor does a vocalization alone produce a vocalization. But if they are embedded in several other behaviors, the likelihood of a matching response is markedly increased. In order to understand which cluster of behaviors will result in a set of responsive behaviors in the other member of the dyad, one must also understand the state of affective attention that exists between them. In other words, the strength of the interaction itself dominates the meaning of each member's behavior. If the mother responds in one way, the interactional energy builds up; if another, the infant may turn away. The same holds true of her responses to the infant's behavior. Predictions of interactive behavior are thus of a complexity several orders greater than those of an infant's attention to an object.

This complexity in the interaction of mother and child is best represented in graphic form (Brazelton et al., 1974). The figures shown are graphs drawn from mother–infant interaction periods. Time is measured along the horizontal axis; the number of behaviors, along the vertical axis. Curves drawn above the horizontal axis indicate that the individual whose behavior the curve represents was looking at his or her partner. Curves drawn below the axis indicate that he or she was looking *away*. Solid lines represent the mother's behavior; broken lines, the baby's. Thus, a deep, broken line below the horizontal axis indicates that the baby was looking away while engaging in several behaviors.

As reflected by Figure 1 (16-second interaction), the mother looks at the baby after the baby turns to her. As they look at each other, she adds behaviors—smiling, vocalizing, touching baby's hand, holding baby's leg—to accelerate their interaction. The baby responds by increasing the number of his or her own behaviors (smiling, vocalizing, and cycling arms and legs) until the peak at point (a). At this point, the baby begins to decrease his or her behaviors and gradually cuts down on them toward the end of their interaction. The mother follows

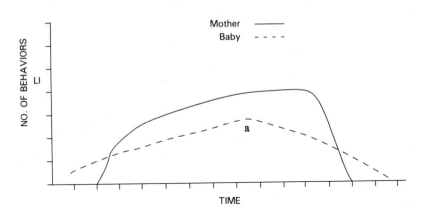

Figure 1

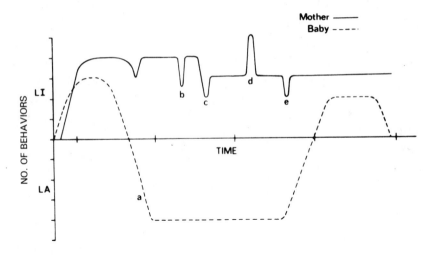

Figure 2

the baby's lead by decreasing her behaviors more rapidly, and she ends her part of the cycle by looking away just before the baby does. Figure 2 (5-second interaction) shows a baby starting a cycle by looking at the mother. She follows by looking at the baby and adding four more behaviors in rapid succession—touching, smiling, talking, and nodding her head. The baby watches her, vocalizes, smiles back, cycles briefly, and then begins to decrease his or her responses and turns away at point (a). The mother stops smiling as the baby begins to turn away, but rapidly adds facial gestures to try to recapture the baby's interest. She continues to talk, touch, nod her head, and make facial gestures until point (b). At this point, she stops the gestures but begins to pat the baby. At (c), she stops talking briefly and stops nodding. At (d), she makes hand gestures in addition to her facial grimaces but stops them both thereafter. At point (e), she stops vocalizing, and the baby begins to look at her again. He or she vocalizes briefly and then looks away again when her activity continues.

In Figure 3 (also a 5-second period), the mother and baby are looking at each other, smiling, and vocalizing together. The baby begins to cycle and reach out to her. At point (a), the baby begins to turn away from the mother. She responds by looking down at her hands, and she stops her activity briefly. This brings the baby back to look at her at point (c). Her smiling, vocalizing, and leaning toward the baby bring a smiling response. In addition, the baby's arms and legs cycle, and he or she coos contentedly while watching her. As the baby turns away, the mother first adds another behavior and gestures. The baby, however, adds activities—ignoring her reminders—and turns away from her. She gradually cuts out all her activity and by point (e), she looks away from her baby. Immediately afterward, the baby begins to look back to her, and the cycle of looking at each other begins again at point (f).

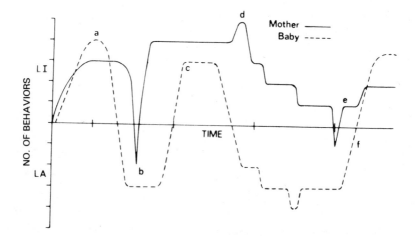

Figure 3

The power of the interaction in shaping each participant's behavior can be seen at many levels. Using looking and not looking at the mothers as measures of attention–inattention, in a 1-minute interaction there was an average of 4.4 cycles of such attention and apparent inattention. Not only were the spans of attention and of looking away of shorter duration than they are with objects, but they are smoother as the attention builds up, reaches its peak, and then diminishes gradually with the mother. Both the buildup, as well as the decrease in attention, are gradual and usually smoothly paced.

A mother's most effective technique in maintaining an interaction seems to be a sensitivity to her infant's capacity for attention and need for withdrawal—partial or complete—after a period of attending to her. Short cycles of attention and inattention seem to underlie all periods of prolonged interaction. Although there appears to be continuous attention to the mother on the part of the infant, stop-frame analysis uncovers the cyclical nature of the infant's looking and not looking. By looking away, infants maintain some control over the amount of stimulation they take in during such intense periods of interaction.

This rhythm of attention–inattention is basic to the homeostatic model described earlier. Mothers must search for and respect their infants' need for the regulation that this affords, or they will overload their infants' immature psychophysiological system and their infants will need to protect themselves by turning the mother off completely (Brazelton et al., 1975). Within this rhythmic, coherent configuration, mother and infant can introduce the mutable elements of communication: smiles, vocalizations, postures, and tactile signals. They can be interchanged at will, as long as they are kept within the rhythmic structure. The individual differences in the pacing of such a structure set the limits. The mother then has the opportunity to adapt her tempo within these limits. If she speeds up her tempo, she can reduce baby's level of communication. If she slows hers down, she can expect a higher level of engagement and communicative behavior from the infant (Stern, 1974a). Her use of tempo to influence the baby's response is probably the basis of the baby's learning about his or her own control systems. As the level of stimulation is gently varied, the baby learns about basic self-regulation.

The mother, in turn, is learning about herself and her role. Mothers must learn how to maintain a calm regulatory base, not overloading the baby with too much stimulation, reducing their own output to synchronize with their babies' need to turn away and regulate themselves. At each state, the mother is learning a great deal about the process of nurturing.

Differences between Mothers and Fathers in Early Interaction

Differences between mother–infant and father–infant interaction are apparent even in the early weeks. The differences are largely qualitative (Yogman et al., 1976). Fathers are more likely to play heightened, stimulating games. They poke and touch, heightening the baby's state of excitement. A baby's response when hearing his or her father's voice, recognizing his face and other cues, will be to raise the shoulders in a pouncelike posture. The baby will watch the father carefully at first, then giggle, cry out with excitement, then withdraw briefly before another period of excitement. A rhythm of higher peaks and longer periods of recovery characterize infants' interactions with their fathers in contrast to their mothers.

These differences are stable over time and are registered in predictable behavioral clusters. They signal to the adult partner that the infant recognizes him or her and expects a certain pattern of response in return. They also suggest different roles on the part of the adult, for example, mother providing an envelope for interactive behaviors, father a base from which play can emerge. The stability of these patterns also implies the infant's need for expectable responses from each parent. Two differing sets of responses will enrich the infants' cognitive and affective expectancy of the world.

The father learns his role on the job, as does the mother. He adjusts his behavior, his own rhythms, to those of the baby, and learns about his capacity to respond and to nurture. The special behaviors saved for him make him feel important and reassure him about his role. A nurturing father develops in much the same set of stages as does the mother. Both parents learn about themselves as nurturers, as they respond to and interact with their infant's nonverbal cues.

12

Still-Face Studies

In contrast to the observation of undisturbed mother–infant interaction, much can be learned from the introduction of a well-defined variation into that interaction. The so-called "still-face" situation is one of the best known of such approaches, and one of the most thoroughly explored. Together with colleagues at the Child Development Unit at Boston Children's Hospital, we [TBB] have investigated and videotaped this situation since 1978 (Tronick et al., 1978).

In the basic study, two video cameras were utilized, one on the baby's face and upper body, the other on the mother's face and upper body. The cameras were fed into a split screen recording, with a second-by-second digital timer recording the real time of their interaction.

The baby, after being soothed and contented, was placed in a reclining infant's seat on a table in a curtained alcove. The mother was asked to enter the alcove to "play with the baby in the chair, as she did at home." She could do everything but take the baby out of the chair. We asked her to play with the baby for three minutes, then to withdraw briefly. After a minute, the mother was asked to return for a second 3-minute period. She was instructed to present a perfectly still face and not to respond to the baby. She was thus violating the expectancy set up in the previous play situation. This situation would test the extent to which the baby relied on the expectancy and would demonstrate the nature of the baby's coping behaviors. Over the past ten years, we have studied and analyzed some hundred dyads, with infants from one to four months. More recently, with Suzanne Dixon and Michael Yogman (Dixon et al., 1981), we have studied fathers and infants in this situation. We have also varied the studies to include blind infants with sighted parents, blind parents with sighted infants (Als et al., 1980), brain-damaged infants, infants with congenital facial anomalies, and more recently, premature infants with their parents (Als & Brazelton, 1981).

In a typical session, a three-month-old baby girl's response to the situation might progress as follows. Before the second 3-minute period, while still alone, the baby might be looking contemplatively down at her hands, fingering the fingers of one hand with the other. As the mother enters, her hand movements stop. She looks up at her mother, makes eye-to-eye contact, and smiles. The mother's masklike expression does not change. The baby looks quickly to one side and remains quiet, her facial expression serious. Her gaze remains averted for twenty seconds. Then she looks back at her mother's face, her eyebrows and lids raised, hands and arms stretching slightly out toward the mother. Finding no response, she quickly looks down again at her hands, plays with them for about eight seconds, and then checks her mother's face once more. Her look is now cut short by a yawn, with her eyes and face turning upward. Her fingers pull at the fingers of her other hand, the rest of her body is motionless. The yawn and neck stretches last five or so seconds. The baby throws out one arm in a slight startle and looks briefly at the mother's face. Her arms move in a jerky fashion. Her mouth curves downward, her eyes narrow and partially lidded. She turns her face to the side, but keeps her mother in peripheral vision. She fingers her hand again, her legs stretch toward her mother and rapidly jerk back again. She arches forward, slumps over, tucks her chin down on one shoulder, but looks up at her mother's face from under lowered eyebrows. This last position lasts for over a minute, with brief looking at the mother occurring almost every ten seconds. She grimaces briefly, and her facial expression becomes more serious, her eyebrows furrowing. Finally, the baby completely withdraws, her body curls over, her head falls. She does not look again at her mother. She begins to finger her mouth, sucking on one finger and rocking her head, looking at her feet. She looks wary, helpless, and withdrawn. As the mother leaves the alcove at the end of the three minutes, she looks halfway up in her direction, but her somber facial expression and curled-over body position do not change.

The consistent pattern of infant behavior in the still-face situation is repeated attempts to elicit mother's response, followed by somber expression, orientation away from mother, and finally withdrawal. All this takes place in less than three minutes. The fact that infants in this situation are so consistently and demonstrably disappointed by the failure in their ability to recapture the mother, and so vulnerable to what they see as her rejection, is evidence of their overriding dependence on a mother's "envelope," on her predictable response to them. After initial efforts and initial protest, they collapse into a self-protective state. First, they try to avoid the need they have to look at their mother. Then they try to "turn off" their environment completely. Finally, they try their own techniques for self-comforting. These sequential behaviors demonstrate both their vulnerability and their powerful expectancy for the levels of interaction their mothers have taught them. The three stages of response have been compared to the stages of behavior seen in hospitalized infants (Bowlby, 1969).

This still-face situation has been tried with many variations. When mothers were asked, while facing their infants, to imagine how they felt when they were overtired and depressed, the infants' displays were significantly changed. They showed increased frequencies of brief positive elicitations, followed by increased proportions of negative responses, such as protest or wariness (Cohn & Tronick, 1983).

When we began these investigations, we expected the infant to demonstrate a reliance on predictable reactions in the parent. However, we were not looking for the meaning to the parents of the baby's obvious disappointment. We found that when the baby became disappointed and withdrawn, the mother became agitated and depressed as well. The mothers in our studies told us of how it affected them. As they sat there, unable to respond to their babies' elicitations, they felt a combination of excitement both at how important they were to their babies and at how competent their babies' elicitations were, coupled with a sense of real personal loss. Each said something along these lines: "It was all I could do, not to respond. I felt as if I were deserting my baby. I felt torn away from her, and I felt as if I were losing a part of myself. I felt sad, angry, desperate in turns. I never want to do it again. When you let me go back and respond, I felt tremendous relief—and a sense of real accomplishment at how much we mean to each other. How much we've learned about each other!"

This short gap in communication at first leaves the mother feeling helpless, ineffective, even frightened. She, too, is still vulnerable and unsure of her capacity to capture and maintain an interaction. When it is going successfully, the feedback from the baby fuels her and rewards her efforts. In the still-face situation, when she sees the baby fall apart in front of her, she realizes both the baby's vulnerability and the shakiness of her own achievements so far. It threatens her own confidence in having achieved these first stages of dialogue. The relief she demonstrates after this condition is over is almost euphoric. She feels how necessary she is and how powerful they are as a team—powerful enough to handle the baby's vulnerability, powerful enough to give her the cues she needs to go on developing as a mother. This "violation" underlines the importance of the work they have already done to reach each other.

Realizing how painful it was for mothers to see their infants' over-reaction and withdrawal, we invited mothers to watch these tapes with us after the experimental situation. When they saw the sequence of behaviors in their babies, they first said, "I never knew I was so important to my baby." Then they rushed back to try to make up for it with the baby. When the normal interaction is recaptured, it has been affected; the infants generally show a period of initial wary monitoring of the mother. Occasionally, they would even arch away. Mothers would generally apologize to their infants, saying things like "I am real again." Within thirty seconds, infants gave in once again to the normal interaction sequence.

As we will see in Part V, depressed mothers often create this violation of their babies' expectancy. When they are able to interact normally from time to time, they set up the expectancy in their babies. At other times, they withdraw because of their own needs, leaving the babies in a state of depression and hopelessness. Such a repeated pattern can account for the classic symptoms of gaze avoidance (because it's painful to allow the expectancy to form again), of gastrointestinal hypermotility (under stress), of autonomic fragility (from the anxiety generated), of inability or unwillingness to interact socially with an eliciting adult. The still-face research helps us to understand these distorted interactions as a magnification of normal processes.

Social interaction is a rule-governed, goal-oriented system in which both partners share actively. The still-face condition violates the rules of this system by simultaneously conveying contradictory information about the partner's goal or intent. The mother, by her entrance and *en face* position, is initiating and setting the stage for an interaction, but her lack of response indicates a disengagement or withdrawal. She is communicating "hello" and "goodbye" simultaneously. Infants, who apprehend this display of intent, are trapped in the contradiction. They respond to the apparent intent and greet the mother, then turn away and withdraw temporarily, only to initiate again. If the infant's efforts fail to get the interaction back on track and to establish reciprocity, complete withdrawal eventually results.

13

Four Stages in Early Interaction

Now that we have examined the nature of early interaction and also how our understanding of it has become more refined, we can begin to outline distinct stages in its development. Elsewhere, we [TBB] have described four stages in mother–infant interaction (Brazelton & Als, 1979). Keeping in mind the feedback model just discussed, and the skills and programming in both parent and infant presented in Parts I and II, we will attempt to identify the progression of achievements these stages represent. The stages can be described as follows: homeostatic control, prolonging of attention and interaction, testing limits, and the emergence of autonomy. Since our work has been with mother-infant pairs, we will describe it as such, although a close father-infant pair will experience a similar development in their relationships.

Homeostatic Control

The first task for infants is to achieve control over their input and output systems. They must be able to shut out as well as to receive stimuli, and also to control their own states and physiological systems. In order to pay attention to adult interactants, infants must control motor activity, state of consciousness, and autonomic responses. Attention to incoming stimuli from an adult demands control over all of these conditions. To achieve a state of attention, infants must learn the preconditions that lead to it, as well as the conditions that surround behavioral responses when they achieve them. This occurs in normal infants in the first week or ten days. The parents' job, as we have seen, is to learn how to contain the baby, how to reduce their own input in order not to overwhelm the fine balance in the infant, and how to fit their own behavioral responses to the particular individual thresholds of their baby. This is the first step in learning how to care for a baby.

A deep sense of empathy puts mothers in touch with their babies' control systems. A mother has described this experience thus: "I felt as if I were inside my baby—as if I were a baby again, as if I were that baby. But then when I look at how competent she is, I know it is more a feeling of experiencing what she is going through in order to control herself and to pay attention. At first I want to do it all for her, but as I watch her, I see that it is so much more important to 'help' her do it for herself. She struggles so hard, and I struggle with her. I can hardly keep from holding her all the time."

The intense identification that we described in Part I helps her understand her baby's struggle to achieve control in this disorganized period. As the mother struggles with her own sense of separation, depression, and disorganization following the major effort of labor and delivery, it must be reassuring to be able to glimpse the emerging competence of the baby. When we share the NBAS with a new parent, we see how meaningful the realization of her baby's competence can be. Her identification with the baby allows her to get on with the often difficult job of accepting the physical separation and also with supporting the needs of a separate individual.

Prolonging of Attention

Having achieved some degree of control, infants can begin to attend to and use social cues to prolong their states of attention and to accept and incorporate more complex trains of messages. In this stage, infants begin actively to prolong interaction with an important adult. As they control their motor and autonomic systems in order to pay attention, they become aware of their capacity to master this process. They learn to utilize cues from the adult to maintain alertness. They also use their own rapidly increasing capacities—smiles, vocalizing, facial behaviors, motor cues—to signal their receptivity and to draw out her responses. They learn how to adapt themselves to the rhythmic give-and-take of a synchronized relationship. This process takes place in the period of one to eight weeks, peaking with social smiling and vocalizing at the end of the infant's second month. By then, each member of the dyad has learned the necessary ingredients of a mutually rewarding and prolonged interactional system.

During this same time, the mother has been learning from the infant and reconstructing a new image of herself. All of the work of pregnancy has heightened her need to learn her new role. The negative side of her ambivalence serves to keep her unsure, self-questioning. It also fuels her search for cues from outside herself. Complacency is not possible at this time. Not only does she turn to everyone around her—her husband, her own mother, a physician, a nurse, friends, and peers—but she is highly sensitive to her baby's responses. Each cue, however slight, a brightening response, motor suppression, not to mention a smile, acts as a reward for her quest. In her hunger for these rewards, she continues to learn her baby's thresholds, her baby's temperament and style of response. She relives her past, greedily observes her own mother or her own peers as they play with her baby. She reaches for any experience, any traditional wisdom to build upon.

As a mother learns that the rhythms of the baby underlie the capacity to attend to her, she synchronizes her own behavior to the infant's. She learns to match the infant's cues, to time her responses. She learns to turn away or to tune down when the baby does. And she learns that she can add a little bit of magnification to each behavior which will lead the baby on. As the baby smiles, she smiles more broadly, teaching the baby how to prolong a smile. As the infant vocalizes, she adds a word or a trill, leading toward imitation. By matching her rhythms, her behaviors to the baby's, she enters the baby's world, offering an incentive to reach for her. As she does all this, her own need to become the longed-for parent begins to feel fulfilled. She can even experience an identification with her own mother.

Testing Limits

With the possibility of an extended dialogue in place, both parents and infants begin to test and stretch the infant's limits. They begin to press the limits of (1) infant capacity to take in and respond to information, and (2) infant ability to withdraw and recover in a homeostatic system. During the third and fourth months, sensitive adults press infants just to the limits of both of these and allow infants time and opportunity to realize that they have incorporated these increased abilities into their own repertoires. The mother has learned her role; the baby is now able to experiment.

In their now-prolonged state of attunement to each other, mother and infant can play serial games of smiling to smiling, or vocalizing to vocalizing, touching to touching. Daniel Stern (1974b, 1977, 1985) has described these games and pointed out that, in them, both mother and baby learn to match the other's intensity, the contour of intensity, the temporal beat, rhythm, duration, and shape of each other's rhythmic behavioral displays. In the process, each member learns about him or herself, as well as about the rewards of socializing with the other. These "games" become a way for the infant to explore inner controls and the ability to attune to the other. For the mother, it becomes confirmation of her ability to understand her child and, especially, to encourage his or her development.

As they play together, mother and baby, both are experiencing mastery. For the baby, it is the ability to sequence controls and the production of signals. The mother is also developing a sense of control—not only over the baby's responses but over herself and her own impatience, over her own need to get away to an adult world. She experiences a sense of being completely available to another being. She tests her abilities as a truly nurturing person—able to identify at several levels with a dependent other. Her fears of being inadequate begin to fade and nearly vanish in these brief game periods. During this same period, a mother often experiences a renewed sense of herself as a loving person. She can afford to love her husband and her own mother more deeply. As she begins to sense her power, her own postpartum depression begins to lift, and she experiences the full exhilaration of parenting. It is this period that mothers remember later as the high point of attachment, of being in love with the baby.

If the interaction does not become rewarding during the third or fourth month, if some of this testing and play does not take place, the parent-infant fit may be at high risk. A sense of joy in this play is the best sign of a good fit. As we will see in Part V, assessment and intervention during this period will depend on such clues.

Emergence of Autonomy

At the point where the mother or father can permit the baby to be the leader or signal-giver, when the adult can recognize and encourage the baby's independent search for and response to environmental or social cues and games—to imitate them, to reach for and play with objects—a vital landmark has been reached. The infant's sense of competence and of voluntary control over his or her environment is strengthened. A most common sign of this development can be seen in normal infants at 4–5 months during a feeding, when they stop to look around and attend to their environment. When a mother can allow this and even foster it, she is encouraging her infant's burgeoning autonomy.

Such initiatives in the baby accompany a spurt in cognitive awareness at 4–5 months. The baby becomes acutely aware of every sight and sound and texture. Aware of the parents' presence and absence, the infant begins to anticipate their leaving by recognizing cues. A baby will now cry "for attention." Object permanence is just beginning, and the baby will look hard at the spot where an object was after it disappears. This increasing sensitivity to the world around makes a baby sense the importance of his or her parents. Coincident with this increased awareness, the baby begins to play games to test out their attachment, tuning them in and tuning them out. Control of their attention enables a baby to begin to separate and become independent.

This fourth stage in our system of parent–infant interaction takes place at about 4–4½ months, after the intense game-playing of the third and fourth month. This stage, called "hatching" by Margaret Mahler, is accompanied by a kind of awareness of the baby's autonomy on the part of both the baby and the mother (Mahler et al., 1975). Up to this point, the mother (or father) has led the interaction. Most of the "games" were shaped by the parent around the baby's behavioral displays. By four months, our analyses show that the baby is leading in setting the game as often as is the parent (Brazelton & Als, 1979).

A typical interaction might proceed as follows: A mother and baby boy sit facing each other: the baby gives a smile or a facial response to her gently initiated overtures. She smiles back appreciatively. They lock onto each other in a brief (10–15 second) set of responses. There is a recognition of each other's rhythms of movement, of attentional involvement. This is then *broken* by the baby. He looks away, as if by chance. Often, he will look at one shoe. The parent tries to capture his gaze by increasing her cues. The baby looks past her at the other shoe. She tries to get into his line of vision. He adroitly shifts past her to look back at the first shoe. In a sequence as long as three minutes, he is in control for the major part of it, leading her back and forth while he examines each shoe. When she gives up to look away, he will snap back to focus on her face and recapture her. Within the safety of their interaction, he has practiced his developing but still fragile autonomy.

Up to this point, the parent has been learning how to "control" the baby and to bring out responses. She has tried out different techniques—probably learned from her own past, but also from trial and error. When they work, that is, by prolonging the baby's state, she has been greatly rewarded. When she can bring the baby to smile, to vocalize "at her," she feels like a warm parent. Controlling the baby's responses gives her a feeling of being in close touch with him. Even the baby's negative responses—of crying, of fussing from internal imbalances—are seen in the balanced light of her ability to help him. During these first four months, the baby's behavior is critical to the mother's sense of herself as a successful nurturing parent.

Now, at this fourth stage in their interaction, as autonomy "hatches," she suddenly becomes unable to predict the baby's behavior. The signals which she has learned to think of as negative, such as gaze aversion, avoidance, and turning away, are likely to come as a shock to her. Until she can see them as a strength, as evidence of the baby's own autonomy, she is liable to feel deserted. Her normal ambivalence will make her question her own self-image. If she takes the baby's manipulation of her seriously, she can experience a kind of rejection. Nursing mothers will call their pediatrician at this time asking, "Isn't it time to wean the baby?" When questioned, they make clear that the infant's new burst of interest in the environment is competing with the feeding situation. For the parent, this competition is a blow. The intense reciprocity, the synchronous messages which have been flowing back and forth between parent and infant have become very important. Needing the feedback, a mother is likely to redouble her efforts to keep the baby close. These redoubled efforts not only reward the infant's game-playing, but by overloading, they make it even more important that the baby "tune her out" now and then. The rejection may revive old feelings of inadequacy or desertion from her own past. Such feelings may lead a mother to withdraw from the baby or else press her to become more aware, more sensitive to the infant's need for "time out," for space.

A parent who cannot tolerate independence will ignore and override this spurt in development in her baby. A mother with problems in her own life, who is under stress—for instance, a single, working parent who feels torn away from her baby—will have difficulty in recognizing this stage of development and will need help in fostering it. If she cannot, the future cost may be great, for the baby will need to rebel or turn away even more forcefully later on. If all goes well, however, the mother (and father) will accept this important stage of development. They will value their child's developing autonomy, even see it as a goal. In psychoanalytic terms, the infant's ego development will then be well on its way.

It is interesting to note that at this same time, the infant's electro-encephalogram depicts a maturational shift (Emde et al., 1976). This signals his or her brain's increasing capacity for storage of cognitive and affective learning. With this shift, there are other signs of rapidly increasing cognitive capacities, such as the first signs of awareness of object permanence mentioned earlier. This is also the age for a first surfacing of stranger awareness, accompanied by clinging to the mother. If a stranger comes into sight and looks the baby in the face too quickly, the baby will break down in crying or sobbing. Motor capacity to reach out, to shape hands in anticipation, and to capture objects in space to bring them into the baby's mouth, or to play with them, comes to real fruition at this time. This is a period when nighttime sleep is also maturing. Most babies now begin to stretch out to an 8-hour sleep period. Learning to sleep, to get from REM cycles back down to deep sleep, is part of increasing autonomy.

All of these—cognitive, affective, and motor capacities—propel the baby toward a whole new level of adjustment, both more independent and acquisitive, but also dependent on the firm base provided by parents. Though a parent can feel rejected, he or she can also feel more needed, needed to provide new experiences and to confirm the baby's competence by reinforcing it with acknowledgement and pleasure.

14

Essentials of Early Interaction

As the parent-infant dialogue develops in these early months, individual differences from one family to the next will become more and more apparent. It is possible, however, to identify several characteristics of any successful relationship during this period. Both clinicians and investigators have found the following concepts valuable in evaluating early interaction.

Synchrony

An immature organism is at the mercy of autonomic requirements for cardiac and respiratory balance. As we have shown, in order to learn how to pay attention to outside stimuli, the infant must become able to regulate various physiological systems. Once a nurturing adult recognizes, intuitively or consciously, this regulatory system, she can help the baby learn how to turn his or her attention on and off. The first step for the adult is to adapt her behavior to the baby's own rhythms. An adult must also find techniques to help the baby reduce or control motor responses that might interfere with the ability to pay attention. By learning the baby's "language," as reflected by autonomic, state, motor, and attentional behaviors, parents can synchronize their own states of attention and inattention to the baby's. They can help the baby pay attention and then prolong this attention within their interaction. In the achievement of synchrony, parents take the first step.

Engaged in the synchronous communication, the infant can learn about the parent as a reliable and responsive being, and start contributing to the dialogue. Through synchrony, the parents, in turn, experience their own competence. In our clinical work, we have found that synchronous attention and withdrawal can be demonstrated and modeled for parents. When they achieve it for themselves, the most insecure parents can feel a sense of control, over their baby's vulnerability and over their own (Brazelton & Yogman, 1986).

Symmetry

Symmetry between adult and baby in an interaction is of course not the same as equivalence. Not only are babies more dependent, but they are more at the mercy of being shaped by an adult. The adult interactant is always more likely to initiate communication, as well as to choose the mode in which communication will occur. Symmetry in an interaction means that infants' capacities for attention, their style, their preferences for both intake and response influence the interaction. In a symmetric dialogue, a parent respects an infant's thresholds. Hence, each member is involved in achieving and maintaining synchrony. In our investigations, we have consistently seen that in successful interaction each member is making a major contribution and an active one. The parent, to be sure, is responsible for this symmetry. A parent must be both selfless and selfish—selfless in being able to see the baby's side, and selfish in desiring feedback from the baby. The parent must be ready to give up a part of herself in the quest for the baby's rhythms and responses.

The importance of recognizing the specific contribution of each member of the dyad will be apparent in Part V. If we, as clinicians, want to assess and help failing pairs, we must be able to help the parent change her role to fit the individuality of her infant. This may require "adultomorphizing" the infant's contribution, translating the dialogue for the parent. The baby's modes of communication, the thresholds beyond which a baby may withdraw, and the behavioral responses that mark them can be spelled out to help a parent understand how to reach her particular infant.

Contingency

As we have seen, the infant's vocalizations, smiles or affective displays, and ability to receive auditory, tactile, or kinesthetic signals are all built on a base of states and autonomic functions. Until homeostasis is achieved, any signal can become an overload as well as an elicitor. Its timing determines its meaning. The effect of a parent's signals is contingent upon the baby's state of attention and needs, as well as the baby's own signals. The baby's capacity for signalling behavior is also contingent upon an ability for self-regulation. It is no surprise, then, that social smiles or vocalizations do not become significant as part of an infant's repertoire for the first weeks of the infant's life. One perceptive mother pointed out to us that her infant was learning about the world when he paid attention, but was learning about himself as he turned away to recover.

In periods of attention, infants can begin to signal their mothers with smiles or frowns, with vocalizations, with motor displays such as leaning forward, reaching, arching the head coyly, and so on. Mothers respond contingently when they can read the messages conveyed in these signals. As a mother responds, she learns from the success or failure of each of her own responses, as measured by the baby's behavior. In this way, she refines the contingency of her responses and develops a repertoire of "what works" and "what doesn't." In the 1960s, studies tried to reflect this contingency with a stimulus-response model (Rheingold, 1961). A goodness-of-fit between the pair was measured by the incidence of smiles by the baby responded to by smiles from the mother. The number of vocalizations from each member was taken as a reflection of how responsive they were to each other. This proved far too simple a technique for evaluating a dyad's interaction. Single behaviors in any one modality are of very secondary importance to the relationship of that one act to the overall rhythms and patterns of meaning in the dialogue between parent and infant. Contingency requires availability on the mother's part, both cognitive and emotional. The result of predictably contingent responses on her part is also related to what has been called selective attunement (Stern, 1985).

Entrainment

The adult and infant who can achieve synchrony of signal and response begin to add another dimension to their dialogue. They begin to anticipate each other's responses in long sequences. Having learned each other's requirements, they can set up a rhythm as though with a set of rules. The power of this rhythm soon establishes an expectancy: both for the results of complying with the rhythm and for interrupting it. So powerful is this expectancy that it seems to carry each member of the dyad along. Each member's contribution seems submerged in a momentum which Lewis Sander and William Condon have called "entrainment" (Condon & Sander, 1974). Like a first violinist, one member can then "entrain" the behavior of the other by instituting the rhythm of attention and inattention which has already been established as the base for their synchrony. Their interaction thus takes on a new level of involvement. Each member of the dyad adjusts to the other, so that the baby is not simply matching the adult's cue, but the rhythms of the adult also tend to look to the movements of the infant.

An example of this kind of entrainment might be as follows. A mother comes up to lean over a two-month-old baby boy. He recognizes her, and his face brightens. His limbs are still as he watches her. His eyebrows raise; his face lifts in anticipation; his mouth forms an "O." She reacts to this by saying softly, "O-o-h, aren't you the bright boy!" As she says the "O-o-h," he watches her mouth, his mouth reacting to imitate hers. He vocalizes a soft "Ooh" very much like hers. She says delightedly, "Ooh, what?" He sighs, turns away briefly to return to look at her mouth and her lifted eyebrows and face. As he looks at her anticipating face, he vocalizes an even more emphatic "Oooh!" She waits a moment until after he has finished, then she returns with a soft, but eliciting, "Oooh, yes." Her oohs are on the same level as his; they match him in intensity and duration. He again averts his eyes, takes a deep breath before he turns back to her eager and waiting face. He says this time, "Oh-oh," with a second sound dropping a third of a scale in a sort of musical trill. Following this, her face lights up even more, her shoulders drop, she reaches out to touch his legs, and she imitates his two-tone cadence exactly, as she says, "Oh-oh, yes!" He recognizes the direct imitation of his production. His face and shoulders lift to almost a peak of investment as he repeats the trill of "Oh-oh." This time the two-tone cadence is clear and emphatic. She is so delighted with this evidence of his recognition of her own vocalization that she changes the sequence to a delighted, "Aren't you wonderful!" He seems overwhelmed by this rising pitch and by her excitement, so he turns away to look at his feet. The sequence is over for the moment.

Within this brief 30-second sequence, each participant has used imitation of the rhythms and vocalizations of the other to capture, hold, and lead the partner on into a richer and richer form of interaction. This entrainment fuels both mother and infant and is a powerful factor in the growth of attachment.

Play

The "games" already mentioned, which Stern (1974b) has described in dyads between a three- or four-month-old infant and his or her parent, are built on entrainment. The repetitious use of signal behaviors and the expectancy for repetition of clusters of interactive behavior are endlessly varied in sequences of "play." The parent expects the baby to be responsive and expressive in several modalities by this age. If one of them initiates interaction in one modality, the other is likely to respond within that modality. If a mother smiles, the baby will smile back; she will widen her smile, the baby will brighten to smile again. By the third smile, the baby may shift modalities to coo back at her. Recognizing that the game has changed, she will coo back at the baby, who then changes the tone of his or her vocalization. She will add a word to her response to mark it. The baby will brighten and repeat the sound. She adds another word; the baby responds a third time. She will try to heighten it even more. Soon the infant will end the sequence by looking away, as if to say, "That's it for now."

When they return to another game, they may shift to an imitative motor game of shrugging or making faces at each other.

These games are likely to occur in sequences of three or four, according to Stern. Within each sequence, there is a set of rules which is quickly established and recognized by each of the participants. The timing, the level of pitch, the intensity, the duration, as well as the modality being emphasized, are all governed by these rules.

Within the games, the infant and parent have the opportunity to enlarge upon their learning about each other. They imitate and model upon each other. Their entrainment allows each of them control over heightening, maintaining, or turning down the level of their dialogue. The infant is learning control over both the parent and the interaction itself. Ultimately, the baby is learning about him or herself. The mother, in turn, is learning about ways to maintain the baby's attention, to lead the baby to increase his or her repertoire, without losing that attention.

Autonomy and Flexibility

The baby's recognition of control leads to autonomy. As synchrony, entrainment, and contingent responses from the parent reinforce different capacities, the baby comes to realize that he or she can control the interaction. As we have seen, by five months of age, many babies begin to dominate the mother's behavior by their ability both to initiate interaction and to turn away from it. They begin testing the situation and their capacity to dominate their captive audience (Brazelton & Yogman, 1986). At this time, after a sequence of synchronized responses has been initiated, the baby is likely to interrupt the dialogue by looking away at another part of the room, at a hand, or at a shoe. So predictable is this at five months that we came to call babies at this age "shoebabies."

The mother's response is also predictable. She redoubles her efforts to bring the baby back into interaction. Feeling deserted, she tries to bring her baby back within her "envelope." At the point where she gives up and subsides, the baby often looks back at her to check her response. While looking, the baby has kept the mother in his or her peripheral visual field. This seems to us to indicate that the baby's goal is autonomy, rather than escaping overstimulation. Since, as we pointed out, this period coincides with burgeoning visual, auditory, and reaching efforts, there are many other stimuli competing for the baby's attention and increasing the need for control.

Autonomy grows out of assurance of predictable responses from the parent. Less secure infants, we have found, come to this level of independence at a later age. Impaired or premature infants whom the parents worried about and hovered over were often seven or eight months old before they dared to reach the same stage of autonomy (Als & Brazelton, 1981). Autonomous behavior on the part of infants at this age is a sign of a healthy relationship and the lack of it, an apparent symbiosis or fusion, is a sign of impaired attachment. Mothers of difficult or disordered infants need help in encouraging autonomy. After all the effort they have made to reach out to withdrawn, easily overloaded infants, they will be less likely to recognize the need on the part of the infant for "hatching" or autonomy.

Implied in the concept of autonomy is another characteristic of healthy early interaction, that of *flexibility*. A dialogue that is too predictable, responses that are too tightly coupled, suggest a relationship arrested in some way. As Louis Sander (1977) has pointed out in describing the regulation of exchange between infants and caretakers, loosely coupled subsystems allow for temporary independence in relation to the larger system. In stable but flexible systems, disturbances in a subsystem need not seriously affect overall stability. However, when a subsystem is inflexible, a disturbance is likely to disturb the overall stability. Such tightly overcontrolled conditions might lead to an overly symbiotic relationship between mother and infant or father and infant, in which the work of autonomy and detachment cannot proceed at a healthy pace.

These six characteristics of parent–infant interaction—synchrony, symmetry, contingency, entrainment, games, and autonomy—make possible the early unfolding of attachment. Without the sense of predictability offered by the first four, and the possibility of detachment demonstrated in play and autonomy, this earliest relationship cannot evolve.

As infants achieve an inner balance and then go on to experience expectation and excitement within a safe, predictable relationship, they begin to discover the capacities for emotion and cognition with which they are endowed. As they learn to elicit and then to reply to the adults around them, they experience the rewards of communication. They begin to recognize emotions within themselves, as well as in others. As they engage, respond to, and enlarge upon the adult's responses, infants learn how to control the emotional environment. Thus, infants become able to recharge both kinds of fueling that we spoke of: from within and from without. They begin to internalize the controls that are necessary for experiencing emotion but they also learn what it takes to produce emotional responses from others. By the end of the fourth month, infants can "turn on" or "turn off" those around them surprisingly effectively. As we will see in the next part, however, there are emotional and historical forces influencing the adult's side of the interaction, which both enrich and complicate the emerging relationship.

PART FOUR

Imaginary Interactions

A book which does not contain its counterbook is considered incomplete.

—JORGE LUIS BORGES
"Tlon, Uqbar, Orbis, Tertius"

Introduction

In clinical work, while the kind of objective observation we described in Part III is vital, it is only one-half of the picture. We must also attempt to understand the private subjective meaning that a child carries for a parent. This is essential in assessing why deviant interactions develop, and in supporting healthy development.

While objective studies of interaction describe the "how" of relationships, studies of the subjective side of interactions provide the "whys." We call the parents' subjective interpretations of their relationship with their child "imaginary interactions." These evolve from the fantasies they carry about themselves, their closest relatives, their ideals and fears, fantasies which originate in their own childhoods. The newborn baby will reawaken certain of these fantasies and thus be cast from birth into imaginary scenarios replayed from an earlier time.

The parental contributions to these imaginary interactions can usually be identified through what parents say about the child, about becoming a parent, and about their emotional life in general. The baby's contributions to imaginary interactions are just as important, but they are very difficult to tap, because young children start to reveal their thoughts through play and words only during the second year. We must extrapolate their subjective version of an interaction through their behavior and symptoms.

In what follows, we will first define certain of the mechanisms behind these interactions, then we will describe some of the turbulent scenarios in which they are played out.

15

Giving Meaning to Infant Behavior

"What a person thinks about a relationship may be more important than the interaction that actually occurs." This quote, surprisingly enough, is from Robert Hinde, one of the leaders in the ethological observation of behavior. The core of a relationship, he suggests, may be closer to the set of private thoughts partners entertain, than to what we observe. Hinde goes on to say: "Mothers perpetually overestimate the element of intent in infant behavior" (Hinde, 1976). Mothers do not relate only to what an infant actually does; they lend enormous meaning to the slightest sound or gesture on the infant's part, and it is to this "injected meaning" that they react (Cramer, 1987).

From the moment of birth and, as we saw in Part I, even during pregnancy, everything the infant (fetus) does is immediately embedded in a maze of significance. One mother said of her newborn: "I think he is going to be stubborn; if he doesn't want to drink, he won't. He sort of puts his bottom lip in. I was stubborn apparently when I was young" (Meares et al., 1982). The importance of this meaning attribution for development has been recognized now in many studies. Jerome Bruner, for example, describes how the mother involves the infant in a sort of adultomorphic process when she reads all sorts of meaning into his or her first sounds. In this way, she introduces the infant to the symbolic world of adults. Bruner sees this as a "language acquisition device" that pulls the infant toward increasingly complex levels of language use (Bruner, 1983).

Infants' perception of their own behavior will be co-determined by such parental attributions. Through meaning attribution, a whole set of values, of reinforcements, of prohibitions, of emotional coloring contributes to shaping an experience, a behavior, or a trait in the infant's repertoire. When parents attribute meaning to an infant's behavior they are led to label it: "good," "bad," "stubborn," "smart," and so on. Their consequent pleasure or anxiety will determine the infants' own set of values about their capacities, their sense of what can and cannot be shared. To a great extent, children's representations of themselves will be molded by parents' expectations, ideals, predilections, and aversions. These are transmitted—in great part—through mimicry, remarks, and actions that reveal to the child how the parents have interpreted his intentions. Through this process the infant "learns how to intend" (Dunn, 1982).

Hinde has suggested that mothers' overestimation of the element of intent in infant behavior is like a delusion. He implies that mothers do not react to the objective aspect of the infant's behavior, but rather to a meaning they inject into it. This meaning stems from their own personal interpretation of the world, of what is good and bad, of what makes people act certain ways. What is at work here is the subjective world of the mother, based on her own past history, her zones of conflict, her values, and so on. We look at meaning attribution somewhat differently. We see it as subjective, but not a delusion. Subjective contributions made by parents to infant behavior are universal. While highly powerful in shaping the interaction, they are not pathological. In fact, one could say that such subjective interpretations by parents of the infant's behavior are an essential ingredient of normal development. How would infants know about themselves if they didn't read in their parents' eyes the meaning of their behavior? How would familial and cultural values be handed down generation after generation, if the process of meaning attribution did not color each bit of infant behavior with a specific value?

Projection

In the psychoanalytic literature, meaning attribution is referred to as projection or as projective identification. In other words, we transfer onto others feelings and images that belong—in fact—to our own selves. Once again, this is not a pathological reaction. In fact, it is socially adaptive: by attributing to others feelings and thoughts that come from inside ourselves, we develop a sense of empathy, a feeling of belonging to a same species.

However, when projections are massive, disregarding the specific individuality of the other, the distortion of reality interferes with relationships. This is particularly true when hostile and aggressive aspects of the self are projected.

In clinical practice with babies, we can see both the adaptive and destructive aspects of projection. A certain degree of projection builds the relationship: the baby is endowed with the characteristics that parents value most and rewarded and loved for any behavior that confirms this positive image.

In pathological projections, on the other hand, parents endow a baby with characteristics that are totally at odds with the baby's nature: the baby is seen as having well-defined intentions or harboring adult characteristics, or even endowed with supernatural forces. The strength and nature of the parents' projections determine to what extent parents are able to recognize the infant's own individuality, whether their unconscious takes over, casting the infant in the role of hero or villain. These characteristics of projections are often revealed in the parent's description of the infant's "problems"; but sometimes it takes a long time before the plot "behind the scene" is uncovered. This is achieved only when parents reveal the link between their perception of these "problems" and their own past. Out of their own history, hidden scenarios emerge in which they act out an imaginary interaction with their infant.

For years, clinicians working with infants have been aware that "symptoms" in the child may be highly expressive of the parent's unconscious conflicts. This is confirmed by almost magical symptom removal in infants when one tackles the corresponding conflicts in their parents. It is as if certain psychic forces in parents had a direct effect on the infant's behavior; this effect is often referred to as "contagion." This deep psychological intermeshing between parents and infants (much less visible later) may be due to two factors.

In the days immediately after childbirth, there is a powerful re-shuffling of psychological forces, with a return of early, infantile modes of functioning in the parents. Their own conflicts and anxieties are thus heightened. This is referred to—by some authors—as a return to the parent's infantile neurosis (Kreisler, 1981).

Symbiotic and fusion phenomena—as described in the infant by Margaret Mahler—may also be at work in parents. Much of what we describe as empathy, reciprocity, "shared subjectivity" relies on the parents' identification with an infant and on unconscious fantasies of being fused with it.

Mahler saw this symbiosis as a first and normal phase, cushioning the early development in the child. Out of this relatively undifferentiated state between parent and infant evolves the infant's individuality. Mahler saw this symbiosis as hard for a mother to give up unless she regresses in fantasy to her own separation from her mother.

This symbiosis does not necessarily preclude a simultaneous objective reading of the infant's messages, and a respect for individuality. While the mother who still maintains a mental representation of the infant as a part of her own self sees the infant's behavior or symptoms as expressing her inner feelings and fantasies, at the same time, she can perceive the "objective" nature of the baby. Those who care for parents must recognize this dual perception: infants are seen as a composite of the feelings and thoughts projected onto them. Yet, at the same time, parents remain able to "read" their child objectively.

In stressing the role of these imaginary interactions, we suggest that children's development is as powerfully determined by parents' fantasies as it is by their innate programs. These various forces are in constant interplay and mutually influence each other; the innate characteristics of the infant (sex, physical appearance, clarity of state, capacity for homeostatic regulation, etc.) shape the fantasies parents develop about the child; infants imprint on their parents' perceptions the individual stamp of their basic characteristics. Simultaneously, parents mold the infant's behavior with reinforcements and inhibitions mediated by their fantasies, expectations, and inner conflicts.

In what follows, we describe some common fantasies and the scenarios in which they can be observed. In each case, we will try to relate the overt interaction that can be observed to the underlying imaginary interaction. Three of the forms parental fantasies can take are:

1. The baby as ghost, representing an important person from the parent's past;

2. The relationship reenacts past modes of relationship;

3. The baby represents a part of the parent's own unconscious.

These fantasies are universal. It is a fundamental fact of human relationships that new attachments are always based on old ones. They also, as will be seen, overlap with one another. Normally, this repetition of the past is seen in discrete signs: the child is said to resemble his grandfather, carries the name of a loved relative, or is thought to be developing the same talent as an admired adult of the parent's childhood. More subtly, a child may evoke the same type of emotional response that the parent had experienced in his or her childhood. This is often a fleeting experience; for instance, a mother suddenly thinks she hears her own mother when—in fact—it is her daughter who is singing. Dreams often allude to this type of filiation in a crude way; a woman might see the face of her son gradually turning into that of her brother.

In clinical work, we see more global and dramatic repetition of the past. Sometimes this appears in the very first words used by parents when they describe a child and especially the child's problems. The clinician may suddenly have the eerie feeling that, when the parents are talking about their child, they are really picturing someone who is absent from the consultation room.

16

The Infant As Ghost

Selma Fraiberg pointed out the presence of "ghosts in the nursery." She called them "visitors from the unremembered past of the parents, the uninvited guests at the christening" (Fraiberg, 1980). Like the good fairy or the threatening witch of fairy tales, these ghosts can cast favorable or malevolent spells on the child. Normally, the child will make such a powerful claim upon the parent's love for his or her individual, unique self, that the ghosts are banished to the background of the nursery. But, at times, the ghosts establish residence at the baby's side, attracting most of the parent's attention. In such situations, *parents relate to the ghost who is interposed—like a screen—between themselves and the child.*

Such an intrusive ghost creates a major source of mismatch between parent and infant. The parents are unable to react to the infant's signals, because they are busy communicating with a ghost. This ghost may occupy the whole space, leaving no chance for parents to see their child, or it may interfere with specific issues: eating, sleeping, discipline. The ghost's intrusion thus reveals a corresponding vulnerability in the parent's past. The child's problems then indicate with great precision conflicts that must be resolved by the parent.

Anyone who works with families soon becomes aware that these imaginary partners are very much a reality. Thoughts, memories, feelings have a life of their own. These actors in the parents' psychological theater cannot be treated like ephemeral fancies. Fantasies become *real* and it is often the role of the child to *materialize* these ghosts.

We have found this to be one of the most amazing characteristics of clinical work with parents and young infants; the past of the parents is replayed in actual interactions, and the infant is cast into a realistic portrayal of a particular ghost. In these scenarios, we can also see the precise and compelling nature of early communication. Recent work on attunement and intersubjectivity contributes greatly to our understanding of these interactions.

As an example, a mother asked for a consultation from one of us [BC], because she was very anxious about her two-month-old boy, Juan, who had regurgitated feedings since birth. In spite of reassuring comments of nurses, who showed that the baby's weight growth was normal, the mother remained convinced that he would die.

Soon after the clinician started talking with this mother, she reported that she was still very upset about the death of her brother, three months before the baby's birth. She was then encouraged to talk more about this event and described her last visit to him in the hospital: he was emaciated, smelt very bad, and kept regurgitating (he was at the terminal stage of intestinal cancer); this impression was so powerful that she fainted. The brother died soon thereafter. She had not felt up to going to his funeral. She didn't cry once. The process of mourning had not taken its normal course.

What was remarkable was that while she was describing this painful scene, Juan suddenly regurgitated. The clinician then simply said: "He regurgitates like your brother did."

This simple establishment of a link had a tremendous impact on this mother; she started crying and was able to elaborate at length on her relationship to her brother. In the next meeting, she expressed that she had been tremendously relieved by this session. She allowed herself to feel sad about her brother (thus entering a true mourning process) and no longer felt so anxious about the child. This, in turn, transformed her relationship to the child and a new beginning was thus made possible. She started enjoying him, having now really buried the ghost of her brother.

Apparently, the way this woman had been able to cope with the loss of her brother was by displacing onto her infant the powerful emotions that predominated in her relationship to the brother. These focused upon the brother's regurgitations which Juan reproduced. This process is well known in clinical work with mourning: the bereaved takes on the characteristics of the lost one; this *introjection* is expressed by an identification with the deceased, and often a particular trait or symptom will be reproduced in the grieving person. It is as if this young woman had sheltered inside of her the image of her dying, regurgitating brother, but instead of reflecting it herself, she projected it onto the child she was then bearing. Since, as we have seen in the part on pregnancy, the fetus is still experienced as a part of the mother's self, it is easily subject to introjections and identifications. Not being able to abandon the link to her dead brother, this mother reproduced it with her infant. Why Juan developed regurgitations after birth (this is a common occurrence, with no necessary pathology), we do not know. We do know, however, that this symptom was immediately interpreted by the mother as evidence that her baby would have the same fate as her brother. This prediction became powerful and malignant, because the brother's ghost had taken residence in the baby. The mother was both denying the pain of his death and inflicting upon herself the anxiety that the baby would die. This mingling of love bonds and fear of death is common in troubled parent–child relationships; it is a mark of painful ambivalence.

Juan's regurgitation might have been a benign, transient problem if the mother had not lent it special meaning. Due to her anxiety, she may have force-fed the child, or—through her activities—somehow interfered with the child's digestion. Selma Fraiberg (1980) gives the example of a mother who burped her baby in such a way (face down) that she actually *induced* regurgitation. Through these types of interaction, a child can be subtly programmed to provide a confirmation of a mother's worst fears.

However, one might still ask, is it mere coincidence that the child regurgitated precisely at the moment when the mother evoked the image of her dying, regurgitating brother? Or has the child the capacity to read some clues that indicate what role he is supposed to play? This is no idle question; clinical practice proves again and again that children will realize in their behavior roles that their parents expect them— unconsciously—to play. The mother who fears that the child will die of starvation has an anorexic baby; the mother who has never tolerated her sibling's assertiveness has a tyrannical son. Because this role assignment is a powerful determinant of child development, we must try to understand how children learn what it is that they are expected to perform.

When Juan's mother evoked the painful memory of her dying brother, there was obviously a great deal of pent-up emotion in her, which must have affected her facial expression, her voice intonation, and her gestures. Even at two months, it is possible that a baby can discern these expressions of emotional states. It is also possible that for this child, regurgitation had become reinforced as a highly charged mode of communication because the mother had loaded this symptom with deep meaning. We may hypothesize that emotional signals in the mother (i.e., her voice, her tears, her facial expressions), when she spoke to the clinician about her brother's regurgitations, triggered a corresponding response in the baby. The baby turned to a channel already developed in their communication: regurgitation.

Such interpretations would seem highly speculative were they not confirmed constantly in clinical practice. Gaze aversion, for instance, becomes almost compulsory in a child whose mother interprets the child's eyes as accusatory or aggressive. Robson tells of a mother who says of her child "he looks daggers" (Robson, 1964). There was gaze avoidance in this couple, because mother feared her son's "aggressive" look. Serge Lebovici reports the case of an infant who suddenly starts crying when his mother evokes the sadness she felt when her husband left her. To him, it is the emotional valence of the mother's words which signals to the baby, triggering his crying when she is sad (Lebovici, 1983).

Robert Emde has filmed children's attentive reading of their mother's facial expression (in what he calls "referencing"). These films show convincingly how the mother's mood signals affect the child's emotional tone and his or her actions. Again, this transmission of emotion is no subtle, ephemeral phenomenon; it produces visible effects on the child's behavior (Emde & Sorce, 1983).

While attunement is easier to describe from the point of view of a mother's empathy with her child's inner state, we have to acknowledge that infants are exquisitely sensitive to their caregivers' moods, and that this is translated into their own behavior. The work of Edward Tronick et al. on the effects of the still-face experiment (described in Part III) leaves little doubt about this.

In Juan's case we assume his mother had selected regurgitation out of Juan's various behaviors because it allowed her to maintain the illusion that her brother was still alive, now in the guise of her child. The symptom was thus actively maintained as a material representation of the mother's denial of her brother's death. It is as if this mother needed a daily reminder of her brother and that Juan complied with her need.

We have described this case at some length, because we wanted to illustrate how the communication of emotion—discussed in interactional studies in Part III—finds application in clinical practice. The case also shows how transmission of emotion can carry thematic elements, bringing a fantasy to life.

The Child as a Reincarnation

In our culture it is normal for parents to endow their children with the features of deceased relatives; this allows the continuation of attachment, the permanence of family traditions, and the maintenance of filiation. In other cultures, a child may be seen as a more literal reincarnation of ancestors. Among the Wolof of Senegal, a child receives the name of a deceased grandparent. The child is experienced as the return—or reincarnation—of this ancestor, and his or her behavior is interpreted as carrying messages from the deceased (Rabain, 1979). This linkage of the infant to ancestors invests the child with power; perceived as smart and powerful, the child thus becomes a source of protection for the family, and this reinforces their attachment. But, in the same way, the child who is seen as the carrier of malevolent intention is feared.

In our Western culture, reincarnation is not labelled as such, and yet a similar belief pervades relationships. Not only is a child a symbolic reminder of past attachments, but the child may replace the deceased in concrete ways, as we have seen. This may be particularly the case when there is coincidence between *death* and *birth*. A child born while the parents are suffering a loss may be used to deny it and delay the pain of mourning.

For example, one of us [BC] was consulted by a mother for severe sleeping difficulties in her two-year-old daughter. This child had been born three weeks after the mother's father died. Experiencing intense feelings of void and loneliness, this mother tried to turn to her baby as a source of comfort but was distressed that the infant couldn't talk back. The desire to replace her father made her seriously misperceive her daughter's communications and fail to respond to the infant's actual demands. The only activity of the child she seemed to care about was her interest in music (displayed by the baby's attending to tunes played on the radio). She explained that her father had been a musician and that her daughter's musical interests were her only link to him. She had even decided to make her child into a musician. In this case, the coincidence of birth and death led to neglect of an infant's needs and signals, and an attempt to shape development. Her defense, against painful mourning, determined their interaction, and narrowed the areas of possible exchange.

While reincarnation may seem too strong a word for cases like this, it serves to evoke the magical, concrete reproduction of a dead person in a child. Though existing only in the parent's imagination, the ghost can affect a relationship in a tragically realistic way.

Fear of an Infant's Death

Practically all overprotective behavior in parents is due to underlying—though often conscious—fears that the infant is threatened by imminent destruction. Many cases of overfeeding are due to fear of starvation; many sleeping difficulties are due to active disturbance of the infant's sleep caused by the parents' need to check that the child is still alive.

There are many possible determinants of this fear of death. An obvious one is the so-called "replacement child" situation, in which a child is born soon after the death of an older sibling. The fear of death then has a clear cause. Another more complex cause is a parent's experience of a child as the reincarnation of someone who was both loved and hated. In one such case, a mother conceived her daughter while her uncle—who had been her father surrogate—was dying of cancer. Soon after birth, the baby developed severe feeding difficulties, leading to a lack of weight gain. It appeared that the mother had force-fed the baby, who then withdrew from all feeding situations. Once this anti-contingent feeding interaction was recognized and explained to the mother, she revealed that she had force-fed the baby because of a constant fear that the baby was sick with cancer and would waste away, just like the uncle. What was more difficult to elicit was that this uncle was not only the object of fond memories; he was also resented tremendously because he had favored the mother's sister. Here, the irrational fear of death revealed a transfer onto the child of love and hate feelings originally directed to a father figure.

The Child As Parent

"Parentification" is described by family therapists as a process through which children are used as a replacement for the parent's own parents. They are thus programmed to give support, guidance, gratifications, or criticism, just as the parents did. This kind of reversal can be seen in many different situations. The commonest is one in which parents have felt deprived by their own parents; they find it difficult to give much to their infant and instead expect gratifications from the child.

When the parents require that infants act in an adult way, their infantile needs are thus denied. For instance, a parent may demand that a small baby show overt signs of affection. Needless to say, this is bound to bring disappointment. The parent then "accuses" the infant of being unaffectionate, unrewarding, and selfish, leading to a continued sense of disappointment for both. In such relationships, there are observable interactive failures: lack of body contact, avoidance of *en face* looking, and a diminished volume of mutual solicitations. When the infant starts roaming about at some distance from the mother, engaging in playful activities, the mother may remark: "You see, he is not interested in me." This is said with a painful emotion. Similarly, when the infant turns to the mother—seeking contact, "refueling"— the mother may miss this sign of attachment, or claim that the infant comes to her "only because he is tired!"

Such problems will become compounded, unless parents come to understand that they expect from an infant what only an adult can provide. This realization can correct the anti-contingency due to misperceiving the child as an adult. Next, a therapist or caregiver must unearth feelings of longing that lead parents to confuse the infant with their own parents. Usually this brings forth a great deal of pent-up feelings and—in most cases—parents will then fully realize how unrealistic are their expectations of the infant.

In very young parents, especially teenage mothers, one finds the same constellation. A teenage girl will often become pregnant when a conflict with her own parents brings about a break in their relationship. The youngster conceives a child to recreate a close mother-child bond, to avoid the pain provoked by growing independence and by the break in the relationship to her own parents. Problems are then inevitable if the teenager unconsciously expects the baby to be the main provider of love. She may resent her baby's cries: "Why should I run to her? What does she do for me?" She may turn away from the baby, or feed the child in a mechanical fashion. It is often difficult for teenage mothers even to understand that their babies need them when they cry. If such a mother allowed herself to perceive the infant's starving for her attention, she would have to accept herself in the role of a mother and—therefore—would have to give up her status as her own mother's dependent child.

In one such situation, a very young mother complained that her nine-month-old daughter was pointing to things as if she wanted mother to bring them to her, as a slave would do for a master. She grew resentful of her child and thought it unjust that *she* should give to her child while the baby "never helps me," as she put it. Unconsciously, she hoped that her daughter would become a giving mother figure, who would make up for her sense of maternal deprivation. The anger at the child developed from this mismatch and from the thwarted hope for parentification of her daughter.

In such situations, the teenager needs to be able to lean on a warm, reliable professional who can be used as a kind of model for mothering. It is only after a long period, during which yearnings for dependency are allowed, expressed, and acknowledged and depressive feelings vented, that the youngster becomes able to consider nurturing someone else: that is, her own baby.

More extreme results of parentification, known by workers in the field, include maternal depression. It is amazing to see how often young children (as young as one to two years of age) will pick up clues of sadness in their parent and will attempt to console the parent. Either they actively care for the parent, or, more generally, they develop a precociously undemanding behavior, so as not to burden the *a₂ ?* depressed parent. Child battering is another extreme outcome. An act of violence against a child can occur when a parent—feeling abandoned and helpless—expects an infant to provide support and understanding. When the child cannot comply, a dangerous anger builds.

The Child As Judge

When a mother or father experiences an infant not only as a parent, but as a *judgmental* parent, a particularly painful cycle is set up. The behavior of an unhappy infant whose needs are not being met is then interpreted as a sign of criticism or rejection. Beebe and Sloate (1982) described a mother who showed great difficulties in interaction with her three-month-old baby girl. When the baby looked at her, she would suddenly loom close to the infant's face; the child developed marked gaze aversion. The mother interpreted this aversion as active rejection by the child. Lack of contingency and attunement were evident (no turn-taking, no baby-talk, no response to the child's change of moods), and the child showed increasing inhibition of responses. The baby also showed defensive movements, as if she were "dodging" the mother. The mother noted only these negative reactions, while she missed the baby's overtures. She assigned a great deal of meaning to the child's behavior, experiencing it as critical, punitive, and rejecting. It appeared that she could not become attuned to the baby, because then she would feel "controlled" by her. Gradually, the therapist helped her understand that she had transferred onto her child accusing and rejecting attitudes that belonged to her image of her own mother.

In the case of Sebastian described in Part V, we will see a parallel case involving the ghost of a judgmental father. Even a very small infant can be powerfully intimidating to a mother who sees in him the reproachful gaze of her own father.

A critical and judgmental attitude is only one of the imagined intentions that can be projected upon a child. Thus, it is not enough simply to determine who is the original model for the ghost; one must also assess the nature of the specific feelings and intentions attributed to the child, and whether these projections are opaque or allow for insight to shine through.

The Child As Sibling

In another frequent scenario, the new infant is experienced as a sibling of the parent. The specific feelings that characterized this former relationship, most commonly, jealousy, are now replayed. When this is the case, the parent unconsciously resents the affection and gratification that the child receives, because it revives the jealousy experienced at the birth of a hated rival.

This can take particularly virulent form when a mother relives, through her son, her jealousy toward a younger brother (especially if these parents clearly preferred a boy to a girl, a still very frequent occurrence!). This powerful jealousy can be expressed in various ways. The child may be experienced as a tyrant who rules the slave-mother with an unbound sense of power. The parent may also overprotect the child, as if he were very vulnerable. In the case of Julian described in Part V, we will describe in detail how much a sibling rivalry scenario can seriously affect the mother–infant relationship.

Good and Bad Ghosts

Since all nurseries have ghosts in them of one kind or another, anyone evaluating a parent–child relationship must be very careful in evaluating what is "normal" or "deviant" in such projections. It is not easy, because—and we wish to stress this again—it is the rule that parents reestablish old ties with their past through their children. Parental love is possible only *because* it has its roots in former attachments; empathy and attunement with a newborn are enhanced by recognition of warm states or feelings familiar from former relationships.

However, jealousy, resentment, and hostility may also be transferred from old to new relationships; we know this only too well from adult psychoanalytic experience. When do such transfers put a relationship at risk?

One useful sign of derailment is a pattern of non-contingent interaction. If the evocation of a person from the parent's past can be linked to this gap in contingency, we can locate the cause of the derailment. This link will reveal an area of conflict for the parent that may need to be resolved. A conspicuous sign of such distortion in a relationship is avoidant and defensive attitudes in a parent toward specific behavior in the baby. In many of the cases we have discussed above, this defensive derailment of interaction is used to ward off painful feelings and thoughts linked to an ambivalent relationship in the past. The parent continues to fight these obsolete conflicts by avoidance and counter-attitudes in the present interaction. In these situations the work for both parent and clinician is to identify the "absent partner," the "ghost," whom the parent interposes between the infant and him or herself. This makes possible redirecting of energies, reemergence of repressed emotion such as mourning or jealousy, and attachment to a more realistically perceived infant. We will see in more detail in the next part how "failures of contingency" are linked with persisting conflictual relationships to "ghosts."

17

Reenacting Past Modes
of Relationship

Another variation of this reliving of the past through a ghost is the reenactment of a preferred mode of relationship. In this case, the infant serves as a "prop" in the playing of a scenario. A mother may thus replay typical scenes from her childhood. If teasing and fighting permeated her relationships with parents, battles may be the order of the day with her baby; if distance and rejection were typical, these may be reproduced. Through this reenactment of former themes parents seek the lost, longed-for relationships of their childhood.

Replaying Food Battles

A mother made an appointment with one of us [BC] because her three-year-old daughter, Dorothy, "didn't eat." The child's weight and height curves were near the lowest percentile. The mother described meals as "real torture"; Dorothy refused to eat and used this negativism to dominate and manipulate her in an intolerable way. She was ready to "throw her out the window."

The more the mother talked, the more it appeared that she contributed much to the staging of the daily "food battles" with Dorothy. The roots of this mutual fighting became evident when she revealed that—as far as she could remember—she had been anorexic and fought daily "food battles" with the grandmother who raised her. Apparently, the mother maintained her attachment to her grandmother through these struggles; she recreated them now with Dorothy, just as others strive to evoke happy memories of long ago.

In this mother's case, the yearning for an exchange involving both refusal and forcing was so powerful that it started *the day* of Dorothy's birth. She reported how upset she felt when Dorothy actively refused her breast after delivery. This perfectly normal averting was experienced as negativism and defiance; it triggered in the mother the will to force the child, so that, since day one, a battle of wills over food was staged, which very faithfully reproduced her relationship with her grandmother.

This "tug of war" type of relationship is common; it appears around issues of feeding, toilet training, and discipline. The basic issue is: "Who is going to dominate whom?" To loosen such conflict, it is necessary that a parent recognize how this pattern of interaction reproduces a past relationship that the parent was not able to mourn and abandon.

Again and again, we are confronted with the fact that the so-called "new" relationship to the baby is in fact powerfully determined by the parent's past. At the same time, it is important to remember that infants bring their own characteristics to the relationship. Not all children will turn away from the breast on day one; not all children will engage in a particular battle of wills set up by a parent. It is the combination between the infant's makeup and specific style of behavior and the mother's interpretation of them that shapes their interaction. In a troubled relationship, however, it is the parent's contributions that may be the easiest target for therapeutic modification.

Evocation of the Past through Its Opposite

Parents often attempt to establish with their child the exact opposite of the relationship they had had with their own parents. This occurs often, for example, when the parents had experienced their parents as overly strict disciplinarians; with their child, they are now incapable or unwilling to impose any frustration or limits. The child is picked up as soon as he or she cries; every whim is gratified. When normal separation experiences should start to occur, these parents remain faithfully ever-present so that the child is spared any distress. Such parents wish to provide the infant with a sense of continuous gratification, avoiding any sense of frustration or limit. The child will then come to expect immediate gratification and may become so demanding as to be experienced as a tyrant. It is when the parents are totally overwhelmed by this merciless creature that they seek help. What they don't recognize is that they have recreated a past relationship to a strict authority; only now, it is the child who rules the parent. Often, the child seems to perceive that the parents "demand" an authoritarian response, and learns to play precisely that role, thus allowing the parents—once again—to live under an authoritarian rule.

Much of the enthusiasm for liberalism in raising children—as had been advocated by Benjamin Spock in his earlier writings—might have, in fact, been based on the wish to spare children from the discipline that an older generation of parents had experienced in their own upbringing. We are now in the next episode of the cycle; parents try to provide "structure and values" to avoid the chaos of permissiveness.

Creation of an Ideal Relationship

There are many other ways to replay old modes of relationship. One common theme is the wish to repair a painful childhood by providing the new infant with what is considered an *ideal* experience. Some of this is present in most parents who try to create with their infant a "perfect" parent–child relation, corresponding to what they wish they had had themselves. In these cases, what parents seek to reproduce is not an actual experience of the past, but an imaginary, ideal version of what their past *should* have been. Again, this is a wish common in many healthy families. The possibility of undoing one's past frustration and helplessness by creating an idyllic, new relationship is one of the most powerful incentives for having a child.

The desire for a perfect childhood can also cause problems, however. As an example, Anthony, fourteen months old, absolutely refused to eat anything during the whole day, while he was in a day-care center. At home, the mother prepared food in a special way; she liquified it in a blender, so that he could take everything in a bottle. She said that he refused food that was not minced in this way, but we soon realized that she contributed much to this preference for a liquid diet.

Once again, the mother's own history revealed the "why" of such an interaction: her father died while her mother was pregnant with her. Her own mother became depressed, placed her in a foster home, went to work in a distant town, and came back to see her only very rarely. Ever since, this woman suffered from an intense longing for a close relationship, which she never encountered until she married and had her baby. Now, she had a chance to create the ideal relationship she had missed and so longed for.

With Anthony, she wanted to experience a very close mother-baby bond, in which he could prolong forever the pleasures of early modes of feeding. When Anthony refused food in the day-care center, he confirmed the mother's condemnation of any baby care other than the mother's own. Her wish was to experience through her child the limitless baby gratifications of which she herself had been deprived.

This type of situation, where problems arise because the mother wants to gratify her baby to the utmost, are extremely frequent; they reveal how much energy parents are willing to spend in order to create an ideal relationship with their offspring, while simultaneously seeking gratification for themselves. How many of us hope to mend belatedly—with our children—what we experienced as missed opportunities in our own childhood!

While such yearnings are very common, if they create an intolerable situation, parent and child need help. Professionals will find that it is not enough simply to point out the exaggerated gratification and the lack of limits imposed on the child. Parents must be encouraged to tell why they believe that their infant needs to be totally gratified and spared any frustration. Very often, parents will then readily report how much they had longed to experience such ideal conditions in their own past. They will talk about their feeling of being deprived and then will usually experience an outpouring of sadness. Only then can the therapist show how they want to repair their own sense of having been neglected through an ideal relationship with their baby. Parents may then also be able to see that their wish to gratify the baby totally is bound to fail; the more they gratify the child's every whim, the more they risk overextending themselves to the point where they feel exploited by their infant. Recognizing this, they are likely to see their child more realistically: less fragile, capable of withstanding frustrations.

The Child As the Potential for Realizing Ideals: King Baby

A baby can also be seen as providing the potential for realizing a longed-for ideal, rather than the realization of a past longed-for relationship. As we saw in Part I, all infants-to-come hold the promise of fulfilling ideals that have been frustrated or kept in abeyance. The newborn is thus embedded in idealizations: he or she is the best, most beautiful, smartest baby, and parents find new evidence of these remarkable talents in each developmental step. This is not only normal, but indispensable for the process of attachment; the child's performance promises rewards to their own pride and need for achievement. Such motivation is needed if parents are to tolerate the many frustrations of infant care and their own ambivalence about a demanding— often ungratifying—baby. Because parents see a projection of their ideal selves, the baby becomes infinitely precious to them.

This scenario of idealization, however, can get out of hand. Parents may foster the infant's sense of omnipotence by gratifying every whim, transferring onto the child an insatiable quest for absolute privilege and continuous satisfaction. If they need to maintain the child's omnipotence at all costs they find themselves abject courtiers in the service of a baby King (or Queen). There can be no frustration of the Royal Will. These parents avoid imposing limits of any kind; discipline or delayed gratification is strictly avoided. The child has a diligent retinue at his or her disposal.

Such parents can go to extremes of personal abdication in order to gratify the child; they may interrupt their sleep all night to console the child. In some food-oriented families, they will gorge the child at the least evidence of discontent. In other cases, this takes the form of submitting totally to the child's aggression. One such mother actually derived pride from a toddler's destructiveness of her belongings; she kept smiling as he repeatedly—and in a testing way—hit her leg with a toy hammer. This mother came from a very traditional, rather strict middle-class family and was in open revolt against her background. She was bitter that her father had not wanted her to go to medical school. She got pregnant, abandoned the child's father, and totally devoted herself to the care of her son. He was allowed to do whatever he wished, as if destined to accomplish her dream of total freedom and make up for her own thwarted ambitions. He would be the carrier of her lost sense of omnipotence; she even encouraged his unbridled aggression to confirm his sense of limitless power. In this imaginary interaction, the mother made her baby play the part of her inflated ego, recognizing no limit.

In Part V, the case of Julian will illustrate these interactions more clearly, and the difficulties in intervention. Such parents find it very hard to accept counselling concerning the need to impose limits, because this implies a curb to their own omnipotence played out by the child.

Such extreme idealization may lead to several problems: the child may be caught in a race for accumulating honors and performances to confirm the parent's dreams of glory. This "Nobel Prize Complex" shows its effects at early ages: the child may be urged to speak and develop cognitive performance before being ready for it. In many upwardly mobile American families, this theme is evident, though usually not to such extremes.

18

The Child As One Part of the Parent

Besides projecting images of their past attachments or ways of relating, parents tend to project on a child parts of their own psyche. It is amazing how often human beings attempt to see in the external world features that really belong to themselves.

Everything and everybody we encounter is thus imbued with characteristics that are generated inside us. While this can make for a feeling of familiarity—allowing contact and closeness—it may also become a source of anguish: if we project "bad parts of ourselves" we will fear in others what we most reject in ourselves.

The psychology of prejudice is illuminated by understanding this phenomenon. In family therapy, such projections are extremely well known: people have called *delegation* the tendency of whole families to lend a particular role to one member. *Scapegoating* is the tendency to assign fault and bad intentions to one family member (the "black sheep") whose function it is to carry projected "bad" aspects of other family members. These projections are very powerful, and family psychiatry has demonstrated that they can lead to serious problems and symptoms.

However, we want to stress again, projective processes are part of normal functioning. *In itself, projection is not pathological;* it is only when it takes certain extreme characteristics that it becomes dangerous.

Empathy is in great part based on the identification we experience with a partner; in turn, this identification is possible because parts of ourselves are projected onto others. The word "projective identification" was coined to describe precisely this phenomenon. For a mother to become attuned to her infant's needs, she must rely on an identification with parts of her own infantile experience, now projected onto the baby. At the same time, if she is really to learn about her baby (experiencing true mutuality), the mother needs also to "pull back" from this identification and respect the infant's objective, individual signals. In other words, successful mothering depends upon a balance between projective identification (finding sameness) and objective reading of the baby (noticing differences). Another way of saying this is that we need fusion-like experiences as well as the ability to separate.

This interplay is reminiscent of the psychological process during pregnancy that we described in Part I. The fetus is first experienced as part of the mother's self but is gradually differentiated and individualized.

The particular balance of these two tendencies is valuable in predicting the course of a parent–child relationship. Anyone trying to understand or help families will do well to examine it carefully. Parents will vary in their tendency to allocate their own psychological traits to an infant. The nature of what they project also varies tremendously. While most parents tend to see ideal, highly cherished qualities in their baby, others project their "bad" characteristics. While some parents lend their child features familiar to them, others project what is most alien. While normal variations of projective identification lead to empathy and attachment, distorted identifications will undermine attunement and contingency. Parents may react exclusively to intentions that they lend to the infant, but which really emerge from their own unconscious conflicts.

The role of the infant must always be kept in mind. The innate characteristics, physical appearance, and gender of the infant may help fixate a particular form of projection. For example, the presence of a visible anomaly may provide material support for the projection of "deficient, weak, abnormal" aspects of the parents' own selves. Even a minor defect in a child may become the cause for severe feelings of low self-esteem in parents, as we will see later when we discuss the "disappointing infant."

The Child As Villain

We have described above how a process of idealization affects the parent–child relationship; the opposite process may also occur. The child may be seen as a villain or monster when parents project "bad" parts of themselves, or when the child exhibits an observable defect. These two situations are closely interwoven. Much of the dynamism of projection is based on the parents' reacting to something they see in the child as embodying their inner tendencies. The child—in turn—may well develop traits that will confirm their projections. Specific behavior in the child may initially trigger off these projections; a passive infant may be labelled as lazy or excessively dependent, if the parents do not tolerate these characteristics in themselves. A child who eats with great gusto may be labelled as voracious or greedy, if the parent is ashamed of his or her own "oral" tendencies. When selected aspects of the child's behavior seem to match an equivalent tendency that the parents despise in themselves, a vicious circle of condemnation and self-fulfilling prophecy may prevail.

With every newborn there is always a potential for disappointment. No baby can match the fantasies parents entertain about their child-to-be. Thus, perfectly normal traits in a baby may also trigger disappointment.

Projections of specific undesirable tendencies will affect the parent–child interaction in that particular area. Parents will overreact to, and discourage or inhibit the corresponding behavior in the child. This is clearly visible in eating difficulties, for example. Stubborn feeding behavior is often attributed to the baby when—in fact—it reveals hidden feeding preference in the parents.

We find many other types of behavior that parents—on the basis of their own unconscious fears and desires—project upon their infants. Fear of separation is a frequent example; a mother will complain of the very clinging, dependent behavior of her infant, when in fact it is she who is afraid of separation.

The mother of baby Julian—who will be described in Part V—exhibited just this problem. She complained that Julian followed her everywhere, that he went into frightening states whenever they were separated. She insisted—in particular—that she could never close a door between them. This mother's history revealed that she had been placed in an orphanage for six months when she was around two years of age; her mother would visit her occasionally, but she could see her only through a glass door (for fear of infectious contagion). It was only when she recalled this period that she was able to experience the sadness linked to this traumatic separation. As these memories became "real," the mother could decontaminate her actual relationship to Julian from these separation fears. Her perception of him changed dramatically. At the same time, she reported that he no longer carried on about separation. There were "no more tantrums" on his part when doors were closed between them.

Since mild forms of this kind of projection are universal, those who work with parents should worry only when parental perceptions are too much at odds with the reality of the child. Such signs are easy to perceive; the parent's description of the child seems farfetched, and the infant is bestowed with qualities, defects, or intentions that simply do not fit in age or character. The infant is seen as harboring motivation that could only belong to an adult. When parents lend very aggressive intentions to a small child, important derailments of the relationship are likely. In Part V, we will discuss other kinds of negative projections and ways of assessing them.

The Disappointing Infant

We are often consulted when the normal process of idealization of the baby breaks down. These are situations where the baby—far from sustaining the parents' self-esteem—becomes a source of disillusionment. As we pointed out earlier, one of the major psychological adjustments after birth is the necessity for the parents to reconcile themselves with the actual baby and mourn the perfect, imaginary one. All parents go through a more or less intense form of disappointment with their baby; this is a normal part of the parenting process. However, when the newborn presents an actual defect, congenital disease, or is premature, the mismatch between the real and imaginary baby becomes much more difficult.

In these circumstances, one can expect a sudden, traumatic breakdown of the parents' self-esteem. The child's defect is unconsciously seen as revealing hidden defects of the parents themselves. It is as if the defect in the child exposed—in a socially glaring way—an inadequacy in the parent. The reaction of disappointment and grief is particularly pronounced if the child carries a visible defect, especially affecting the face (like a cleft lip), or a disease affecting the central nervous system or the eyes. The child is like a mirror to the parents; his or her defect reflects their deficiencies. An Italian immigrant, for example, who had worked hard to become successful in his country of adoption, reacted with severe shock to the birth of his Down syndrome son. He reported that—upon hearing the bad news—he rushed back home, looked at himself in the mirror, and kept shouting, "But I am not a monster!" For this man, the child's facial features necessarily reflected his own self-image, and he needed help to reassure himself that his face did not match the deviant features (the "monster") of his child.

In Part V, we will describe the case of a child with a congenital cataract (Antonio). A therapeutic intervention which recognizes this disappointed idealization will be explored.

19

Assessing Imaginary Interactions

Imaginary interactions can come in many forms, but they are always powerful. We hope that this brief overview of different scenarios will serve as a frame of reference for assessing the manifold variety of projections that can color early parent–infant interaction.

When looking at troubled relationships, we must always keep in mind this basic fact of *all* parent–infant relationships, normal or less normal: what we feel about our children, the way we care for them, the style of education we "choose," all this is heavily determined by the reenactment of long-buried patterns. While raising a child is indeed a creation, it is fueled by the *re-creation* of long-forgotten experiences. Whenever we observe parents and infants, we must constantly ask ourselves: Whom does this child represent? What old patterns are being repeated? Into what old scenarios has this child been cast? If we try to answer these questions, our observations become a therapeutic process, one that goes far beyond counselling or reassurance. As we will see in the next part, this work of *assessment* becomes in itself an *intervention*.

PART FIVE

*Understanding
the Earliest Relationship:
A Complementary Approach to
Infant Assessment*

. . . often, when you get to know patients, they lose their diagnosis, you know.

—ELVIN SEMRAD
Semrad: The Heart
of a Therapist

Introduction

In the earlier parts of this book, we have attempted to show the nature of the parents' and infant's contribution to their earliest relationship, and how this relationship evolves both from an objective and a subjective point of view. Now, using nine actual cases, we will show how these complementary observations and insights can be applied to assess parents and infants, and how this assessment becomes, in itself, a kind of therapy.

An Indian sage once remarked, "The first step is the last." When parents choose to make an appointment with a pediatrician or nurse for a "routine" check-up, or to consult a psychiatrist, psychologist, or social worker about a problem they perceive as their child's or their own, they are also choosing a certain approach to diagnosis and treatment. Pediatricians, for instance, are trained to assess babies. In a hospital setting, they concern themselves with somatic problems (low birth weight, congenital anomalies, diseases, etc.). In a "well baby" consultation, pediatricians and nurses focus on growth, vaccinations, diet. It is only fairly recently that they have seen the treatment of behavior problems and troubled parent–child relationships as part of their work. Academic psychologists are also more geared to assessing the child alone and have usually not been trained to make relationships an object of assessment.

Professionals working in social agencies, in guidance centers and facilities that deal with families (psychiatrists, psychologists, social workers, etc.), on the other hand, are more used to considering relationships as their object of inquiry and intervention. They are trained to deal with conflict, emotion, and fantasy. Usually, however, they have little experience in assessing babies, especially normal babies.

These various professionals also differ according to their interest, on the one hand, in competence and so-called "normal" development, and failure of development and pathology on the other.

People trained in the mental health field are more attuned to "deep" and pathological material. They are vigilant concerning failures of adaptation and the signs of anxiety, insecurity, depression. In intervention, they often seek to eradicate pathology by first unearthing— mostly through verbalization—hidden (often unconscious) thoughts, fantasies, and fears. Their training does not stress the positive forces in development, tendencies for self-correction and compensation.

Pediatricians, especially those trained in child development or in the emerging field of behavioral pediatrics, stress the normal unfolding of developmental achievements and the cognitive and perceptual competence of babies. However, when confronted with a behavioral problem, they tend to minimize its pathological implications and will usually reassure parents, stating: "He will grow out of it." Such an outlook can neglect maladaptive patterns of development and underestimates the powerful impact of unconscious forces, especially parental fantasies about children, as described in Part IV.

It is our belief (and the *raison d'être* of the present book), that only a combination of these approaches can accurately understand, and thus support and treat, the problems of infancy and the parent–infant relationships. This is true whether the issues are minor developmental ones, such as sleep or crying, or severe problems, such as maternal depression or serious birth defects. Also, with such a complementary approach, the opportunity to prevent minor problems from becoming more serious is great.

20

Combining Developmental Observations and Analytic Insight

"Causes" in the field of infancy are circular in nature. The combined forces of the infant's makeup and of the parents' reactions and fantasies interact with each other in continuous feedback. An interdisciplinary approach is thus needed; we must take into consideration the infant's stage of development, parental fantasies, *and* the complex interaction of these.

The majority of problems in infants are now seen first by pediatricians and nurses, and by the staff of day-care centers. Traditionally, only the most pathological cases were referred to people trained in psychiatry. There is a trend now for a more comprehensive approach to all cases, whether light or severe. Workers in the field of pediatrics and early education can profit from the insights of psychological and psychiatric studies. Conversely, workers in the mental health field should profit from knowledge gained in pediatrics and in studies of normal infant development.

When dealing with parents and infants, all caregivers—whatever their discipline—need insights from other fields. Ideally, they would work in a team setting, in cooperation with pediatricians, psychologists, nurses, social workers, and psychiatrists. Teaching programs should include techniques of assessment of infants, of parents, and of interactions.

In the nine case histories that follow, we show both pediatricians and psychiatrists working with parents and infants. Using the cases, we try to illustrate the particular contributions of each profession and of other disciplines in understanding the cases and helping the families. While we see interdisciplinary settings as ideal, our case commentaries offer a model of how a "bi-focal" approach can be used by any individual caring for parents and infants, regardless of professional background.

We try to see each symptom as the result of multiple forces, including the individual characteristics of the infants and parents and parental fantasies. These shape the system that we subsume under the term *interaction*. We consider all problems as relational (Emde & Sameroff, 1989). This is true even when clear-cut organic pathology—such as a birth or congenital defect—is present; as we will see, the prognosis of such children depends a great deal on how parents perceive and experience the defect, and how they deal with it. Concepts derived from experimental child psychology, such as reciprocity, synchrony, and contingency, also help us assess the quality of interaction (Cramer, 1987).

21

Assessing Interaction

Diagnosis in the field of infant psychiatry is still at the pre-experimental stage. Such diagnostic schemes as the DSM III are not very useful for infants or parent–infant relationships. What we sorely need is a classification based on the nature of the interaction (Kreisler & Cramer, 1983). This is by no means easy because, interactions being processes, they are difficult to define, unlike physical symptoms, such as pneumonia, or psychological problems, such as a phobia. A long-term goal in the infancy field would be for a professional to be able to observe a parent and child, talk with the parents and then arrive—within a reasonably short time—at a diagnostic formulation of that particular interaction (Cramer, 1986).

For the time being, we have some reference points and basic criteria, which include:

Developmental Stage

Developmental stages are particularly vital in understanding interaction in infancy, when needs and abilities are changing so rapidly. The younger the infant, the greater the need for repeated assessment. This has been amply proven with prematures. Early unfavorable evaluations have uneven prognostic value since, in many cases, compensating factors (especially linked to parental adjustment) can bring about much better scores later on (Parmelee et al., 1975; Lester et al., 1987). Since parenting is also affected by the developmental stage of the child, it changes over months and cannot be evaluated in a one-shot assessment (Robson & Moss, 1970; Coleman et al., 1953).

We need thus to judge all interactions with developmental status in mind. Some broad stages of development as they affect interaction were outlined in Part III.

Any reliance of diagnostic considerations on developmental status, however, must be done with caution. The postpartum period, first of all, is a period of intense change (a "crisis" in every sense of the word). All sorts of symptoms may appear transiently during the first year after birth; they change easily and their presence or disappearance is not a safe anchor for a diagnosis. It is the underlying curve of development that has diagnostic value. Even so, predictions in infancy are hazardous. Signs which seem ominous just after birth may become much less alarming later on, just as an absence of overt problems early does not necessarily preclude later problems. Finally, professionals should be very cautious in using diagnostic labels because of their well-known self-fulfilling nature.

Observation of Behavior

Because infants cannot relate their inner states through verbalization or symbolic play, their overt behavior must be scrutinized as an expression of subjective experience. Observation of the baby's behavior is thus central to assessment. Techniques of observation are described in Part III. Video recordings are an irreplaceable tool in this endeavor, and microanalytic analysis has refined their use. Assessment scales (such as the NBAS, described in full in Part II) are valuable both as quantitative evaluations and as interventions. A clear description of the infant's actual symptoms is also part of the assessment of interaction, inasmuch as functional disorders (such as insomnia and anorexia) can be seen as communication of inner states.

Observation of an infant's behavior should never be seen as purely "objective," however, for the observer is an active presence and influence. Transference is at work, and reactions appear that would not be seen in a "neutral" setting. The use of video equipment also influences what goes on, although in our experience, it does not usually inhibit the spontaneity of parent and child. The observer, though, is always part of the system. His or her involvement can modify family interaction. Given skill and experience, this influence can be for the better.

Subjective Experience

As we saw in Part IV, the parents' inner experience of the child and the projections they cast on the child will powerfully shape the infant's experience of him- or herself. Anyone trying to understand early interaction must tap these parental fantasies.

The Complementary Approach

It must be obvious now that our model of assessment is based on a complementary pooling of data based on both observation and subjective reports. The value of such an approach has been pointed out: S. Fraiberg (1980) was a pioneer in the attempt to integrate psychoanalysis and developmental studies. Together with one of the authors, Daniel Stern has published a case in which both the contents of the mother–infant psychotherapy and the objective measurements of the interactive patterns are presented. They show how subjective factors in the mother interact in a specific way with the characteristics of the baby, creating distorted interactions that shape the child's behavior (Cramer & Stern, 1988). Stern also has used both psychoanalysis and developmental psychology to explore the ways infants develop a sense of self (Stern, 1985).

A complementary approach also serves to remind us that so-called "normal" development is fueled by such unconscious forces as anxieties, ambivalence, and conflicts, usually acknowledged only in a pathological context. Normal development and pathology intermesh and interact all the time, and both must be included in any assessment of interaction. In our work with infants, we have constantly been impressed with the resilient resources in both parents and babies. Self-correcting tendencies and energy for adaptation are probably stronger in this early period and in young parenthood than they will ever be again (Brazelton, 1981). This is why we believe that infancy is an ideal period for brief intervention (Cramer, 1989). Support and insight offered at this time can unleash powerful positive forces for attachment and growth. In brief, the clarification of projections, anxieties, and ambivalences will often suffice to allow the normal maturational process to resume between parents and children. The process of assessment itself—if it communicates to parents the many-sided understanding we describe—can be a powerful force for change as well as an effective measure to prevent future problems.

In the cases that follow,* we hope to illustrate our combined approach, and also to show how assessment and intervention, understanding and healing, go hand in hand.

---

*Each of these cases (with names changed) was drawn from the practice of one of the authors, who is the "I" speaking in the case history. The commentary is by both authors.

22

Lisa:
"Angry Already"

Mr. and Mrs. J. brought three-and-one-half-month-old Lisa for a consultation because of her "relentless" crying. They reported that she cried for eight to ten hours a day and on into the night. No one could stop her, they maintained, and neither parent was able to stand it any longer. They had seen three different pediatricians, all of whom assured them that "it's just colic," and that if they would only "relax," so would Lisa. "Anyway," they were told, "it will be over when she's twelve weeks old." Now she was more than twelve weeks, and the crying hadn't stopped. They were frantic. Her grandmother had come to help out when the mother went back to work after Lisa was six weeks old. When she arrived, she commented that Lisa was just like her mother as a baby, and she'd been desperate at the time. Mrs. J. found that remark soothing, but also disturbing. She really didn't want her daughter to be like her. Could we help her change her while she was little?

When I asked her what was disturbing about having a daughter just like her, she said, "She's so angry. I don't want her to spend her life fighting to keep control over her anger. Here she is, just a tiny baby, angry already."

Mrs. J.'s remark reveals a typical projection of the type we described in Part IV. This mother perceived Lisa's crying as a sign of anger; this meaning attribution created a distorted interpretation of the child's signals; her crying may have had nothing to do with anger, may have revealed discomfort, a need for discharge or some other communication.

Crying, as we pointed out in Part II, serves many purposes for babies. At least four cries (pain, hunger, boredom, discomfort) are distinguishable early in the baby's life. Mrs. J.'s interpretation of Lisa's crying as revealing anger makes it clear that her own anger will have to be dealt with in order to help comfort the baby.

The grandmother's contribution is also very revealing; it shows how imaginary interactions can be carried from one generation to the next. Mrs. J.'s plea to the doctor is an effort not to relive with Lisa the conflict that must have caused much distress between herself as a child and her own mother.

Mrs. J. was a pretty, rather heavily made-up, well-dressed young woman, a successful partner in a law firm. Her calm-looking husband looked a bit younger than she, although he claimed to be "her age." As he remarked, "I don't get involved in all of this as my wife does," his wife looked at him with a mixture of envy and of scorn. She mumbled, "Maybe if you did, I wouldn't have to be so involved." I sensed a certain amount of tension between them, and just as I realized it, Mrs. J. said, "It's only Lisa that has brought about the tension between us." I realized how sensitive she was to any disapproval. Her carefully made-up face and appearance began to have more significance to me.

They told me more about their family. Their older boy, Tim, was two years old now and had always been so different. He'd been so easy from the first, hadn't given them a moment's concern. "He's like his Dad," said Mrs. J. He'd been so easy that she had felt no pangs about going back to work when he was one month old. In fact, she felt that if she'd stayed home longer, she'd have gone stir-crazy. Mothering just wasn't any challenge, and she thrived on challenge. He'd adjusted to everything—the sitters, the day care, and more recently, to Lisa. He never even acted as if he were jealous. As she recounted this, her husband nodded, interjecting little bits of reminiscence about his son's infancy. He seemed more involved and eager to talk about this boy as a person than she was. As she talked about him, I noted a kind of detachment that was different from her involvement with Lisa. At one point, as if justifying herself, she said, "I was glad to leave him to others; I felt as if I might ruin that beautiful disposition." I commented, "It's almost as if you didn't trust yourself to be his mother." She stiffened a bit and said, "Or maybe I felt he didn't need me. He was already so easy with himself. I never feel like *he* (pointing to her husband) really needs me either—or knows I'm there."

Mr. J. smilingly replied, "Of course you're there, but we're so different." It turned out that he was an insurance salesman, only moderately successful, with more flexibility about his schedule. He was able to stay at home more, and he "managed all the crises." "Except this one with Lisa," she quickly interjected.

Mrs. J. seemed resentful to have the responsibility for her baby, as if this were a hindrance for her professional ambitions. She appeared to regard commitment to success in work as incompatible with competent mothering; in fact, she hinted that her boy was better off if she did not take care of him, leaving this to others. The conflict between professional achievements and mothering capacities appeared to fuel this mother's distress, and yet suggested the strength of her caring.

She knew she'd been lucky with Tim. Somehow she'd been aware that this next baby would be a challenge. Before Lisa was born, she said she knew that she would be "a hellion." She was active most of the day even as a fetus. When she arrived, Lisa was a bit "scrawny" and long. She looked "angry from the first." I commented that being angry seemed to be something that Mrs. J. had attributed to Lisa before. She said, "Well, why else would she cry so much?"

Clearly, Mrs. J. was "predisposed" to read anger into Lisa from the word go. That this was the case with Lisa, and not with Tim, must be due to gender; Mrs. J.'s image of an angry girl comes from her own past experience.

Crying may feel particularly unbearable because the mother experiences it as a reproach directed at her by her daughter; guilt may then torment a mother who feels incompetent. Her resentment against Lisa can be seen as embodying her sense of maternal "failure."

I asked Mrs. J. a bit more about Lisa as a newborn, because I sensed that this "scrawny" newborn might have been somewhat undernourished in the uterus. Mrs. J. told me she was a hypersensitive, hyperactive newborn, who was difficult to organize from the first. She not only overreacted to stimuli, but she was very difficult to feed, spitting up her feedings, "if you fed her too much. You had to hit it just right or she'd never settle down, even after a feed." This overreactive newborn had indeed been hard to understand or to feed, and her responses, which looked negative to her overly sensitive mother, confirmed her fears of herself as an inadequate mother.

Here we see the interplay between the characteristics of an individual baby and the mother's history. Lisa's overreactive nature contributed in a decisive way to materialize—and justify—the mother's fantasy that her baby incarnated the angry part of herself.

As Mrs. J. talked about Lisa, the baby began to stir in her father's arms. It was as if she sensed we were now talking about her. She woke up abruptly to start screaming. Mrs. J. immediately grabbed Lisa from her husband, began to pat her, to rock her vigorously up and down, anxiously searching for a bottle or pacifier to try to stop her crying. I commented on how difficult it seemed for her to hear Lisa crying. She said testily, "Doesn't it bother you that she cries all the time?" I replied, "I think I can understand it in her. She's a very hypersensitive little girl. There may not be an easy solution to her crying. However, I think I can help you. Instead of just trying to stop her crying, I'd rather we aimed at a different goal. I'd like to help you understand her as a person. That may be more critical to her future and yours than just to stop her crying."

Mr. J. leaned forward, as if he understood what I was saying. Mrs. J. began to jiggle Lisa even more frantically. Lisa looked strained and overwhelmed. Mrs. J. said, "I just want to find out how to handle this crying, so we can live like human beings again. These three months have been a real nightmare." I asked her whether she was afraid of anything in particular. She said seriously, "At times, I've been afraid of either losing my mind, or of doing something terrible to Lisa." I said I knew how she felt, for most people feel out of control when a baby cries relentlessly. She said incredulously, "They do?" I commented that she seemed to feel as if she were unusual in her responses. At first, she started to protest, then she said softly, looking at her husband, "I know, I am an easily upset person. I have so little self-control. This baby makes me feel helpless and so angry at times that I'm afraid of her. I wish *he* would take over." I went on to say that it was almost as if she didn't trust herself as Lisa's mother and reminded her that she'd said that about Tim, too. "I am not a motherly type. I could feel OK about Tim, because I knew my husband and Tim could make it together. With Lisa, no one likes her, not even my mother. She wants to leave us to go back to Florida, because of Lisa's temper." I said, "You do keep calling her crying anger or 'a temper' in Lisa. Does it remind you of yourself as a child? You told me that you were angry when you were little." Mrs. J.'s voice softened and became almost childlike. "I was a terrible little girl. I was angry all the time. My mother would just walk away and leave me, she got so exasperated. I felt she hated me at times. And I hated myself, until I could learn to control myself. Now Lisa is going to be just like me. Oh God!"

She was so close to tears that I wasn't sure about whether I should pursue this, but her husband leaned over to pat her hand. Her baby had now settled down and was nuzzling into her breast. "You know," I said, "it's almost as if Lisa knew it was good for you to let off steam about your feelings. Look how she's cuddling into you." Mrs. J. looked down at her, as if she was seeing her for the first time. "Do you think she knows already how I'm feeling?" "Perhaps it frightens you for Lisa to be like you and so sensitive, but, you know, it really could be a wonderful asset." I paused. "Why do you suppose you're as worried as you are?" "I've never felt I should be a mother," she replied. "I feel competent as a person at work. But not at home!" I asked her whether she'd like to talk more about that if we could arrange a time to talk about it. She looked surprised. "I thought I was going to get help for Lisa, not for myself."

This was an important turning point. First, the mother felt able to express her fear of battering her child. This is a crucial aspect of psychotherapeutic work: the therapist indicates that such painful and guilt-inducing impulses can be shared; the mere fact that the mother voices her fear of hurting the baby has a powerful, soothing impact. The mother senses that if such impulses are told to a trusting partner, the chances of acting on them is lessened.

In this dialogue, one also sees how important it is to bring the past into the present; to be able to remember how "terrible" she was as a girl helps Mrs. J. decontaminate the present relationship from the angry ghost of her childhood. Then, she can start seeing Lisa in a new light, as if—indeed—she is seeing her for the first time.

Despite the realization that it is the parent's problem as well as the baby's, there will be strong resistance to exploring the parent's role. "I thought I was going to get help for Lisa, not for myself." A nurse or pediatrician will need skill and tact to shift the focus to the parent. All professionals working with infants need to have such psychological skills.

I assured Mrs. J. that I did intend to help her with Lisa but that that might also mean helping her with her own reactions to Lisa. Being an extremely sensitive baby, Lisa was sensitive to her mother's moods and feelings. We wanted this to become an asset, not a hindrance in their relationship. Her mother nodded as if she were agreeing with me.

I examined Lisa. There were no signs of other problems. She was indeed very sensitive to any kind of handling. I had observed Lisa all the time we were talking, and as I began to examine her and to play with her, I was able to point out certain things that I felt might help her parents understand her better. I had waited to do this until we had established an understanding between us that it wasn't just Lisa who was at stake, but also her mother's image of herself as a competent parent.

Lisa, already a well-rounded baby, was no longer long and lean. But she had a worried gaze as she surveyed the room. When I looked at her, her eyes widened to stare at me. I was reminded of a caged, wild animal. They seemed to contain both fear and longing. As I talked softly to her, she winced and her frown deepened. Now her eyes avoided mine.

I realized that talking to her and looking at her at the same time created too many stimuli for her. She pulled away to arch in her mother's arms. Her mother, too, stiffened as Lisa did; the interaction between them, which a moment ago had been so rewarding, was turning into a stiff, unyielding one. Mrs. J. turned Lisa's body outward, away from hers, as if she couldn't stand Lisa's rejecting posture. In a matter of minutes, she handed Lisa to her father. Her father started to embrace her, felt her stiffen, waited until she softened, then began slowly to rock her in his arms. He never looked at her or spoke to her. I asked him softly if he'd learned this way of comforting her because he knew how easily overloaded she was. He nodded silently, as if he were saying, "If I speak now, she'll fall apart." Mrs. J. said scornfully but with envy, "He knows how to handle her. She prefers him to me already." When Lisa started to cry a little while later, her mother looked as if she had expected it. She said, "This is how she is at least eight hours a day. If he's at home, he can calm her some, but when I am at home, she can't stand me. I'm afraid I may hurt her—or leave her for good." By now, I was seeing the same wild, trapped look in Mrs. J.'s eyes that I'd just seen in Lisa's.

Indeed, they were alike. I felt it critical to help this woman see Lisa as a separate individual. I felt obligated to try to explain what I'd just seen, although I knew that an understanding of Lisa's hypersensitivity was only a part of their problem. I tried to explain that I'd seen many babies like Lisa, who'd developed a kind of physiological hypersensitivity to stimuli, even before birth. We don't know exactly what causes it, but we see it in babies who are long for their weights at birth, and who are relatively skinny and depleted of sugar and fat stores. It is thought that the placenta may not have fed them adequately at the end of pregnancy. As a result, I explained, they are jumpy and irritable, overreactive as newborns, moving from a sleep or quiet state to a screaming, irritable one in a matter of moments. Lisa's frown was that of a wary baby who knew how difficult it would be for her to handle any noise or visual stimulation. Her arching was an attempt to protect herself from becoming overloaded.

Lisa's mother and father listened intently as I described this syndrome to them. Mrs. J. said, "You seem to know Lisa, all right. Why do you suppose she was like that at birth? Had I done something to her in the uterus to make her that way?" I assured Mrs. J. that as far as we knew that probably wasn't the case, for she'd already assured me that her diet had been adequate, she didn't smoke or drink or take medications, and she was not hypertensive. She said, "Was it because I was tense? I didn't want to be pregnant with her, you know. Did I ruin her from the first?" I said that I didn't think that was possible in the uterus, but that I felt that it was affecting her handling of Lisa now. She bristled and said, "Anyone would react to a screaming baby the way I do." I said, "That's absolutely right. They would, and I don't blame you for your reactions to her. The only trouble is that Lisa is so sensitive to your own anguish that I fear she overreacts to that, too. Did you see how she stiffened just then when you got tense? It's almost as if you two had already developed a sort of pattern of oversensitivity to each other. She senses when you get tense, she stiffens and starts to cry, then you really feel desperate."

A distorted interaction had developed; the child's tenseness was symmetrical to the mother's. A communication (one could almost call it contagion) of tenseness kept occurring. The mother may unconsciously have induced this tenseness as if needing to prove that her mothering must fail with Lisa.

Then Mrs. J. said again, "Well, you can *see* how inadequate I am. I can't even hold her. She's better with her father. What kind of success is that!" I nodded in agreement and said, "But since it's a problem, can't we work on it together? Lisa needs your help to become less sensitive, and to become easier with herself and her world. She was as difficult for me to handle as she is for you. She needs the quiet kind of approach which you gave her a few minutes ago. When she begins to fall apart, maybe you could just rock her or give her something to suck on, soothing her until she calms herself, which is your real goal. When you see that you can't be of any help to her, she may be better off left alone, to cry it out for a little while. Perhaps she needs to cry to let off an overload of stimulation. I'd try only one thing at a time—

looking at her, or singing to her quietly, or holding her or patting her. More than one may be too much."

I suggested that they try several approaches: (1) feeding Lisa in a quiet, darkened room several times a day; (2) playing with her quietly, watching for signs of overloading, such as frowning, arching, hiccoughing; (3) when she overreacted, instead of doing more to quiet her, try a single soothing and containing maneuver; (4) then, try to leave her alone to quiet herself. They could let her cry ten to fifteen minutes at a time. (5) Last of all, they could keep a diary, so that we could evaluate her pattern of crying on their next visit.

Two weeks later, Mr. and Mrs. J. were cautiously joyous. Lisa was quieting down, her crying was already reduced to a two-hour stint at the end of the day. But their big achievement, said Mrs. J., was that "We think we now know Lisa. She's a real person to us. We can see how she works. Instead of feeling frightened of her, I now see her as a challenge. When I do the right things, she no longer frowns at me, she looks grateful. I can't believe it!"

When a mother's projection of anger onto a child is withdrawn, she can begin to discover the actual nature of her child. The interaction becomes more gratifying.

The mother had lost her own worried look. She looked younger, happier, and much more relaxed. As she held Lisa, she held her tenderly, glancing down briefly as she talked. I asked them to tell me what they'd done. They recounted a period of learning how to handle this sensitive baby. Many things had not worked, but in general, as their diary showed, their attempts were gradually calming her down. She was now reachable. They showed me how she would smile, coo with them, if they started very gradually and let her lead them to build up to a satisfying interaction. Her mother's confidence as she handled her was heartwarming. The baby, too, looked happier, softer, and more relaxed.

I congratulated both parents on their success and wondered whether we could talk more about their reactions to her when she was difficult. "For," I said, "there'll be some more tough times. Can't we think about how her crying makes you feel, so that when difficulties come again, you'll have some insight into your reactions to her?" I asked Mrs. J. whether she had any idea why she felt so fragile, for, I assured her, "You aren't, really. Here you've turned a very difficult baby around and are beginning to enjoy her. You told me that you rushed back to work after your older boy was born. Did you feel a similar fear of failure with him?" She nodded and said, "I felt I really shouldn't have tried to be a mother. Lisa proved it to me." "Can you tell me anything about these feelings? They must come from somewhere." She said, "I was six years old when my little sister was born. My mother was so relieved to have another baby and this was a good baby, that she kept pointing out the contrast between me and my sister. When I'd try to help her with my sister Elizabeth, she'd push me away, saying, 'You'd just ruin her if you handled her. She'd get to be just like you. I'll take care of her!' When Lisa came, it was like a prophecy come true. She was like me, and I'd done it. When I saw my mother with her, it was as if I could see how she'd felt about me. She looked at Lisa as if she couldn't stand her, and I realized how much she'd hated me. There, I've said it!" Her husband started to protest, but I stopped him and said, "I think it's critical that you hear and understand how deeply her sense of failure with Lisa and Tim can go at times. You were helpful to her in the bad times with Lisa and sensitive to Lisa's needs as well. They may need you again in other crises."

The ghost in this nursery is the mother herself, watching her mother's love go to a baby sister. Lisa's birth recreated a painful time, the "trauma" of the sister's birth and the feelings of being the troublesome bad child who drove away her own mother.

Mrs. J. said, "You know, I've never dared face how upset I was then. I just wanted to run away. Now that I am beginning to get on Lisa's wavelength, sometimes I feel as if I could mother the world." I joined her in her feelings of euphoria and conquest over some basic self-doubts, while reminding her that there was more ahead. But there would be fun together, for Lisa was likely to be a spirited baby in the future and would be able to give and take in a relationship that would continue to test them both. Mrs. J. finished our interview with, "Thank you for helping us. Now I won't have to work *just* to get away from her."

In this short-term, rather superficial intervention, we can see how understanding of a baby's hypersensitivity and a mother's projection of anger helped defuse a painful situation. Mrs. J. needed this cognitive understanding of her baby before she could feel anything but overwhelmed and resentful. With this knowledge and with some taste of success, she could begin to face the imaginary interactions that recreated her own past. Having verbalized this in front of her supportive husband, she may have an easier time and more self-confidence in the future. Certainly, her relationship with this baby has a better chance of developing well, now that she has made progress with this initial difficulty and learned to see her as a separate person.

To sum up, this intervention pooled two approaches: first, observation of the baby helped explain to the parents why she was so easily upset and upsetting to them. The real difficulties of parenting such a baby were acknowledged. Next, it was necessary to help the mother verbalize her feelings of anger, of guilt, and of failure. This led to unveiling her projection of her "bad self" onto the baby. Lisa had to be separated from the angry ghost of the past.

23

Sebastian: "Reproachful Eyes"

Sebastian, three-and-one-half months old, was brought for a consultation because of feeding difficulties. His mother was very concerned, saying that he hardly ate and was not gaining weight. As they sat in my office, his mother, Mrs. M., avoided the *en face* position; she turned Sebastian away from her on her lap and never gazed into his eyes. Her avoidance of body contact was evident. When the baby sought closeness, reaching to nestle against her, she would start some activity which made intimate contact impossible. Even when she gave Sebastian a bottle, she held him facing away from her. When she had to hold the baby against her—for instance, when she burped him—she was very rigid and her movements were totally mechanical. When the infant again showed an attempt at body contact, she remained motionless, seemingly impervious to his needs.

In conversation, over several visits, she mentioned that breast-feeding had not "worked" at all, and that she had given up very early. When asked why she did not look at Sebastian as she fed him, she stated that his glance intimidated her. Later, she described it as "reproachful." I asked her what she meant by that, and she replied that she was sure that Sebastian judged her as a bad mother, incapable of fulfilling her role.

Later, when asked about her own childhood, she volunteered that her father had spent several years away from the family when she was young. On the occasions when he would appear, she was frightened. His eyes made her feel incompetent and ridiculous. There had never been physical closeness in her family, and she could remember feeling intensely ashamed when allusions were made about her body. Puberty had been very difficult. When she found herself close to her father, she would freeze completely.

In this case, the correlation between the past relationship to the father, and in the present to Sebastian, was offered by the mother herself. Despite her insight, the projection was so powerful as to force the mother to avoid her baby's eyes altogether and to forego affectionate body contact. The result was constant anti-contingency and increasing symptoms. The baby was becoming very irritable, at times impossible to soothe; he was visibly caught between the wish to be close to his mother and the fear of being pushed away. In some sessions, the infant actually cried and fussed for an hour solid, attempts at consoling him remaining fruitless.

What is so striking—in this case—is the concrete nature of the projection; the mother needs to avoid Sebastian's eyes as if they *actually* are her father's; body contact is avoided as though with her father. Almost tangible distortions of the child's "real" signals make a fulfilling interaction impossible.

Sebastian and his mother illustrate several characteristics of projection that put an early relationship at risk. First of all, Sebastian is experienced as *too accurate* a reproduction of his maternal grandfather. As we have seen, all parents see aspects of family members in their babies. But when this identity is too literal, the child becomes a prisoner of the parent's own past. Unless parents can separate the real personality of the baby, emerging from the confusion with the image of their own parents, true contingency is not possible and the interaction remains distorted. When the feelings that link the infant to the parent's own parent are mostly *negative*, the interaction is more at risk; in this case, for example, there is shame and the fear of being judged. Finally, a sense of *conviction* that attributed characteristics really belong to the infant makes therapy more difficult. While the mother could see a link with her childhood, she did not have enough insight to see that the characteristics she saw in the child were of her own making. If this deeper failure of insight is not recognized, a clinician might be content to give advice to an apparently understanding parent or merely to attempt to correct misperceptions by stressing that, in reality, the child does not correspond to a parent. Such a pedagogical approach is insufficient when projection and conviction of its reality is so strong.

After four months of weekly therapy, Sebastian and Mrs. M. still had much to overcome. His mother still appeared immobilized by him. Sebastian was delayed in motor development, still on his belly, unable to sit well alone. When he elicited a response from his mother, she stiffened, or her body sagged, as if it were too much for her to reach out to him. He, too, was rather limp. He rarely got interested or excited. He protested weakly, and his features sagged also, as if he weren't sure that his protests were worth it. When his mother finally picked him up, she held him like a statue in her lap. When he reached up briefly to touch her face, she winced and pulled away momentarily. Finally, she looked down at him with a smile, but he had given up and turned to a toy to play with. Restless in her arms, he seemed to signal that he'd rather be put down to play, but she ignored or seemed unconscious of these behaviors. He resigned himself to playing with the toy. His play was monotonous and joyless. He batted it over and over, never exploring it or mouthing it.

Since feeding was still an issue, Mrs. M. handed Sebastian to me to feed. He was vigorous in his refusal. He cried inconsolably as I tried to feed him. His mother took her wailing child, but again she seemed insensitive or afraid of him. She tried to feed him immediately, without an attempt to console or comfort him first. Of course, he refused and spit out the nipple. His cry was hollow and rather empty. He looked up into her face briefly. She didn't return his look, and he looked away.

When he drooled from the feeding, Mrs. M. took this as an opportunity to repeatedly dab at his lips with a cloth. She kept trying to catch his mouth with her cloth. He turned his head from side to side. Their most vigorous encounter ensued as she pursued and he refused to let her close to him. They both giggled briefly. I had the feeling that their most passionate interaction was based on intrusive behavior on the mother's part with strong negativism on his.

Despite this glimpse of closeness, Mrs. M. seemed generally unable to respond to her baby's short-lived bids for attention. Had she responded, he'd have gotten more involved and more excited about his world. As it was, he seemed low on energy, playing perfunctorily but without any real pleasure. He seemed most excited when she rallied with intrusive behavior. I had the feeling that this pattern might begin to shape his interactions with adults. He was too frightened to play with me, but I was sure he could still respond to a sensitive adult. Sebastian's feeding refusal was part of an overall pattern. Since his most vigorous response was a negative one, it did not surprise me that he refused unwanted food in an ungratifying feeding interaction.

The avoidance of visual and body contact continued to distort this relationship. When Sebastian was eight months old, we were able to quantify the mother's and infant's behavior during their interaction. The position held longest while we observed them was characterized by the following features: Sebastian was held five to twenty-five inches away from his mother's chest with his back turned toward her, looking away. Mother and baby adopted this position fifty percent of the observed time; it was four or five times more frequent than any other positions (Cramer & D'Arcis, *in press*). On the basis of this microanalysis, we could demonstrate the interactive expression of the mother's personal fears, based on past experience.

Around Sebastian's first birthday, we came to realize that this mother–infant pair was locked into patterns of extreme contact avoidance, leading to very ungratifying exchanges. Sebastian was very fretful with many other signs of distress. The mother was constantly complaining about him and she berated herself as a "bad mother." We then embarked on a dual form of intervention. On one hand, we had to "treat" the relationship; we did this through weekly joint sessions during which we showed to this mother how her fear of close contact interfered with any reciprocal interchanges. On the other hand, we realized that the mother's inhibitions were so strong that much time would elapse before her behavior would change. Her rapidly developing baby needed a gratifying partner. Therefore, when Sebastian reached the age of eighteen months, he was involved in play therapy by himself.

At the age of two-and-a-half, Sebastian was still quite hyperactive; his speech was delayed and he showed marked difficulties in play. By that time, his mother had grown quite despondent about her ability to mother him. Through our weekly encounters, however, she gradually found new ways of relating to Sebastian. She particularly enjoyed reading to him, which fostered their relationship. Nevertheless, she still avoided body contact.

When Sebastian reached the age of five, he was developing fairly well. His speech was now excellent; he was less hyperactive and was able to play. His mother was still complaining about her failures as a mother, but we felt she had come a long way.

In retrospect, we felt it likely that had we not intervened, Sebastian might not have been able to come out of his hyperactivity and that other more severe symptoms might have developed. At the time of this writing, he would not be considered a high-risk child if seen now for the first time in evaluation. This is an example of early assessment leading to specialized psychiatric help which—probably—prevented a very poor outcome.

24

Peter:
"Wild Man"

Peter, nearly four months old, was brought by his mother to our clinic, because he was "unhappy, constantly crying, and fussing." Mrs. S. had already sought help from many sources: from her obstetrician, from her own pediatrician, who called the behavior "colic" and assured her Peter would outgrow it, and from her own parents, who blamed her for the baby's crying. She was hysterical, weeping, and even threatening that she might "hurt the baby" if she were sent home without relief.

Peter was assessed as normal physically. Mrs. S. looked depressed and dishevelled. She came alone, assuring me that her family (including her husband) couldn't see any of this as a problem. She felt deserted by them. Though she said she "knew" that his crying "jags" were "just" colic and were all her fault, that didn't help. She still didn't know what to do about it and was so depressed that she was afraid—for herself and for the baby.

While she talked, Peter's little face looked pained and he frowned off into the distance. He held his body stiff, jumping from time to time as his mother talked and as her emotions came to the surface. He winced when I tried to speak directly to him. When, with some difficulty, I engaged him in eye-to-eye contact, he frowned as I drew close, then looked off into the distance. When I made the mistake of trying to hold him, Peter immediately began to scream in a piercing, hopeless wail. His mother sighed deeply, took him back into her wooden arms. He quieted and resumed his empty staring off into space.

The most disturbing aspect of this case was the complete lack of positive interaction; the faces of mother and baby were strained and tight. They looked away from each other; there was withdrawal on both sides. There were many signs of failure of contingency and reciprocity. Both partners showed signs of emotional distress. The baby was withdrawn and reacted negatively when the examiner tried to reach him. It is striking that this case was not regarded as serious by the first doctors who were involved. When a mother says that she might hurt her baby, this should necessarily lead to intervention.

At birth, Peter had weighed eight pounds, two ounces and seemed just fine. Apgars were 8-9-9, "almost perfect." But Peter soon began to have difficulty breathing and had to be put in oxygen for twenty-four hours. Mrs. S. said she knew something would be "wrong," and this problem confirmed her expectations. Peter had mild *hyperbilirubinemia* (jaundice), and his mother was sure that this was evidence of future problems. He was discharged with her after four days, but one of the nurses mentioned in passing that he was a "wild man," so she knew she was headed for trouble.

During his first months at home, Peter seemed to have difficulty in virtually every area of functioning. Mrs. S. said he had "been fussy since we got him." It was always difficult to soothe him, though an automatic swing and bouncing carriage rides seemed to help for a while. Peter's fussing worsened over the first three months to the point where he seemed to cry continually except for about twenty minutes after a feeding. Both feeding and sleeping were difficult for Peter. He squirmed during feedings, often arching his back. His formula was switched again and again. Mrs. S. became further upset by her difficulties in interacting with Peter. She felt he often seemed to ignore her attempts to interact with him.

In such a context, when a caregiver makes a remark, however casual, such as, "He is a wild man," this will be taken by the mother as an official confirmation of her projection. The label sticks to a child, bringing about a self-fulfilling prophecy. Every word from a professional will be fastened onto by parents at this raw, sensitive stage, and caregivers should word very carefully what they say about a baby, whether or not parents seem unduly anxious.

Despite his mother's fears, Peter was a well-nourished, healthy-appearing boy. He seemed alert and even smiled occasionally at me when I looked at him from a distance of about six feet. He sat quietly in his mother's lap but was visually exploring the environment while I talked with his mother. His mother was anxious, both in his care and in conversation with me.

Throughout the developmental assessment and physical exam, both of which showed him to be entirely normal, Peter demonstrated a hypersensitivity to stimuli. When he became upset, it was very difficult to console him, though he eventually quieted down if his mother held him still in her lap. Walking and rocking and patting did not help at all.

My impression was that Peter clearly showed a constellation of temperamental characteristics labelled "difficult" by Stella Chess and Alexander Thomas (1984), among others. He was hypersensitive to stimuli, easily upset, difficult to console, and had a history of irregularity in sleeping and feeding schedules. Mrs. S., however, blamed herself for all this, which she interpreted as Peter's "unhappiness."

My discussion with the mother initially focused on Peter's temperament. A few specific suggestions were made: provide a quiet room for feeding to diminish competing and disturbing stimuli; diminish nearby noises during naps by closing his door and having his sisters play elsewhere; interact with him gently, providing gradually modulated stimuli and looking carefully for signs of overload, like turning away or tension in the extremities.

Mrs. S. was urged to call as needed, and a follow-up appointment was made for one week later.

At this point, the intervention focused on helping the mother by showing that Peter is a "difficult" baby. This might somewhat lessen her self-blaming tendencies. As we pointed out earlier, however, it will no doubt be necessary to go deeper if we want to get at the roots of this mother's guilt.

There were no telephone calls from Mrs. S. between the initial visit and the next visit one week later, when Peter was four months old. She told me the child had improved, though he was still difficult and cried and fussed at length. He was sleeping through the night, and she was beginning to have some success in reaching him.

My observations showed that Peter remained hypersensitive and tense but had progressed in his ability to cope with stimuli. His face was not quite as anxious. He could look at me for a short space of time.

Mrs. S.'s face was softer, less angry-looking. She kept saying something like the following: "What you showed me about him was such a help. I couldn't tell you how guilty I felt about him. I realized that I'd resented him from the very first. And I'd been blaming him for all the misery that I was feeling." She went on to tell me how good she felt about him when he relaxed in her arms "in the quiet, dark room you told me about." In fact, he seemed almost to be able to let her hold him just for fun. She had gotten herself a rocking chair "like you have here in the clinic." And she'd found that if she just rocked him quietly for a period, she could then talk to him gently and feel by his body's relaxation when he could take her voice. As she got closer to Peter this way, feeling for his reactions in her arms, she found she could even turn his body into hers, and he could take it. "However," she said, "he still won't let me look him in the face." She expressed to me the evolution of her apparently rejecting wooden posture with the baby. He had been so unaccepting, so easily overloaded by her face and her voice, that she had ended by holding him facing away from her as a compromise. She now expressed her longing to get close to this baby. She told me of her longing and how no one before had helped her.

"What had I done differently?" I asked. After some thought, she said that she felt I had not judged her as overanxious. It also became clear as we talked that the observations we shared about Peter's behavior during my interactions with him, including the physical exam in the first visit, had increased her confidence that I was seeing what she saw.

What is it that helped this mother? The main ingredients of these two office visits were:

1. The pediatrician allowed the mother to express herself, to voice her fears and guilt. He did not simply reassure the mother that nothing was wrong with the baby. His empathy showed the mother that she had the right to feel overwhelmed and distressed. This capacity for listening and for respecting the seriousness of the "symptoms" seen by the mother is of major therapeutic value. It allows for a working alliance between the caregiver and the mother-infant couple.

2. The actual difficulties in handling a particular baby are spelled out. This helps a mother from feeling alone in her "inadequacy."

3. Once again, the important turning point is the moment when the baby is no longer seen as a dangerous enemy and the focus of the dialogue becomes the mother's own feelings. She could now start talking

about herself, which should lead to an understanding of deeper sources
of difficulty.

After she told me of her longing to get close to her baby, Mrs. S. told me
that despite her improved relationship with him, she still felt that she was
failing with her child. She was unable to accept praise for the excellent
developmental gains Peter had made cognitively and socially. She had had
thoughts of running away and deep anger that further increased her guilt
and loss of self-esteem. Relationships with her husband and other relatives
and friends were becoming strained.

During this discussion, Mrs. S. began to talk about her childhood, her
feelings that her parents were not close to her, and her determination to
reverse that with her own children. Mrs. S. had felt rejected as a child. She
longed to be like an older sister who was pretty and popular. But she felt
that her parents hated her. Now, with Peter, she was feeling the same rejection
she had felt as a child. As she unloaded this in a real surge of emotion, her
eyes filled with tears. She said, "I know I'm unreasonable, but I don't know
how to handle the feelings that come up in me when Peter cries."

It became clear to Mrs. S. that at least some of Peter's fussing represented
a sort of distress from overstimulation, and yet she could not help feeling
that Peter was using his distress manipulatively to gain her attention. This
made her feel more guilt. We talked about that openly, which was fortunate,
because without any input from me, Mrs. S. assumed that I too had blamed
her for the continued crying. This led us to a discussion of feelings she had
had during one of Peter's episodes of prolonged crying in my office.

Since Mrs. S.'s attention was focused so much on negative, fussy behavior
from Peter, I tried to find a way to break into this vicious circle. I suggested
regular play sessions of about ten minutes each, several times a day, when
Peter had her undivided attention. In these sessions, she was to respond only
to positive eliciting behavior from him. The purpose was twofold:

1. To give Mrs. S. confidence that she could have positive interactions
with Peter; and

2. To teach Peter that behaviors other than fussing could elicit attention.

I also suggested that Mrs. S. step back when she felt the desperate
feeling of guilt or helplessness overwhelming her and get some control
over them before interacting with Peter to comfort his distress.

By the time they came in one month later, Mrs. S. and Peter were in better shape. Peter's bewildering crying episodes had ended. When he cried now, "it was for a purpose." His mother said that when he did cry, she took my suggestions and put them to work. She tried to step back from him "and from myself" to see what he was crying about. Usually, he'd gotten over-loaded with too much stimulation. She could then sit down with him in a quiet room, rock him, talk quietly to him, and "teach" him how to accept her and her ways of reaching him.

I wondered aloud whether she was looking for reassurance from someone we hadn't spoken of yet. At this, Mrs. S. broke down in deep sobs, saying how she longed for her mother, who had stayed away from her and the baby. She felt her mother was staying away in exactly the same way she had when Mrs. S. was growing up, with rejection of her for her failures. Suddenly she sat up, holding Peter closer to her, looked down at him tenderly, and said: "But I do think you understand, and that's a big help." She seemed to be talking to her baby and to me at the same time.

As Mrs. S. found an understanding ally who valued her feelings and as she was allowed to express her longing for a "good, understand-ing mother," she became able to develop some understanding of her baby, too. Like many mothers, she needed to feel a sense of being mothered herself before she could become more nurturing to her infant.

In this case, we see how a relatively brief involvement in a devel-oping mother–infant relationship, at a critical time, can bring about change. Mrs. S. had had anxious feelings about her developing fetus during pregnancy, and separation from her infant during the perinatal period confirmed her sense of herself as an incompetent mother who had damaged her baby. These experiences led the new mother to overreact to Peter's crying and fussy behavior and see it as rejection. Fortunately, Mrs. S.'s mounting desperation led her to seek help early; she also had the ability to look below the surface and to understand the reasons for her overreactions. Early intervention gave the family the chance to reorganize itself before failures in the relationship could cause lasting damage. In such situations, continuing support from receptive caregivers will be important.

The child's own hypersensitivity to external stimuli contributed much to this troubled early relationship. As it was explained to her,

Mrs. S. could begin to see Peter as a sensitive individual separate from herself. As long as she saw the hypersensitivity and the crying only as symptoms of her own failure, she was unable to see her child as a person. Her confusion between him and herself tended to build on itself, increasing her anxious handling of the baby, which reinforced trying behavior. As soon as Mrs. S. could begin to look for the more positive responses in her son, which emerged when she reduced her stimulation, Peter could learn how to reach her. As his nervous system matured, as he learned to adapt to his mother's stimulation, the need for crying decreased. Each learned from the other, and soon Mrs. S. began to feel that Peter could be a source of the loving response and the sense of herself as a successful person for which she had always longed.

25

Clarissa:
"No Matter What"

Clarissa D. was born prematurely to a thirty-one-year-old mother who had had several miscarriages. She had her cervix sutured in order to carry this baby. When she went into labor at twenty-seven weeks, the sutures were removed and the two-pound baby was delivered. The infant survived despite many complications. She was in severe distress with Apgar scores of 5 at one minute, 7 at five minutes, requiring oxygen for resuscitation. Respiratory distress ensued and, for seven weeks, Clarissa was given constant artificial respiratory support with a tube in her throat and numerous medications. Jaundice appeared and, on the second day, an exchange transfusion was necessary. She received phototherapy for five more days. She required pulmonary surgery and developed an infection and pneumonia, for which she received antibiotics for fourteen days. Despite all of these complications, Clarissa survived and was placed in room air at the age of thirty-five weeks, eight weeks after her birth. At this time, we were able to start following her with our assessment techniques. She still had respiratory problems and evidence of cerebral hemorrhage, which we suspected might have left her with mild neurological damage.

During this period her mother had visited her fifty-one times, her father forty-nine. When we asked them to join us as we assessed Clarissa, Mrs. D. was very happy, because she hoped we would find that, as she firmly believed, Clarissa "could do things for which no one seemed to credit her." She quickly added that she had seen a normal, full-term baby girl and realized how different she was from Clarissa. She knew it would take a long time, but the fact that the infant had survived and was already doing better made her feel that she would get stronger over time. Mrs. D. was back at work as an editor but planned to take time off when Clarissa came home. Both Clarissa's parents had formed a very intense relationship with the staff of the neonatal intensive care unit; the eagerness with which they cooperated bespoke their deep need for support.

As part of an ongoing study, we administered the Neonatal Behavioral Assessment Scale every two weeks from thirty-six to forty-four weeks of gestational age. Both mother and father took off time from work in order to be present on each occasion. The nurses had taught them how to administer necessary oxygen when Clarissa became too stressed, and they appeared to know when and how to handle her. But when she became stressed with our stimuli as we tested her, both parents would look discouraged and depressed. During the examination at thirty-six weeks, Clarissa became agitated, and as her color worsened, the exam had to be discontinued. However, the baby brought her right hand to her mouth and calmed herself. Mrs. D. noticed this and virtually beamed with delight. As Clarissa briefly watched the examiner's face to follow it, her mother could hardly contain herself. Despite the extreme fragility of this baby, despite her marginal respiratory status, which caused her to become blue and breathless whenever she was stimulated, despite poor motor tone of her arms and increased tone in her legs (raising the possibility of a neurological deficit), despite inadequate state control, which caused her to shoot from a quiet state to an agitated crying state in a very short time, Clarissa's attempts to control herself and her transient responses to auditory and visual stimuli were noted by the examiners. Her parents seemed to be aware of all of her deficits but were able to pay attention to her attempts to control herself and other strengths. They tried to understand the limits of her responses—the narrow margin between her threshold for response and the level of stimuli above which she would be overwhelmed.

Even when a major problem like severe prematurity is present in a baby, assessment must focus on parent–infant interaction. When special therapy is needed, parents benefit by feeling part of the therapeutic team at all times. What these particular parents needed at this point was a demonstration of their infant's particular strengths as well as deficits, and a model for interacting with an easily disorganized infant.

At forty weeks of gestational age, Clarissa went home. She was still quite difficult to reach. She could console herself more easily than we could. The parents confirmed this, calling her a challenging baby, whom they just had to "wait to reach." On the next visit, Mrs. D. told the research team about their trouble with infertility and their determination to have a baby. Clarissa was a "special" child as a result. They were determined to see that Clarissa came along as well as possible now, "no matter what." The mother had maintained her breast milk for twelve weeks and was trying hard to feed Clarissa, despite all of these odds. The baby's neurological score was still only 5 out of 14 on this visit, with inadequate reflex behavior throughout, inconsistent muscle tone, abnormal eye movements, and less than adequate state behavior. Her cry was very high and strained, with a piercing quality. She showed little improvement over the four weeks of exams, and we felt that her recovery was still uncertain. Her parents were bravely cheerful and found it difficult to admit that they had real worries about Clarissa's future. Though they reported the worries expressed by the neurologist about possible "brain damage," they usually just watched quietly as we examined their baby.

Pre-term infants show a variety of characteristics: at one month, they are awake a shorter period of time and spend a greater percentage of that time fussing and crying (up to eight months); they are also less easily soothed (Als, 1982). Even when ready for discharge, pre-term infants are less alert and responsive than their full-term counterparts (Di Vitto & Goldberg, 1979). Initially, parents show less body contact with their infants, spend less time face to face, smile less and talk less to their infants. During early feedings, parents of full-term infants touch, cuddle, and talk to their babies more than parents of pre-term infants. These differences diminish with time, but at eight months, a play period shows that pre-term infants play less, fuss more, and receive more parental attention than full-terms. This difference may begin to disappear by twelve months (Goldberg et al., 1988).

On the whole, interactions with prematures are more taxing for parents, testing their capacities to attune to a less responsive, less well put together infant. This is also true for "professional" infant handlers; as examiners, we need to maintain and support the pre-term infant much more than with a term infant. The pre-term infant easily overreacts to environmental inputs, is more easily stressed and overstimulated, requires more finely tuned structuring and techniques of assessment (Als, 1983).

Parents will tend to compensate for these inadequacies; mothers tend to become hyperactive, while the infant tends to avert his gaze.

This is a good example of failure of contingency. The mother becomes intrusive, because she does not receive adequate messages and feedback from the infant. When mothers are taught to imitate the baby's behavior, they will slow down; infants then become more able to maintain gaze contact (Field, 1979).

These assessments of premature infants have enhanced our research into early interaction in general. Studying the premature infant's capacity to organize around positive interaction with a nurturing adult has helped us to understand more about normal recovery processes from labor and delivery and the amazing plasticity in recovery from insults to the nervous system in all newborn babies.

The efforts of the research team gradually met with a little more success, and by forty-four weeks, Clarissa was less fragile, less easily overloaded, and a bit more reachable for auditory and visual responses. She still had to be very carefully swaddled and offered stimuli very quietly and slowly.

The parents watched us hungrily for cues as to how to handle her, and for encouragements. They talked uncomplainingly about the fact that they could never take her out, and watched her almost day and night. They met her frequent, uncontrollable crying periods with swaddling, frequent feedings, and all the techniques they had seen us apply. They used our visits as opportunities for support and reorganization for themselves, as well as for opportunities to watch for progress. The mother had decided to stay home with Clarissa indefinitely, and the father came home each night to relieve her. They supported each other through it all, each praising the other to us, but they also openly wished for an extended family which was nearby and could support them.

At the five-months visit, Clarissa's postural performance was worrisome enough that the research team decided to refer her to a nearby cerebral palsy intervention program for evaluation and treatment. In meetings with a psychiatrically trained social worker who was a member of our team, the parents voiced many questions regarding this referral and indicated their anger and frustration over the lack of definite answers to their questions about the child's long-term outcome.

Physical therapy was started at eight months. By nine months, Clarissa's ability to maintain an active playing period was increasing, and her responses to those around her were better. She no longer cried as intensely as at five months, but she was still difficult to regulate in her play and in sleep–wake transitions, and still needed to be fed at least every three hours day and night. She had also developed severely crossed eyes.

Her parents looked exhausted. After a long discussion of Clarissa's feeding and sleeping problems at nine months, the parents asked openly about her prematurity and the questions they had stored up about brain damage. "Would she ever completely recover?" This question had always been foremost on their minds, but they had not dared to admit it to each other, they said, until we "forced them to." It seemed a relief to be able to talk about it. They very quickly added that they were enjoying Clarissa and were aware of all the emerging skills that she showed. Indeed, on our assessments (the Bayley scale), at nine months she was performing at her age, although the exam had required a low-keyed, patient approach on the part of the examiner, who was willing to spend twice as long as usual on her.

The contribution of dynamic psychiatry in such a situation consists essentially of two kinds of encouragement. Parents need license to voice concerns, fears, questions that they don't dare to bring up spontaneously. They need to feel that these can be shared with the medical team. Very often, parents of sick children experience tremendous relief when a professional allows them to voice their fear of poor outcome, their fear of death, their ambivalence about the treatment, and so on. Communication in itself becomes therapeutic.

Parents also need to express feelings about the situation, accept their own sadness, grief, and anger. Although this need seems obvious, in our joint work between psychiatrist and pediatric teams, we are impressed to see how often professionals are afraid of emotional displays, especially tears and sadness. Professionals tend to rush toward a comforting reassurance, which tends to obliterate the tragic aspects of the situation and to block the work of grief.

On a return visit at eighteen months, we were impressed by the continued recovery in this child. She was still potentially disorganized, but she appeared to know her own capabilities and could defend herself from "falling apart." She now slept through the night and fed herself. She played by herself creatively. Her mother talked at some length about how difficult it had been to let Clarissa learn to play alone and to ignore her constant demands. At night, she had first let Clarissa cry for a while and then, to her surprise, Clarissa had begun to sleep through the night. In the daytime, she had found that Clarissa could be independent and resourceful, if her initial whines were ignored. This was hard for Mrs. D., but she had been shown by the physiotherapist that Clarissa could be more outgoing and independent than she had realized. The child's vision had improved markedly with the aid of glasses. She spoke now in three- and four-word phrases, and her receptive language was entirely adequate.

When she was examined physically, she had an extended temper tantrum, which ended when her mother picked her up to comfort her. Tone and reflexes in her lower extremities were only slightly higher than normal, as was her sensitivity to auditory stimuli. She still walked with a slightly wide base. On the Bayley exam, she now performed somewhat above her age, with above-average scores on energy level and coordination of fine and gross motor skills.

Her parents described her as "fun, talking all the time, and rewarding." Indeed, she was delightful, determinedly stubborn, and charming in a social situation. When she had trouble with a task, she kept at it, repeating it over and over until she completed it. When she finally failed at a task, she quickly looked to her mother or father for support, as if failure could be very disappointing for her. We felt that her parents' determination to help this child recover was now reflected in her determination to succeed.

The parents were grateful for our care but felt that we had not "told them enough." Although they now had no real concern about her recovery, they would have liked to have been kept better appraised of each step in that recovery and what to expect. They seemed to feel that they had been struggling in a rather lonely way. But after this statement, they began to recount in detail their memories of each of our assessments and how much they'd learned from each one. While the physical examinations made the parents defensive, they enjoyed watching Clarissa perform on behavioral exams. They could see and feel that she'd learned from one time to another.

In our work of assessing premature infants, the effect of sharing the developmental processes of the infant with the parents and enlisting their energy to bring the infant to his or her best potential has been even beyond our expectations. As we demonstrate ways to produce the most developed behavior in the infant, the parents are able to reproduce our methods and to work toward their infant's optimal recovery. Hence, our assessments of premature infants have become a window for us and for parents into organization and ongoing development. Within the assessment of any small baby, one can observe not only present capacities, but also what infants do to parents and how they react. By sharing this observation with them, we give parents an opportunity to identify an infant's positive potential in addition to deficits.

Repeated observations shared with parents are a powerful kind of intervention. They fuel the parents' perceptions of the infant as a competent and developing individual, even through all the complications of prematurity. Even after identifiable damage, recovery is strengthened. The timing of such assessments in earliest infancy and the sharing of the information with parents as it is being demonstrated seem to be the important factors in this therapeutic effect.

26

Bob:
"They Took Him Away"

Bob was born prematurely in a suburban hospital, weighing about four-and-one-half pounds. He was brought to our high-risk nursery for observation because of suspected pulmonary problems, although he seemed generally in good condition.

When his mother failed to visit him during the week after delivery, our staff became very worried. When called in for an appointment, the young woman, Mrs. R., expressed great anguish because her child had been taken away from her; she feared the doctors would perform harmful operations on him and was convinced that she would not see him alive again. This lethal prediction had set off feelings of anticipatory grief; she did not want to attach herself to a child doomed to early death.

Both the nurses on the floor and her obstetrician explained to her that her conviction was unrealistic. Bob showed only minor pulmonary problems, and the staff had no concerns about his prognosis. This reassurance, however, was to no avail. When I went to speak with her, the mother revealed the source of her fears. When she was six years old, her mother gave birth to a boy. She often played at mothering him herself. When he reached the age of nine months, he developed acute pneumonia. The doctor who was called "took him away" in an ambulance, and the girl only saw her brother again several days later, in a casket.

When her own baby was taken away by doctors and transferred by ambulance to a special unit, Mrs. R. was sure the same scenario was being replayed. Her son now had become her brother; he too would die from a pulmonary disease. This mother was in an acute state of anxiety. She avoided becoming attached to Bob to protect herself from the anticipated grief if he were to die.

As in any such case, our first task was to provide the mother with an opportunity to talk, without jumping too fast to reassuring maneuvers. It was essential to let this parent vent feelings of grief in the past and anticipation of loss in the present. Most helpful was the unfolding of a detailed account of past tragedy. When Mrs. R. told us what happened with her brother, a great deal of pent-up feeling was liberated. It then became easier to suggest to her that the parallels she had drawn between past events and the present situation were largely imaginary.

When this confusion between past and present was clarified, Mrs. R. experienced relief. Then—and then only—she became receptive to our explanations of Bob's minor pulmonary problem. His symptoms were described. His X-rays were shown, and she was encouraged to visit the child. At that point, she finally "discovered" him. It was as if Bob were then born. A true attachment began to develop.

On a follow-up when Bob reached the age of nine months (the age when the brother had died), Mrs. R. became fleetingly anxious again, but we were able to reassure her.

This failure of attachment—which might have had very serious consequences—was primarily due to the mother's fantasy life, with some contribution from the circumstance of Bob's birth. Mrs. R. related in a very intense way to the image of her dead brother, in the past, but failed to interact with the real baby. This is in no way an unusual or rare situation; reactions to the birth of a premature baby often churn up past grief and, in any case, are always powerful. Such a fear of attachment is not necessarily "abnormal" or "pathological" per se.

This case of a particular maternal reaction to the birth of a premature has been presented to illustrate again a basic tenet of assessment in infancy: even when a well-defined problem is inherent in the infant, creating difficulties in itself, the assessment of interaction needs to take into account, simultaneously, the parental contributions to failure or distortions of reciprocity.

Intervention, in other words, is more effective when these "imaginary interactions" are given as much attention as the premature baby's problems. An increasing number of programs for premature babies and parents take into account these two sides of intervention. Marshall Klaus and John Kennell, who have done pioneering work in this field, have offered guidelines for such intervention with preemies (1982). Others have also attempted to pay attention simultaneously to the infant's "deficiencies" and to the parent's contribution to possible interactional failure (Minde et al., 1980; Parmelee et al., 1983; Samaraweera et al., 1983).

27

Antonio:
"A Bad Eye"

Antonio was born to a thirty-four-year-old mother, her first and very much wanted baby. Mrs. Q.'s husband accompanied her through her labor, and they were delighted when she delivered a healthy, vigorous boy. He was alert as they examined him on the delivery table. When his eyes widened as he followed their faces, his mother noted a cloud over the left pupil. This immediately frightened her. When the pediatrician examined the baby in her room, he quickly reassured her that it was probably a congenital cataract which could be removed in the future by an operation. At the time, she seemed to accept this, but later on each office visit, she asked the doctor to reiterate his opinion. Since by then the cataract had been confirmed by an ophthalmologist, it was easy to do so. Mrs. Q., however, became a bit teary whenever she discussed this "minor" defect. She blamed herself openly and questioned everything she had done during her pregnancy. Had she eaten something wrong? Could she have had an infection no one knew about? Was it her genes or her husband's—she knew of no blindness or serious eye problems? Could this be related to her own nearsightedness?

On each office visit, she had discussed his eye problem. The pediatrician tried to reassure her by demonstrating his excellent visual development. At six months, he'd developed an understanding of object permanence. This was early. He looked down when a toy was dropped under the table, as if he knew where it had gone and he wanted to retrieve it. His rapid motor development was also advanced. He crawled at six months, sat alone and played with toys at seven months. He stood at chairs by eight months. All of his development was accompanied by an apparent urge to "get going." He was a beautiful, brown-eyed baby, who took in the world around him avidly. He played vigorously, chortled as he played. He demonstrated his wonderful sense of humor as he played "peekaboo," laughing when he hid his face. The pediatrician was delighted with his development, his charm, and his exuberance and hoped his mother could fully enjoy them.

A sense of humor and a charming approach to others usually implies an inner richness and competence. These attributes promise well in a baby.

At each visit, however, his mother seemed to be growing more anxious. As Antonio developed, she seemed to take less and less pride in his achievements. She worried about how wide open his eyes were and how noticeable his left eye appeared. "Won't other people notice his defect; won't they tease him about it later?"

Although Antonio's motor development was going so well, his mother was unusually worried about whether he'd hurt himself. She was afraid he would fall when he pulled himself up on furniture. Antonio was intensely interested in exploring and playing with his food. Yet Mrs. Q. couldn't allow him to finger feed small bits of food "for fear he'd choke on them." At night, she could not stay out of his room. She admitted that she went in several times each night to check on his breathing. When he roused to a light sleep and tossed and murmured, as all babies do every four hours or so, she *had* to go to him. She could not take the doctor's advice to let him learn to get himself back to sleep. She said she had to rock him to sleep in her arms, often moaning, "Poor baby." According to Mr. Q., when Antonio stirred in his sleep, she'd rush to waken him, pick him up, and weep with him. As his sleep got worse and worse—waking every two hours—the pediatrician could see that reassurance and efforts to help her let him learn to handle his own sleep patterns were not working. She was unable to accept Antonio's relatively minor problem, and was beginning to hover over him. The doctor grew afraid that she would pass on to him a sense of vulnerability that would dampen his delightful, outgoing temperament. He could foresee Mrs. Q. making him a "vulnerable child," anxious and fearful of inadequacy. The loss of an expected perfect baby had been such an injury to her that her anxiety and guilt could not be handled in the usual pediatric relationship. In order to protect him and his future development, and in order to help Mrs. Q. free herself of this fixed image of her baby as defective, the pediatrician referred her to me for a more intensive psychotherapeutic approach to their problems.

Even when a baby's personality and total development are not yet affected, unresolvable issues such as these need attention. The problem, the lack of autonomy in feeding and in motor development, could become worse due to unresolved grieving. In cases like this, it was time to focus on the deeper issues which fuel unrealistic fear.

In psychiatric interviews, Mrs. Q.'s concerns continued to grow. Antonio's "handicap" was very upsetting to her; she kept ruminating about it, wondering why it happened to her, and became increasingly depressed. Her low mood was aggravated by exhaustion; she never allowed herself to sleep deeply. She remained vigilant to Antonio's voice all night. The sleeping difficulty, in particular, caught my attention; it was due to excessive anxiety, and we needed to understand its source. Mrs. Q. explained how shocked she was when told of Antonio's problem. When she was told he would need an operation, this frightened her terribly. She thought he would die under anesthesia.

The more she talked, the more it became clear that Mrs. Q. experienced sleep itself as a threat. Her fear prompted her to check Antonio repeatedly; she wanted to make sure that no harm would occur to him during sleep. This particular anxiety needed further clarification, which gradually emerged.

Mrs. Q. recalled that when she was eight years old, her older sister, twelve years old, suddenly developed a paralysis of the facial nerve, resulting—among other symptoms—in paralysis of her left eyelid. She remembered with pain the family's grieving reaction, the care given to the "bad" eye (Scotch tape was used to keep the eyelid closed) and the mocking comments from her sister's classmates. The similarity between the sister's and Antonio's eye symptoms was striking. More striking even was the fact that the mother had until then not consciously made this link. Now, as we encouraged her to see how Antonio's symptom must have reawakened painful memories, the mother was "illuminated." She then remembered that her sister's paralysis occurred suddenly *during the night*. She was well when she went to sleep and showed the paralysis upon waking up. Again, this led to further confusion between past and present. Her fear that the night would bring harm to her child, as it had done to her sister, explained her vigilance during Antonio's sleep and her fear of anesthesia.

Here, the unfolding of the mother's history in itself had a therapeutic effect; the crucial insight came from "link-making:" Antonio's symptom is like the sister's. His sleep disturbance is due to the mother's fear that he would become ill at night, like the sister. The ghost that had to be exposed to daylight was the reincarnation of the sister in Antonio, due to the similarity of their eye symptoms.

Later, the mother revealed that she harbored protracted ambivalent feelings toward that same older sister. She was jealous of her as the father's favorite child. Now Mrs. Q. feared—in unconscious retaliation—that her son would suffer the same fate as the rival sister.

The clarification of these unconscious patterns of feeling dating from the past and now replayed in the present fostered change. Mrs. Q. felt tremendous relief. She stopped waking up each time Antonio moved, and his sleep disturbance disappeared. More important, her depression lifted, and she started to see Antonio differently. His "handicap" now appeared minor. She became much more hopeful about the possibilities of surgical treatment and cooperated more with the physicians.

On follow-up, we noticed two encouraging factors. She showed no more anxiety as Antonio sped about the office, and she had decided to go ahead with another pregnancy. During the second pregnancy, she showed no anxiety about the future child's health; she had a baby girl with whom she interacted well.

The reaction to the birth of a baby with a defect follows certain patterns (Solnit & Stark, 1961). The initial period of shock is due to an abrupt realization that the child does not correspond to the ideal image of the baby fostered during pregnancy. The parents must also mourn the loss of their self-image as people capable of duplicating themselves with a beautiful baby. A wound has been inflicted, re-awakening old vulnerability to the parents' self-esteem.

All those who care for parents of a newborn child with a defect must recognize this mourning in order to intervene preventively. Several developments in particular must be avoided:

- The parents may become entrenched in a denial of the child's problem, interfering with medical and educational corrective measures;

- The parents may berate themselves as being the cause of the problem, with the development of guilt, depression, and conflict in the couple;

- The parents may assign the "fault" to the medical staff;

- The parents may reject the child.

In all these cases, the major problem is the breakdown of the parents' self-image, mirroring the child's defect. Attachment may fail to develop because the child, far from being a source of pride, has become the proof of parental failure.

As we pointed out in Parts I and IV, idealization of the child is normal in new parents. When this fails to take place, the parent–child interaction is at risk. If mourning and reorganization cannot take place, various scenarios can develop. The parent can become overanxious and fearful, as we saw above. In another scenario, the child is cast in the role of scapegoat of the family; he or she is used to focus and represent the "bad" characteristics of other family members. Each person projects inner feelings of inadequacy onto him; the visible defect serves to materialize the evidence of badness, yet protects the self-esteem of the other family members. Self-fulfilling prophecies then accentuate the child's potential for further failure, and parents relate to those expectations of failure, rather than to the child's inherent potential for development. In other cases, where guilt over the creation of the defect predominates, parents may develop attitudes of atonement by total devotion. They must sacrifice their life, as in punishment for causing the defect.

Early intervention, as we have suggested, can avoid these scenarios. While the birth of a defective child always represents a major emotional upheaval and tests the capacities for attachment of any parent, several factors can help mitigate the severity of the wound to parental self-esteem. Among these is an accurate understanding of the defect. It is interesting that in cases where a defect is detected during pregnancy, the parents' fears and expectations are much worse than the feelings parents report once they see the child at birth and perceive the damage realistically (Drotar et al., 1975; Johns, 1971).

Mothers who knew they were carrying children with missing limbs due to thalidomide abandoned thoughts of institutionalizing these children when they first saw them and discovered they could love them. Even a child with a severe defect can trigger strong attachment (Roskies, 1972).

These data indicate that fantasies about a defect can be much worse than the realistic perception of it; also, a child's capacity to elicit attachment and parenting may powerfully counteract the disappoint-

213

ment and grief. The rewards of the relationship counterbalance the pain of the wound to self-esteem.

Several intervention programs have also indicated that support of parenting can be efficient, especially when it is accompanied by demonstrations of the child's individual characteristics (Bromwich & Parmelee, 1979). Modelling interaction with a defective child can also bolster the mother's attachment and help fight depression (Als, 1982).

Whatever technique is used (guidance, support, psychotherapy), the clinician should be very attentive to the problem of self-esteem. Attachment to a "disappointing infant" can develop only if parents can resolve the wound to their self-image. This often requires special help. One should never forget that a baby begins inside the mother. As such, a newborn represents in a visible way the innermost part of her self.

28

Sarah:
"Malina"

Sarah is the second child of Mrs. L., an Hispanic mother, who was referred to our child guidance clinic by her pediatrician. A quiet little girl, rather immature-looking for seven months, she sat on the floor somewhat unsteadily in front of her mother. She played in a monotonous way with two toys she was given. She banged one endlessly, mouthed it, but without any real interest. As she dropped it, she picked up another to repeat her disinterested banging and mouthing, as if she were just killing time, waiting for something else to happen. She showed a minimum of interest in either of these toys. She never explored them, nor did she look around at us to see whether we were watching her. She seemed almost in a world of her own, without interest or excitement.

In the middle of our interview, her mother began to weep. As if she were waiting for this and were completely in tune with her, Sarah turned immediately to look at her teary mother, real concern on her face. In fact, it was the first evidence of any change in her expression. As she turned, she fell over from her sitting position. After a short delay, her mother jumped up to catch her. Sarah vocalized brightly, looked at her mother. For one brief second, they communicated in a reciprocal way. Then, Sarah looked away; her mother returned wearily to sink into her chair and talk to me. Sarah resumed her dull banging of the toys around her. Once only, she tried to pull her mother away from me, but she gave up easily. She returned lifelessly to her dull monotonous play, as if accustomed to this lack of communication.

In work with infants, we are frequently confronted with mothers showing various degrees of depression—from postpartum blues to protracted, actual depressions. While severe cases—such as puerperal psychosis—are rare, many first episodes of psychiatric crisis—in women of childbearing age—occur within the first month after birth (Paffenbarger, 1982).

While in the case of a premature baby it is primarily the infant's problems which cause difficulties in achieving attachment and reciprocity, in the case of a depressed mother, her withdrawal and inhibition will be the major factor in a troubled relationship. As we have pointed out, however, both parties are always involved.

Mrs. L. had been quite depressed since the birth of her daughter. She was upset to have had a girl: "I don't want her to become sad like me." Sarah hardly ever looked at her mother. She often turned her body away from mother. When I asked the mother to engage the child face to face, they still did not look at one another. The baby kept playing with a toy.

In marked contrast was Sarah's reaction to her five-year-old brother, who came along on the next visit. As soon as he called her, she brightened up, smiled, and became excited. She did the same with me. It was as if she "saved" herself for more rewarding partners. The mother said that this difference in response was usual for Sarah, who "preferred" her father and her two brothers.

I observed that the mother had a very particular way of communicating with Sarah; she sat on the floor at some distance from the baby, hardly touched her, and talked in a very low, whispering, voice. When asked why she spoke like that, she explained that a loud voice would frighten Sarah.

When the mother tried to call Sarah—and the baby would not answer— she would do two things: first, she would call her daughter "Malina" ("bad girl" in Spanish), and then she would wave "bye-bye" to her. In this way, she conveyed two things to Sarah: "You are bad when you don't take me into account," and "We will leave each other when you don't pay attention to me."

It was striking how sensitive this mother was to any sign that could be interpreted as Sarah rejecting her. In fact, it was mostly to these aspects of the baby's behavior that she reacted. In other words, she could not tolerate her show of autonomy, interpreting it as active rejection. As soon as the baby turned away from direct contact (as when playing with a toy), the mother severed all contact and reinforced the distance between them (waving "bye-bye"). The mother's very low level of solicitation further contributed to lowering the intensity and frequency of communication.

After a break due to holidays, we began therapy two months later. At nine months, Sarah had made very little progress. She still sat and played monotonously, with no interest in her toys. She was steadier in sitting now but immobilized when she fell over. She was too "good." She tried, but only briefly, to elicit any interaction with her depressed mother. When they did interact, it was brief and Sarah seemed to end it by looking away, as if she already needed to maintain control over the duration of their close interaction. She now looked as depressed as her mother. She was slow-moving, quiet, and seemed to expect little from her environment. At one point, Mrs. L. picked Sarah up. She banged on her mother in an effort to get her attention; then, when mother finally responded, Sarah turned away as if it were either painful or she wasn't accustomed to it. She squirmed to be put down. Later, when she was picked up again by her slow-moving, depressed mother, Sarah bit her face, kissed her violently as if trying to rouse her. When the mother finally paid attention, their interaction was flat and there was no real play. Mrs. L. began to try to wipe Sarah's nose and Sarah squirmed rather vigorously to get away. After this sequence, Sarah grabbed at her mother's nose, poked at her eyes, her face, with the same aggressive determination that her mother had demonstrated in nose wiping. As her mother held her tight, Sarah tried to dig into her, as if this kind of aggressive burrowing were her only access to this depressed woman. The entire sequence was a mixture of sad and aggressive tactile interaction with no playful affect displayed.

During this visit, the mother began to talk about herself. She explained that she had wanted a baby, because she hoped for a companion who would not leave her. Very poignantly, she expressed her distress to see Sarah becoming independent, "I wish she would stay in my tummy." She then explained that each time Sarah turned away or did not respond, she actually felt abandoned. This is why she called her "Malina" and waved "bye-bye." She went on, saying: "Each time I love someone, they leave me." (Two weeks later, she announced she was pregnant again, and it became clear that she wanted again the experience of a baby as a part of herself.)

Once again, those reactions are typical in certain depressive people; they are not able to perceive overtures made to them and only register what can be seen as signs of rejection.

After much dialogue I learned that Mrs. L. was a "replacement" child, born one year after a brother died at age nine in a car accident. During her whole childhood, she saw her father depressed because of the brother's death and felt powerless in her attempts to console him. She compared herself unfavorably to the brother and felt increasingly rejected, "knowing" that her father preferred, forever, the deceased brother.

Now, she is caught in a similar scenario with Sarah; she "knows" that Sarah does not love her and necessarily prefers men (the father, the brothers, and even me), just as her father preferred her brother.

This is the central feature of the actual failure of contingency between mother and Sarah; it was when we assessed it and linked it to what actually happened in interactions that treatment was possible.

Sarah herself became a powerful ally in the treatment. In spite of mother's turning away when Sarah played alone, the baby kept trying to reengage the mother. When we were able to demonstrate Sarah's continued overtures to her, the mother started to perceive her attachment. This, in turn, fueled the repressed capacity for attachment in the mother. Our work consisted in allowing such a reinforcing system to develop. We brought the mother's attention to the infant's overtures and simultaneously helped her to distinguish the ghosts of her past from the present relationship.

Gradually, we witnessed a change in the interaction; the more this mother perceived Sarah's attempts at engaging her, the more she became confident that Sarah wanted her. We then witnessed a growing reciprocity between them. Within a few months, the mother no longer thought that Sarah preferred men; she stopped calling her "Malina" as she became convinced that Sarah was attached to her.

It took two years, however, before this mother actually came out of her depression with therapy and medication. Our goal, meanwhile, was to make sure that the relationship between mother and daughter was not severed.

Maternal Depression and Early Intervention

In Part III, we defined contingency as a pattern of appropriate responses to a partner's signals, needs, and emotional communications. Contingency is an expression of availability; it reveals empathy and a capacity to be affected by the inner state of the partner. This implies what Robert Emde has called emotional availability and what Daniel Stern called attunement. The pediatrician, or nurse working with pediatric patients, will be most alert to the ways congenital diseases or abnormalities or deviant temperamental traits in an infant interfere with contingent responses. Child psychiatrists or social workers in guidance clinics will be more attuned to how problems in the parents, such as ambivalence, anxiety, lack of identification with parental roles, and unresolved grieving can produce contingency failures.

Among the various problems in the child or in the mother that may interfere with contingency, maternal depression is one of the most frequent and severe. Sarah's case illustrates many instances of noncontingent behavior, that is, behavior addressed to the partner but in no way tailored to the partner's concurrent signals or communications. For instance, Mrs. L. whispered, as though to herself, sitting at some distance from Sarah, impervious to the infant's attempts to reach her.

Manifestations of noncontingency or anti-contingency can be described according to frequency, and according to the activities in which they occur (feeding, looking, physical approach, etc.), and also according to which partner of the dyad is contributing the most to them.

There is now experimental evidence that contingency failures due to even minor forms of depression or depressive behavior can affect infants. The most widely known of such experimental evidence is drawn from the "still-face experiment" described in Part III. Edward Tronick, who has worked extensively with this "still-face" situation, proposes that it is the infants' sense of impotence—when trying to elicit the mother's active involvement—that most contributes to what can in turn be described as a form of depression developing in them (Tronick et al., 1978). The lack of response to their attempts at reestablishing contact is the crucial factor in the reaction of the infant to this experiment and, clearly, to an infant's reaction to a depressed mother. Even such minute—experimentally induced—disruptions of contingency have been shown to provoke changes that persist beyond the experiment (Tronick et al., 1984).

If such minor—time-limited—breaks in contingency can have such clear-cut and relatively lasting effects on infants, we should not be surprised to find that maternal depression has more complex and lasting effects, even in the first months. James Robertson reports the case of a two-month-old baby whose mother became depressed when she learned that her husband might have cancer. The mother became withdrawn, did not respond to the baby's smiles and vocalizations, and hardly talked to him. Within a week, a marked setback in development was observed, with bodily activity decreased and smiles difficult to elicit. Although the diagnosis of malignancy was ruled out within a few days, the baby remained sober and unresponsive and this setback on development remained evident for several months. He remained passive, undemanding, and at twelve months, his development was still two months delayed (Robertson, 1965).

Other work pools the advantages of both clinical and research methods. Tiffany Field tried to test whether depressive affect can be identified in infants and whether this can be linked to interaction with a depressed mother (Field, 1985). The results showed that three- to four-month-old infants, in interaction with mothers suffering from postpartum depression, showed significantly fewer positive facial expressions and vocalizations when compared with infants of nondepressed mothers. All in all, research on the effects of maternal depression in infancy has so far suggested that even very small deficiencies in contingency in the mother's behavior are perceived by the young infant. When they are soon reversed, the infant may learn to cope with them. If they persist, the effects on the infant may be long-lasting. This is more likely to occur when the mother's behaviors are frequent enough and when violations of expectancy affect all aspects of their relationship. Negative, hostile, or withdrawn responses are likely to create a negative learning model, leading to withdrawal or depression in the baby. Finally, the infant's inability to produce a contingent response in the mother may contribute to the child's own developing "depression." Babies who receive little confirmation or reinforcement of their own behavior are likely to turn inward, to withdraw, in an effort to conserve their limited energies.

When there is manifest, severe depression in mothers with emotional inhibition and withdrawal, deficits in emotional availability, noncontingency to the infant's solicitations, and lack of stimulation become pervasive. In cases of serious depression in parents, children appear to develop a high incidence of psychiatric problems, especially of the depressive form. Early infancy and adolescence seem to be the stages in which children are particularly vulnerable to parental depression (Beardslee et al., 1983).

29

Mary:
"Time Out"

Mary, eight months old, and her parents, Mr. and Mrs. A., were referred for a consultation because of her frequent regurgitation. She had been born "small for date;" her growth curve showed some delay. The pediatrician had repeatedly told the parents that she was a "light-weight" and even mentioned the word "dwarf." This problem was now compounded by the fact that Mary spit up her food several times a day, sometimes with frank vomiting. There was anxiety that this might further hamper her growth.

Mary's parents are both teachers. They seemed very involved with their baby and wanted to give her "many kinds of experience." In my office, they attempted to make her walk, they talked to her in a very adult way, explaining why they had made this appointment. They constantly engaged her in activity with no provision for "time out," for recharging.

On the other hand, Mary appeared to be a rather passive child. She had a rather starved, skinny look. She was "plugged" with a pacifier and played with a toy in a monotonous fashion. She couldn't explore it with her mouth because of the pacifier. Nor did she really explore the toy either visually or manually. Her play had the quality of space-filling. Her father held and jiggled her almost constantly; she seemed to be waiting for him to look at and talk to her. Both parents spent a lot of time pressing toys on her, and demonstrating how they work. When her parents passed her back and forth, she never looked back at the parent who had just given her away. This curious lack of attachment behavior made one fearful that she did not "expect" a satisfying interaction. She seemed never to receive it in our office.

When she tried to stand up on her own, her father took over and threw her into the air until she spit up. He continued to hold her but without looking at her, talking to her, or playing with her. There was a continuous distancing from her. Although she seemed to ask for more and more motor activity, she seemed a rather dull baby. On one occasion, when she was allowed to stand on her own, she cruised around the chair, brightening and vocalizing. When the parents did not respond, she banged her head on the chair. She bit her mother's leg, and mother picked her up to sit passively in her lap again. The father then took her and handed her a toy, without any interpersonal interaction. She vocalized into the distance but without any apparent expectation for a response. When she finally broke her monotonous play with a fussy protest, Mr. A. shifted her around vigorously in his arms, but again without really interacting. Then she started to play with her pacifier. This was the richest play we observed as she lovingly turned it over and over to inspect it, mouth it, insert it, pull it out to make a popping sound. Her face brightened. This object seemed to be her most reliable source of interaction.

At one point in the visit, Mrs. A. seemed sensitive to Mary. When she banged a toy rhythmically, her mother imitated her unconsciously. But she appeared inhibited with Mary and reinforced Mary for interactions with toys, rather than people. In some ways, she seemed afraid of her.

When Mr. A. held Mary, it was without tenderness or sensitivity. He acted wary of any mood swing in her and overwhelmed her few attempts at autonomous behavior.

Throughout the first office visit made by the family, several striking features of their behavior emerged. First of all, the father took the lead in most interactions with the baby. He pressed her into motor activity, walking "exercises," and overstimulated her constantly with new toys, but in a didactic manner, not playful or humorous. At one point, the father pointed to a picture in a magazine and used the word "bonsai" in describing it. Neither parent spent much time talking lovingly to the child, cuddling her, or even looking at her in a relaxed, affectionate fashion. Mary often appeared greedy for more stimulation, but did not show signs of attachment to her parents.

Since this unusual interaction aroused our curiosity, we asked the parents' permission to videotape the office visits. We then submitted these to microanalysis and were able to quantify certain features of this family interaction.* We found that indeed the father spent considerably more time interacting with Mary than the mother. Study of the tapes showed also that many of the father's responses or approaches to the baby were anti-contingent. Few of the mother's were so judged. Most conspicuous was the fact that almost

*This microanalytic study was conducted in collaboration with Nathalide Zilkha.

all of the interaction was done through direct physical contact (and not through voice or gaze).

Within this interactive pattern, Mary had no time to recuperate from long bouts of physical stimuli. She was "forced" to react, and her father kept offering her activity that she was not asking for, nor ready to integrate. Her only escape from all this inappropriate barrage of stimuli was through regurgitation.

In a later visit, the father spoke about his educational "ideology." He explained that he wanted Mary to be smart and autonomous; he thus was constantly challenging her intellectual and motor abilities. He saw his role as a father as a "teaching" one, constantly challenging her skills.

We then gave the father our impressions of his particular style and asked him why he felt that Mary should be stimulated in such a constant way. He then unravelled a tragic story: he had had a twin brother who showed early signs of mental retardation and of mild neurological problems. Tests eventually revealed that he suffered from a rare progressive disease. This sick brother became the center of the family's devoted attention, causing a great deal of jealousy and suffering in Mary's father, until the brother died at age twenty.

This disease turned out to be hereditary. When Mary was conceived, both parents were very concerned, fearing that she might turn out to have the same problem. Since Mary's birth, the father had wanted to reassure himself—through continuous stimulation—that she was not retarded intellectually nor handicapped in her motor development. With his compulsive and anti-contingent activity, he was struggling against the reappearance of his handicapped brother's ghost and was unable to recognize or adapt to Mary's needs.

Once Mr. A. gave us this background, we asked him directly about his fears that Mary would turn out like her deceased uncle. He explained that before she was born, he was so afraid of transmitting the disease to a child that he had actually considered resorting to artificial insemination, using donated sperm.

In this case, as in others we have described, the parents' acknowledgement of a "ghost" and recognition of their child's individual needs was accompanied by gradually changing behavior. When we were able to point out a link between the overstimulation of Mary and her regurgitation, the father began to pay attention to her needs. We were also able to show the parents how Mary had no choice but to become entrained into ever higher levels of stimulation and that her own initiative and motivation were being overwhelmed. With this guidance, given after the father's ghosts had been unveiled, these intelligent parents were able to relax and to learn to stimulate Mary less.

Later microanalytic analysis of the videotaped sessions showed that there was a reversal in the parents' roles: while at the beginning, Mary was engaged in interaction with her father three times as much as with her mother, by the last session, she was spending triple the time with her mother. The number of interactions that were visibly anti-contingent also diminished markedly. Especially interesting was the fact that the time Mary spent alone and did not engage with either parent was also more than tripled. During this same time, the regurgitations had gradually ceased and the parents' anxiety diminished. Follow-up sessions will help to make this change lasting.

30

Julian:
"The Tyrant"

Julian's mother, Mrs. C., consulted me in a state of exhaustion. She said she could no longer cope with her fourteen-month-old boy. She complained that he was exceedingly demanding and very domineering; she didn't dare oppose him. In fact, she said she was so intimidated by what she experienced as a display of superior force that she obeyed him like a slave. She often complained about the misery of her servitude. Her description seemed exaggerated from the start; for example, she said that unless she kept constant watch, he would destroy everything in his room. She also had to make sure he did not seriously hurt another child.

While she was talking, Julian inspected our toys, roamed about the room, but showed little evidence of what she saw in him: violence and the wish to dominate. He was a sturdy, vigorous boy, but did not appear to be particularly unruly.

Mrs. C. was in her mid-thirties, a successful executive. Julian's father was also in business and successful, too, but not to the same degree as his wife. Julian had been "planned" for several years. When he arrived, his mother was completely "head over heels in love with him." She had postponed her return to work so that she could continue to breast-feed him and ended up staying at home with him until the time of our consultation. She pointed out that she had given up her career for Julian. When he was six months old, he was still waking every two to three hours through the night "to be breast-fed." She had been afraid that she didn't have enough milk to satisfy him and had to go to him whenever he cried. She had finally taken him into her bed, to sleep between her and her husband. In this way, she had hoped to nurse him as often as he wanted it, and get some sleep herself. However, this arrangement had left her exhausted. At the time of our visit, she was still breast-feeding night and day every three to four hours.

After Mrs. C. had recited her tale of the exhausting year, she paused to check on Julian. He looked at her petulantly, and she rushed over to find out what he was doing. He became a bit restless, going from one part of the room to another, calling out to her with each step. When I tried to talk to her about the need to set limits, "for his sake," she seemed unable to hear me. Julian's demands then became more vocal as we tried to talk, and she leapt to comply with them. A rather frantic interplay ensued. I sensed anger and desperation in Mrs. C. and a certain distractibility and discontent in Julian.

This mother's description of selfish domination and violence, to which there seemed little contribution on the part of her son, reflected the possible influence of past history more vividly than usual.

Gradually I learned from Mrs. C. that she had been cast into a maternal role while still a young girl. She was the elder sister of six boys. Her mother was overwhelmed by successive pregnancies and required her daughter to become a surrogate mother. Most of her childhood had been spent caring for her younger brothers. While doing so, she experienced a deep feeling of being exploited by these selfish boys, as well as a sense of being deprived of motherly love. She had essentially given up the privileges of being a child.

With Julian now, she again felt forced to play the maternal role, and resented this, although the resentment had emerged only gradually. She was now jealous of the advantages she gave her son, just as she had been jealous of her siblings in the past.

It took some time before Mrs. C. could acknowledge a constant fear of hitting her child, an aggressive tendency she had kept in check through the mechanism of reversal; oversolicitude and overprotection disguised her aggression.

This forced oversolicitude contributed to her exhaustion. She thus protected herself against the potential effects of her jealousy; her fear of battering really belonged to her past anger at her brothers. The potential for violence she saw in Julian was a projection of the violent anger she perceived in herself. Her fantasy was thus a protection; a powerful baby was less likely to be harmed by her. The role of a devoted, altruistic mother who slaved to the point of exhaustion was preferable to that of a vengeful, battering mother.

Once we learned the hidden scenario which fueled the mother's complaints about Julian (selfish domination, violence, etc.) and were satisfied through observation that he was no more demanding and violent than is normal at this age, our task became clearer. In the following sessions, we helped Mrs. C. compare her representations of Julian as excessively demanding against the reality of what he was actually doing at any particular moment. Simultaneously, we helped her verbalize the pent-up resentment against her status as an indentured caretaker for spoiled brothers. This helped her recognize that the "real" target of her anger was in her past, and not in her baby.

This recognition gave Mrs. C. tremendous relief, as no mother can tolerate anger against her own baby without the most painful feelings of guilt.

Mrs. C. was also helped to link her fear of violence (she was really afraid that Julian would turn into a delinquent) to her own unconscious violent anger, stemming from a sense of being neglected by her mother since early childhood. Throughout our sessions, the "red thread" of our insight was the paradoxical situation in which this mother had placed herself: she slaved for her son, and simultaneously resented his privileges. Her anxiety and over-protectiveness gradually diminished as she modified her perception of Julian as violent and a "tyrant." Julian's own independence and self-confidence also increased.

At a follow-up visit, when Julian was four-and-a-half years old, the mother again expressed her relief that her fears had been unfounded. Julian seemed to be progressing well.

31

Assessment As Intervention

In presenting the foregoing cases in some detail, our purpose is to show how the dual perspective outlined earlier in the book (observational/interpretive analytic, developmental/psychoanalytic) applies to clinical work. While there is no attempt to exhaust the variety of clinical situations, these nine cases were chosen to represent common issues and typical problems in assessment and intervention. Since the cases were drawn from the very different types of practice of the two authors, they may also suggest the variety of orientations typical among those who care for new parents and young children. We have also tried to balance the cases between those that present themselves as the infant's problem (prematurity, feeding problems) or that of the parents (depression, anxiety). In making this initial distinction, we recognize that both partners always make a contribution and that the symptom which brings parents to us may not be as significant as the underlying conflict or "imaginary interaction."

In conclusion, we would like to stress again that the process of understanding the dynamics of this earliest of all relationships is *in itself* an intervention. From the administration of a brief behavioral test of a newborn baby in the presence of parents to the most elaborate and long-term unveiling of childhood "ghosts," the act of assessing parent–infant behavior and putting it into words is a powerful agent of change.

With this dual outlook and respect for the impact of assessment in mind, we offer four simplified guideposts for clinical work with parents and infants, whether a routine "well-baby" check-up or long-term psychotherapy. Since each has been illustrated in the preceding cases, they are highly condensed.

Setting. Parent and child must be seen together. The atmosphere should be free enough so that the parents will interact "normally" with the baby. A playful atmosphere with toys will often facilitate this process.

The caregiver's approach should favor the parents' verbal report of their experience. Intrusive questioning and authoritarian direction inevitably stifle such openness. The caregiver must divide his or her attention between the interaction that is occurring and the verbal reporting by the parents. This is easier said than done.

Video recording is useful and often frees up the clinician, allowing retrospective analysis of interactive patterns. Often only during this reviewing process does the coincidence between verbal reports and corresponding interactive patterns emerge. On occasion, the tapes can be shared with the parents in a safe, understanding manner.

Objective assessment. A thorough evaluation of the child's developmental level is needed to supplement close scrutiny of the interaction. These objective assessments not only help the clinician arrive at a diagnosis; they also become a means of intervention, when they are shared with the parents in a tactful way.

Subjective reports. The parents' subjective representation of their relationship to the child and memories of the parenting they received while growing up can be elicited in tandem. We have seen again and again that the way parents perceive themselves, in their parenting, the meaning they attribute to their child's behavior becomes a determinant of future behavior and development. Every clinician will find comfortable ways to facilitate the parents' reports of their feelings, thoughts, fears, and hopes. The projection of these often must be untangled from the child's actual behavior.

In this process, where sharing of yet-untold feelings is paramount, "active listening" gradually becomes active intervention.

Focus on relationships. In the case of young infants, our only arena of intervention is a relationship. Actually, we deal with three relationships. First of all, as we have seen, when we examine newborns, the relationships we achieve with them become interventions. Secondly, understanding and explaining to parents the nature of their relationship to the child is the main avenue for change. Last, but not least, the relationship achieved between the family and the clinician can fuel trust, relief, and growth.

REFERENCES

PREFACE

Winnicott, D. W. *The Child, the Family, and the Outside World* (1964). Reading, Mass.: Addison-Wesley, 1987.

Winnicott, D. W. "Communication between infant and mother, and mother and infant, compared and contrasted." In *Babies and Their Mothers*. Reading, Mass.: Addison-Wesley, 1986.

Winnicott, D. W. *Human Nature*. New York: Schocken Books, 1988a.

PART I: Pregnancy: The Birth of Attachment

Barnard, K. E. Reported in F. A. Pedersen, "Father influences viewed in a family context." In M. E. Lamb (ed.), *The Role of the Father in Child Development*, 2nd edition. New York: John Wiley, 1982.

Bell, D. H. *Being a Man: The Paradox of Masculinity*. New York: Harcourt Brace Jovanovich, 1984.

Bibring, G. L., J. F. Dwyer, and A. F. Valenstein. "A study of the psychological processes in pregnancy." *Psychoanalytic Study of the Child* 16(1961):9–72.

Boddy, K., G. S. Dawes, R. L. Fisher, S. Pinter, and J. S. Robinson. "Foetal respiratory movements, electrocortical and cardiovascular responses to hypoxaemia and hyperpnea in sleep." *J. of Physiology* 243(1974):599.

Brazelton, T. B. "Behavioral competence of the newborn infant." *Seminars in Perinatology* 3(1979):35–44.

Brazelton, T. B. "Precursors for the development of emotions in early infancy." In R. Plutchik and H. Kellerman (eds.), *Emotion, Theory, Research, and Experience*, Vol. II. New York: Academic Press, 1981a.

Brazelton, T. B. *On Becoming a Family*. New York: Delacorte Press, 1981b.

Brazelton, T. B. *Infants and Mothers*, 2nd edition. New York: Delacorte Press, 1982.

Brazelton, T. B. *Neonatal Behavioral Assessment Scale*, 2nd edition. Philadelphia: Lippincott; London: Blackwell, 1984.

Coddington, R. D. "Life events associated with adolescent pregnancies." *J. of Child Psychiatry* (April 1979).

Cramer, B. "Sex Differences in Early Childhood." In *Child Psychiatry and Human Development*, Vol 1:3(1971):133–151.

Deutsch, H. *The Psychology of Women*, Vols. I and II. New York: Grune and Stratten, 1944.

Freud, S. *The Interpretation of Dreams* (1900). New York: Basic Books, 1955.

Gottlieb, G. "Ontogenesis of sensory function in birds and mammals." In E. Tobach, L. R. Aronson, and E. Shaw (eds.), *The Biopsychology of Development*. New York: Academic Press, 1971.

Granat, M., R. Lavie, D. Adara. "Short-term cycles in human fetal activity." *Amer. J. of Obstetrics and Gynecology* 134(1979):696–701.

Grossman, F. K., L. S. Eichler, and S. A. Winickoff. *Pregnancy, Birth and Parenthood*. San Francisco: Jossey-Bass, 1980.

Gurwitt, A. J. "Aspects of prospective fatherhood." *Psychoanalytic Study of the Child* 31(1976):237–273.

Hahn, S. R., and K. E. Paige. "American birth practices: A critical review." In J. Parsons (ed.), *Psychobiology of Sex Differences and Sex Roles*. Washington, D.C.: Hemisphere Publishing, 1980.

Herzog, J. "Patterns of expectant fatherhood: A study of fathers of a group of premature infants." In S. Cath, A. J. Gurwitt, and J. M. Ross (eds.), *Father and Child: Developmental and Clinical Perspectives*. Boston: Little, Brown, 1982.

Hon, E. H., and E. J. Quilligan. "The classification of fetal heart rate II: The revised working classification." *Connecticut Medicine* 31(1967):779–783.

Janniruberto, A., and E. Tajani. "Ultrasonographic study of fetal movements." *Seminars in Perinatology* 5, 2(1981).

Kakar, S. "Fathers and sons: An Indian experience." In S. Cath, A. J. Gurwitt, and J. M. Ross (eds.), *Father and Child: Developmental and Clinical Perspectives*. Boston: Little, Brown, 1982.

Keller, E. Personal communication, 1981.

Klaus, M. H., and J. H. Kennell. *Parent-Infant Bonding*, 2nd edition. St. Louis: C. V. Mosby, 1982.

Kohut, H. *The Restoration of the Self*. New York: International Universities Press, 1977.

Korner, A. F. "The effect of the infant's state, level of arousal, sex and ontogenic stage on the caregiver." In M. Lewis and L. A. Rosenblum (eds.), *The Effect of the Infant on Its Caregiver*. New York: John Wiley, 1974.

Leonardo da Vinci. *Literary Works of Leonardo da Vinci*. O. P. Richter (ed.) Oxford, England: Oxford University Press, 1939.

Maccoby, E. C., and C. N. Jacklin. *The Psychology of Sex Differences*. Palo Alto, Calif.: Stanford University Press, 1974.

Mahler, M. S., F. Pine, and A. Bergman. *The Psychological Birth of the Human Infant*. New York: Basic Books, 1975.

Milani Comparetti, A. "The neurophysiologic and clinical implications of studies on fetal motor behavior." *Seminars in Perinatology* 5(1981).

Money, J., and A. A. Ehrhardt. *Man and Woman; Boys and Girls*. Baltimore and London: Johns Hopkins University Press, 1972.

Papousek, H., and M. Papousek. "Early ontogeny of human social interaction: Its biological roots and social dimensions." In M. Von Cranach et al. (eds.), *Human Ethology*. Cambridge, England: Cambridge University Press, 1979.

Parke, R. "Fathers." In M. Yogman and T. B. Brazelton (eds.), *In Support of Families*. Cambridge, Mass.: Harvard University Press, 1986.

Parmelee, A. H., and E. Stern. "Development of states of infants." In C. D. Clemente, D. P. Purpura, and F. E. Meyer (eds.), *Sleep and the Maturing Nervous System*. New York: Academic Press, 1972.

Pedersen, F. A. *The Father-Infant Relationship: Observational Studies in the Family Setting*. New York: Praeger, 1980.

Pedersen, F. A., R. L. Cain, M. J. Zaslow, and B. J. Anderson. "Variation in infant experience associated with alternative family roles." In L. Lassa and I. Sigel (eds.), *Families As Learning Environments for Children*. New York: Plenum Press, 1982.

Pines, D. "In the beginning: Contributions of a psychoanalytic developmental psychobiology." *Int. J. of Psychoanalysis* 8(1981):15–33.

Roberts, A. B., D. Lille, and S. Campbell. "24–hour studies of fetal movements and fetal body movements in normal and abnormal pregnancies." R. W. Beard and S. Campbell (eds.), *The Current Status of Fetal Heart Rate Monitoring and Ultrasound in Obstetrics*. London: The Royal College of Obstetricians and Gynaecologists, 1977.

Rosen, M. G., and L. Rosen. *In the Beginning: Your Brain before Birth*. New York: New American Library, 1975.

Sadovsky, E. "Fetal movements and fetal health." *Seminars in Perinatology*. 5, 2 (1981):131–143.

Samaraweera, S., and S. Cath. "Fostering the consolidation of paternal identity: The Tufts Family Support Program." In S. Cath, A. J. Gurwitt, and J. M. Ross (eds.), *Father and Child: Developmental and Clinical Perspectives*. Boston: Little, Brown, 1982.

Soulé, M., and L. Kreisler. *Les Bons Enfants*. Paris: Editions E.S.F., 1983.

Sterman, M. B. "Relationship of intrauterine fetal activity to maternal sleep stage." *Experimental Neurology*. 19(1967):98–106.

Stoller, R. "Primary femininity." *J. of the Amer. Psychoanalytic Assn.* 24(1976):59–79.

West, M. M., and M. I. Konner. "The role of the father: An anthropological perspective." In M. E. Lamb (ed.), *The Role of the Father in Child Development*, 2nd edition. New York: John Wiley, 1982.

Winnicott, D. W. "Transitional objects and transitional phenomena." In *Collected Papers of D. W. Winnicott*. New York: Basic Books, 1958.

Winnicott, D. W. "Communication between infant and mother, and mother and infant, compared and contrasted." In *Babies and Their Mothers*. Reading, Mass.: Addison-Wesley, 1986.

PART II: The Newborn as Participant

Adamson, L. "Defensive reactions to visual and tactile barriers during early infancy." Unpublished doctoral dissertation, University of California, Berkeley, 1977.

Als, H., E. Tronick, L. Adamson, and T. B. Brazelton. "The behavior of the full-term yet underweight infant." *Developmental Medicine and Clinical Neurology* 18(1976):590.

Barnard, K., and T. B. Brazelton. *The Many Facets of Touch.* Johnson and Johnson, Skillman, N.J., 1984.

Boukydis, C. F. Z. "Adult response to infant cries." Unpublished doctoral dissertation, Pennsylvania State University, University Park, 1979.

Bowlby, J. "The Nature of the Child's Tie to His Mother." *International Journal of Psychoanalysis.* 39(1959):350–373.

Brazelton, T. B. *Neonatal Behavioral Assessment Scale,* 2nd edition. London: Spastics International Medical Publications, 1984.

Brazelton, T. B., M. L. Scholl, and J. S. Robey. "Visual responses in the newborn." *Pediatrics* 37(1966):284.

Brazelton, T. B., G. G. Young, and M. Bullowa. "Inception and resolution of early developmental pathology." *J. of the Amer. Academy of Child Psychiatry* 10(1971):124.

Butterfield, P., R. Emde, M. Svejda, and M. Neiman. "Silver nitrate and the eyes of the newborn." In R. Emde and R. S. Harmon (eds.), *The Development of Attachment and the Filiative Systems.* New York: Plenum Publishing, 1982.

Cairns, G. F., and E. C. Butterfield. "Assessing infants' auditory functioning." In B. Z. Friedlander et al. (eds.), *Exceptional Infant,* Vol. II. New York: Brunner/ Mazel, 1975.

Condon, W., and L. Sander. "Synchrony demonstrated between movements of the neonate and adult speech." *Child Development* 45(1975):456–462.

Dayton, G. O., M. H. Jones, P. Ain, R. A. Rawson, B. Steele, and M. Rose. "Developmental study of coordinated movements in the human infant." *Archives of Ophthalmology* 71(1964):865.

Dixon, S., M. W. Yogman, E. Tronick, H. Als, L. Adamson, and T. B. Brazelton. "Early social interaction of infants with parents and strangers." *J. of the Amer. Academy of Child Psychiatry* 20(1981):32.

Dubowicz, L. M. S., V. Dubowicz, and C. Goldberg. "Clinical assessment of gestational age in the newborn infant." *J. of Pediatrics* 77(1970):1–10.

Eisenberg, R. *Auditory Competence in Early Life: The Roots of Communicative Behavior.* Baltimore, Md: University Park Press, 1976.

Engen, T., L. P. Lipsitt, and H. Kaye. "Olfactory responses and adaptation in the human neonate." *J. of Comparative Physiological Psychology* 56(1963):73.

Fantz, R. "The origins of perception." *Scientific American* 204(1961):66–72.

Goren, C., M. Sarty, and P. Wu. "Visual following and pattern discrimination of face-like stimuli by newborn infants." *Pediatrics* 56(1975):544–549.

Gorman, J., D. Cogan, and S. Gellis. "An apparatus for grading the visual acuity of infants on the basis of opticokinehe nystagmus." *Pediatrics* 19(1957):1088–1092.

Johnson, P., and D. Salisbury. "Breathing and sucking during feeding of the newborn." In M. Hofer (ed.), *Parent-Infant Interaction.* Amsterdam: Elsevier, 1975.

Kaye, K., and T. B. Brazelton. "The ethological significance of the burst-pause pattern in infant sucking." Paper presented at meeting of Society for Research in Child Development. Minneapolis, MN, April, 1971.

Klaus, M., and J. Kennell. *Parent-Infant Bonding.* St. Louis: C. V. Mosby, 1982.

Kluckhohn, C., and H. Murray. *Personality in Nature, Culture and Society.* New York: Knopf, 1948.

Korner, A., and E. B. Thoman. "Relative efficacy of contact and vestibular-proprioceptive stimulation in soothing neonates." *Child Development* 43(1972):443.

Lacey, J. I. "Somatic response patterning and stress." In M. Appley and R. Thumbell (eds.), *Psychological Stress*. New York: Appleton-Century-Crofts, 1967.

Lester, B. M., J. Hoffman, and T. B. Brazelton. "The rhythmic structure of mother-infant interaction in term and preterm infants." *Child Development* 56(1984):15–27.

Lester, B. M., and P. S. Zeskind. "A biobehavioral perspective on crying in early infancy." In H. Fitzgerald et al. (eds.), *Theory and Research in Behavioral Pediatrics*, Vol. I. New York: Plenum Publishing, 1982.

Lipsitt, L. P. "The study of sensory and learning processes of the newborn." *Clinical Perinatology* 4, 1(1977):163–186.

MacFarlane, A. "Olfaction in the development of social preferences in the human neonate." *Parent-Infant Interaction*. CIBA Foundation Symposium 33. New York and Amsterdam: Elsevier, 1975.

Madansky, D. Personal communication, 1983.

Milani Camparetti, A. "The neurophysiologic and clinical implications of studies on fetal motor behavior." *Seminars in Perinatology* 5(1981).

Peiper, A. *Cerebral Function in Infancy and Childhood*. New York: Consultant's Bureau, 1963.

Saint-Anne D'Argassies, C. *Le Développement Neurologique du Nouveau-Né à Terme et Premature*. Paris: Masson et Cie, 1974.

Salapatek, P. H., and W. Kessen. "Visual scanning of triangles by the human newborn." *J. of Experimental Child Psychology* 3(1966):155.

Sigman, M., C. B. Kopp, A. H. Parmelee, and W. Jeffrey. "Visual attention and neurological organization in neonates." *Child Development* 44(1973): 461.

Thoman, E. B. "Early development of sleeping behavior in infants." In N. R. Ellis (ed.), *Aberrant Development in Infancy*. New York: John Wiley, 1975.

PART III: Observing Early Interaction

Aldrich, C. A. *Cultivating the Child's Capacities*. New York: Macmillan, 1928.

Als, H., and T. B. Brazelton. "Assessment of the behavioral organization of a preterm and full-term infant." *J. of the Amer. Academy of Child Psychiatry* 20(1981):239–263.

Als, H., E. Tronick, and T. B. Brazelton. "Affective reciprocity and the development of autonomy: The study of a blind infant." *J. of the Amer. Academy of Child Psychiatry* 19(1980):22–40.

Bell, R. "A reinterpretation of the direction of effects in studies of socialization." *Psychological Review* 75(1968):81–95.

Bower, T. G. "Perceptual functioning in early infancy." In R. J. Robinson (ed.), *Brain and Early Behavior*. London: Academic Press, 1969.

Bowlby, J. "The nature of the child's tie to his mother." *Int. J. of Psychoanalysis* 39(1958):350–373.

Bowlby, J. *Attachment and Loss*, Vol. I. New York: Basic Books, 1969.

Brazelton, T. B. "Early parent-infant reciprocity." In V. C. Vaughn and T. B. Brazelton (eds.); *The Family: Can It Be Saved?* New York: Yearbook, 1976.

Brazelton, T. B. "Behavioral competence of the neonate." *Seminars in Perinatology* 3(1979):35–44.

Brazelton, T. B. "Precursors for the development of emotion in early infancy." In R. Plutcik and H. Kellerman (eds.), *Emotion: Theory, Research and Experience,* Vol. II. New York: Academic Press, 1981.

Brazelton, T. B., and H. Als. "Four early stages in the development of mother-infant interaction." In A. Scluit et al. (eds.), *The Psychoanalytic Study of the Child,* Vol. 34, 1979.

Brazelton, T. B., B. Koslowski, and M. Main. "The origins of reciprocity: The early mother-infant interaction." In M. Lewis and L. Rosenblum (eds.), *The Effect of the Infant on Its Caregiver.* New York: John Wiley, 1974.

Brazelton, T. B., E. Tronick, L. Adamson, H. Als, and S. Wise. "Early mother-infant reciprocity." *Parent-Infant Interaction.* CIBA Foundation Symposium 33. New York and Amsterdam: Elsevier, 1975.

Brazelton, T. B., and M. W. Yogman. "Reciprocity, attachment and effectance: Anlage in early infancy." In T. B. Brazelton and M. W. Yogman (eds.), *Affective Development in Infancy.* Norwood, N.J.: Ablex, 1986.

Brazelton, T. B., M. W. Yogman, H. Als, and E. Tronick. "The infant as a focus for family reciprocity." In M. Lewis and L. Rosenblum (eds.), *Social Network of the Developing Child.* New York: John Wiley, 1979.

Bruner, J. S. "Eye, hand, and mind." In D. Elkind and J. G. Flavell (eds.), *Studies in Cognitive Development.* New York: Oxford University Press, 1969.

Cohen, L. B., and P. Salapatek (eds.). *Infant Perception: From Sensation to Cognition,* Vols. I and II. New York: Academic Press, 1975.

Cohn, J. F., and E. Tronick. "Three-month-old infant's reaction to simulated maternal depression." *Child Development* 54(1983):185–193.

Condon, W. S., and L. W. Sander. "Synchrony demonstrated between movements of the neonate and adult speech." *Child Development* 45(1974):456–462.

Connolly, K., and P. Stratton. "Developmental changes in associated movements." *Developmental Medicine and Child Neurology* 10(1968):49–56.

David, M., and G. Appell. "A study of nursing care and nurse-infant interactions." In B. M. Foss (ed.), *Determinants of Infant Behavior.* New York: International Universities Press, 1961.

Dixon, J., M. W. Yogman, E. Tronick, H. Als, L. Adamson, and T. B. Brazelton. "Early social interaction of parents and strangers." *J. of the Amer. Academy of Child Psychiatry* 20(1981):32–52.

Eimas, P. O., E. R. Siqueland, P. Jusczyk, and J. Vigonto. "Speech perception in infants." *Science* 171(1971):303–306.

Emde, R. N., T. J. Gaensbauer, and R. J. Harmon. *Emotional Expression in Infancy: A Biobehavioral Study.* Psychological Issues Monographs 37. New York: International Universities Press, 1976.

Freud, A. "The ego and the mechanisms of defense." In *The Writings of Anna Freud,* Vol. II. New York: International Universities Press, 1936.

Hartmann, H. *Ego Psychology and the Problems of Adaptation.* New York: International Universities Press, 1958.

Hinde, R. "On describing relationships." *J. of Child Psychology and Psychiatry* 17(1976).

Kaye, H. "Infant sucking and its modification." In L. P. Lipsitt and C. C. Spiker (eds.), *Advances in Child Development and Behavior*, Vol. III. New York: Academic Press, 1967.

Kaye, K., and T. B. Brazelton. "The ethological significance of the burst-pause pattern in infant sucking." Presented at the Society for Research in Child Development, Minneapolis, Minnesota, 1971.

Kobre, K. R., and L. P. Lipsitt. "A negative contrast affect in newborns." *J. of Experimental Child Psychology* 14(1972):81–91.

Lorenz, K. "Der kumpan in der umwelt des vogels" (1935). In C. H. Schiller (ed.), *Institutive Behavior*. English translation. New York: International Universities Press, 1957.

Mahler, M. S., F. Pine, and A. Bergman. *The Psychological Birth of the Human Infant*. New York: Basic Books, 1975.

Maratos, O. "Trends in the development of imitation in early infancy." In T. G. Bever (ed.), *Regressions in Mental Development*. Hillsdale, N.J.: Lawrence Erlbaum, 1982.

Meltzoff, A., and M. K. Moore. "Imitation of facial and manual gestures by human neonates." *Science* 198(1977):75–78.

Piaget, J. *Play, Dreams and Imitation in Childhood*. New York: E. P. Dutton, 1951.

Piaget, J. *The Construction of Reality in the Child*. New York: Basic Books, 1954.

Provence, S., and R. Lipton. *Infants in Institutions*. New York: International Universities Press, 1963.

Rheingold, H. "The effect of environment and stimulation upon social and exploratory behavior in the human infant." In B. M. Foss (ed.), *Determinants of Infant Behavior*, Vol I. New York: John Wiley, 1961.

Robertson, J. *Hospitals and Children*. New York: International Universities Press, 1962.

Sameroff, A. J. "The components of sucking in the human newborn." *J. of Experimental Child Psychology* 6(1968):607.

Sameroff, A. J., and M. Chandler. "Reproductive risk and the continuum of caretaking casualty." In F. D. Horowitz et al. (eds.), *Review of Child Development Research*, Vol. 4. Chicago: University of Chicago Press, 1976.

Sander, L. "The regulation of exchange in the infant-caregiver system and some aspects of the context-contest relationship." In M. Lewis and L. A. Rosenblum (eds.), *Interaction, Conversation and the Development of Language*. New York: John Wiley, 1977.

Siqueland, E. R., and L. P. Lipsitt. "Conditioned head-turning behavior in newborns." *J. of Experimental Child Psychology* 3(1966):356–376.

Spitz, R. "Anaclitic depression." *Psychoanalytic Study of the Child* 2(1946):313–342.

Spitz, R. "The derailment of dialogue: Stimulus overload, action cycles and the complete gradient." *J. of the Amer. Psychoanalytic Assn.* 12(1964):752–775.

Spitz, R. *The First Year of Life*. New York: International Universities Press, 1965.

Stern, D. "A microanalysis of mother-infant interaction." *J. of the Amer. Academy of Child Psychiatry* 10(1971):501–517.

Stern, D. "Mother and infant at play." In M. Lewis and L. A. Rosenblum (eds.), *The Effect of the Infant on Its Caregiver*. New York: John Wiley, 1974a.

Stern, D. "The goal and structure of mother-infant play." *J. of the Amer. Academy of Child Psychiatry* 13(1974b):402–421.

Stern, D. *The First Relationship*. Cambridge, Mass: Harvard University Press, 1977.

Stern, D. *The Interpersonal World of the Infant*. New York: Basic Books, 1985.

Trevarthan, C. "Descriptive analysis of infant communicative behavior." In H. R. Schaffer (ed.), *Studies in Mother-Infant Interactions*. New York: Academic Press, 1977.

Tronick, E., H. Als, L. Adamson, S. Wise, and T. B. Brazelton. "The infant's response to entrapment between contradictory messages in face-to-face interaction." *J. of Child Psychiatry* 17(1978):1–13.

Tronick, E., H. Als, and T. B. Brazelton. "Maturity in mother–infant interaction." *J. of Communication Information Processing*, 27(1977):74–79.

Walcher, D. N., and D. L. Peters. *The Development of Self-Regulatory Mechanisms*. New York: Academic Press, 1971.

Watzlawick, P., H. J. Beavin, and D. Jackson. *The Pragmatics of Human Communication*. New York: Norton, 1967.

Winnicott, D. W. *The Child, the Family, and the Outside World*. London: Penguin 1964. Reading, Mass.: Addison-Wesley, 1987.

Winnicott, D. W. "The mother-infant experience of mutuality." In J. Anthony and T. Benedek (eds.), *Parenthood*. Boston: Little, Brown, 1970.

Winnicott, D. W. "The newborn and his mother" (1964). In C. Winnicott et al. (eds.), *Babies and Their Mothers*. Reading, Mass.: Addison-Wesley, 1986.

Yogman, M. W., S. Dixon, E. Tronick, L. Adamson, H. Als, and T. B. Brazelton. "Father-infant interaction." Paper presented at meeting of American Pediatric Society, St. Louis, Missouri, 1976.

Zelasco, P. R. "Smiling and vocalizing: A cognitive emphasis." *Merrill-Palmer Quarterly* 18(1972):349–365.

PART IV: Imaginary Interactions

Beebe, P., and P. Sloate. "Assessment and treatment of difficulties in mother-infant attunement in the first years of life: A case history." *Psychoanalytic Inquiry* 1, 4(1982).

Borges, J. L. "Tlon, Uqbar, Orbis, Tertius." In *Labyrinths*. New York: New Directions, 1964.

Bruner, J. "Thought, language and interaction in infancy." In *Frontiers of Infant Psychiatry*, Vol. I, 1983.

Cramer, B. "Objective and Subjective Aspects of Parent-Infant Relations: An attempt at correlation between infant studies and clinical work." In J. Osofsky (ed.), *Handbook of Infant Development*, 2nd edition. New York: John Wiley, 1987.

Dunn, J. Comment: "Problems and promises in the study of affect and intention." In E. Tronick (ed.), *Social Interchange in Infancy*. Baltimore, Md.: University Park Press, 1982.

Emde, R., and J. Sorce. "Emotional availability and maternal referencing." In *Frontiers of Infant Psychiatry*, Vol. I, 1983.

Fraiberg, S. *Clinical Studies in Infant Mental Health: The First Year of Life*. New York: Basic Books, 1980.

Hinde, R. "On describing relationships." *J. of Child Psychology and Psychiatry* 17(1976):1–19.

Kreisler, L. "L'enfant du désordre psychosomatique." *Recontres Cliniques*. Privately printed, 1981.

Lebovici, S. *La Mère, Le Nourisson et Le Psychanalyste: Les Interactions Précoces.* Paris: Paidos/Le Centurion, 1983.

Mahler, M., F. Pine and A. Bergman. *The Psychological Birth of the Human Infant.* New York: Basic Books, 1975.

Meares, R., R. Penman, J. Milgom-Friedman, and K. Buker. "Some origins of the difficult child: The Brazelton Scale and the mother's view of her newborn's character." *British J. of Medical Psychology* 55(1982):77–89.

Rabain, J. *L'Enfant de Lignange.* Paris: Payot, 1979.

Robson, K. "The role of eye-to-eye contact in maternal-infant attachment." *J. of Child Psychology and Psychiatry* 8(1964).

PART V: Understanding the Earliest Relationship

Als, H. "The unfolding of behavioral organization in the face of a biological violation." In E. Tronick (ed.), *Social Interchange in Infancy.* Baltimore, Md.: University Park Press, 1982.

Als, H. "Infant individuality: Assessing patterns of very early development." In *Frontiers of Infant Psychiatry,* Vol. I(1983).

Beardslee, W. R., J. Bemporad, M. B. Keller, and G. L. Klerman. "Children of parents with major affective disorders: A review." *Amer. J. of Psychiatry* 140(1983):825–832.

Brazelton, T. B. *On Becoming a Family.* New York: Delacorte Press, 1981.

Bromwich, R. M., and A. H. Parmelee. "An intervention program for pre-term infants." In T. M. Field (ed.), *Infants Born at Risk.* Holliswood, N.Y.: Spectrum, 1979.

Chess, S., and A. Thomas. *Origins and Evolution of Behavior Disorders: From Infancy to Early Adult Life.* New York: Brunner/Mazel, 1984.

Coleman, R. W., E. Kris, and S. Provence. "The study of variations of early parental attitudes: A preliminary report." *Psychoanalytic Study of the Child* 8(1953):20–47.

Cramer, B. "Assessment of parent-infant relationships." In T. B. Brazelton and M. W. Yogman, (eds.), *Affective Development in Infancy.* Norwood, NJ: Ablex Publishing, 1986.

Cramer, B. "Objective and subjective aspects of parent-infant relations: an attempt at correlation between infant studies and clinical work." In J. Osofsky (ed.), *Handbook of Infant Development,* 2nd edition. New York: John Wiley, 1987.

Cramer, B., and U. D'Arcis. "Body contact avoidance in mother and baby: correlation between clinical and microanalytical data." *In press.*

Cramer, B., and D. Stern. "Evaluation of changes in mother-infant brief psychotherapy." *Infant Mental Health Journal* 9, 1(Spring, 1988).

Cramer, B. "Les thérapies spécifiques et la consultation thérapeutique." In S. Lebovici and F. Weil-Halpern, (eds.) *Psychiatrie du Bébé.* Paris: Presses Universitaires de France, 1989.

Drotar, D., A. Baskiewicz, N. Irvin, J. Kennell, and M. Klaus. "The adaptation of parents to the birth of an infant with a congenital malformation: A hypothetical model." *Pediatrics* 56(1975):710–717.

Di Vitto, B., and S. Goldberg. "The development of early parent-infant interaction as a function of newborn medical status." In T. M. Field et al. (eds.), *Infants Born at Risk*. Holliswood, N.Y.: Spectrum, 1979.

Emde, R., and Sameroff, A. *Relationship Disturbances*. New York: Basic Books, 1989.

Field, T. M. "Interaction patterns of preterm and term infants." In T. M. Field et al. (eds.), *Infants Born At Risk*. Holliswood, N.Y.: Spectrum, 1979.

Field, T. M. "Perinatal risk factors for infant depression." In *Frontiers of Infant Psychiatry*, Vol. II, 1985.

Fraiberg, S. *Clinical Studies in Infant Mental Health*. London: Tavistock, 1980.

Goldberg, S., S. Brachfield, and B. Di Vitto. "Feeding, fussing and play: Parent-infant interaction in the first year as a function of prematurity and perinatal medical problems." In T. M. Field et al. (eds.), *High-Risk Infants and Children*. New York: Academic Press, 1988.

Johns, N. "Family reactions to the birth of a child with a congenital abnormality." *Medical Journal of Australia* 1(1971):247–282.

Klaus, M., and J. Kennell. *Maternal Infant Bonding*. St. Louis: C. V. Mosby, 1982.

Kreisler, L., and B. Cramer. "Infant psychopathology: guidelines for examination, clinical groupings, nosological propositions." In J. Call et al. (eds.), *Frontiers of Infant Psychiatry* I. New York: Basic Books, 1983.

Lester, B. M., Z. Boukydis, J. Hoffman, M. Censullo, L. Zahr, and T. B. Brazelton. "Behavioral and Psychophysiological assessment of the pre-term infant." In B. M. Lester and E. Tronick (eds.), *Defense of the Premature Infant: The Limits of Plasticity*. Lexington, Mass.: Lexington Books, 1987.

Minde, K., P. Manton, D. Manning, and B. Hiner. "Some determinants of mother-infant interaction in the premature nursery." *J. of the Amer. Academy of Child Psychiatry* 10(1980):1–21.

Paffenbarger, R. S. "Epidemiological aspects of mental illness associated with childbearing." In I. F. Brockington and R. Kuman (eds.), *Motherhood and Mental Illness*. London: Academic Press, 1982, New York: Grune and Stratton, 1982.

Parmelee, A. H., L. Recknith, S. E. Cohen, and M. Sigman. "Social influences on infants at medical risk for behavioral difficulties." In *Frontiers of Infant Psychiatry*, Vol. I, 1983.

Parmelee, A. H., M. Sigman, C. B. Kopp, and A. Haber. "The concept of a cumulative risk score for infants." In N. R. Ellis (ed.), *Aberrant Development in Infancy*. New York: John Wiley, 1975.

Robertson, J. "Mother-infant interaction from birth to 12 months: 2 case studies." In B. M. Foss (ed.), *Determinants of Infant Behavior*, Vol. III. New York: John Wiley, 1965.

Robson, K., and H. A. Moss. "Patterns and determinants of maternal attachment." *J. of Pediatrics*, Vol. II(1970):916–985.

Roskies, E. *Abnormalities and Normalities: The Mothering of Thalidomide Children*. New York: Cornell University Press, 1972.

Samaraweera, S., F. Moylan, C. J. Larroque, A. Patterson, K. Angoft, and V. Katzenskin. "Earliest intervention in neonatal intensive care units: A team approach." In *Frontiers of Infant Psychiatry*, Vol. I, 1983.

Semrad, E. *Semrad: The Heart of a Therapist*. S. Rako and H. Mazer (eds.). New York: Aronson, 1983.

Solnit, A., and M. H. Stark. "Mourning and the birth of a defective child." *Psychoanalytic Study of the Child* 16(1961):523–537.

Stern, D. *The Interpersonal World of the Infant.* New York: Basic Books, 1985.

Tronick, E., H. Als, L. Adamson, S. Wise, and T. B. Brazelton. "The infant's response to entrapment between contradictory messages in face-to-face interaction." *J. of the Amer. Academy of Child Psychiatry* 17(1978):1–13.

Tronick, E., J. Cohn, and E. Shea. "The transfer of affect between mothers and infants." In T. B. Brazelton and M. W. Yogman (eds.), *Affective Development in Infancy.* Norwood, N.J.: Ablex, 1984.

INDEX

ABOUT THE AUTHORS

T. Berry Brazelton, M.D., founder of the Child Development Unit at Boston Children's Hospital, is Clinical Professor of Pediatrics Emeritus at Harvard Medical School. Currently Professor of Pediatrics and Human Development at Brown University, he is also President of both the Society for Research in Child Development and the National Center for Clinical Infant Programs. Dr. Brazelton is the recipient of the C. Anderson Aldrich Award for Distinguished Contributions to the Field of Child Development given by the American Academy of Pediatrics. The author of over 150 scholarly papers, Dr. Brazelton has written twenty books, for both a professional and a lay audience, including the now classic *Infants and Mothers* and *To Listen to a Child*. The Brazelton Neonatal Behavioral Assessment Scale is in use in hospitals throughout the world.

Bertrand G. Cramer, M.D. is Professor of Child Psychiatry at the University of Geneva and a practicing psychoanalyst. He is a pioneer in infant psychiatry and trains doctors, psychologists and nurses in this field. Dr. Cramer is Vice-President of the World Association for Infant Psychiatry and Allied Disciplines. A graduate of the New York Psychoanalytic Institute, he has trained elsewhere in the U.S. and in Europe. In 1982–1983 he was Visiting Professor at Harvard Medical School. In addition to over seventy scholarly papers, Dr. Cramer is the author of two books: *Psychiatrie du Bébé* and *Profession Bébé*.